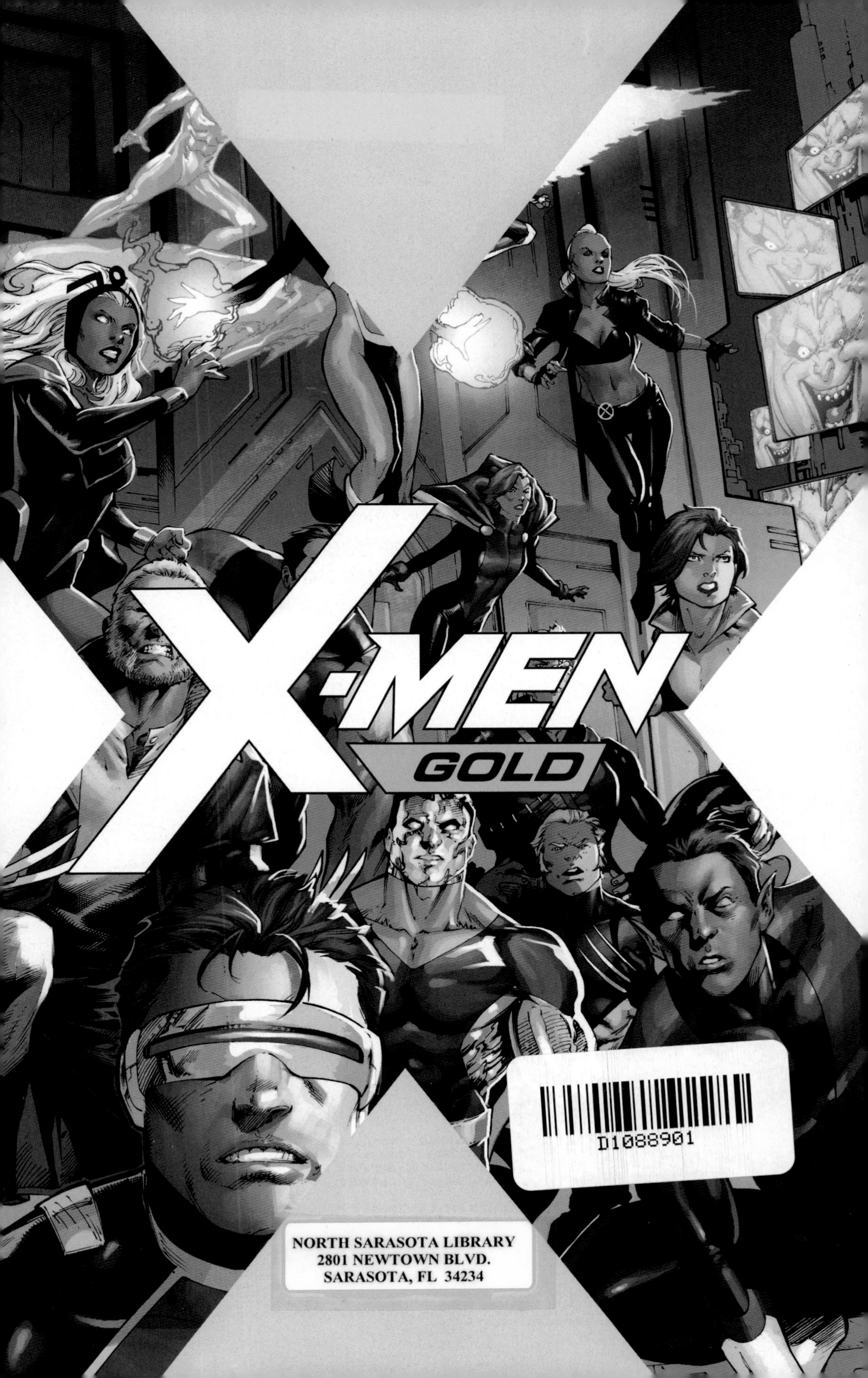
X-MEN
GOLD

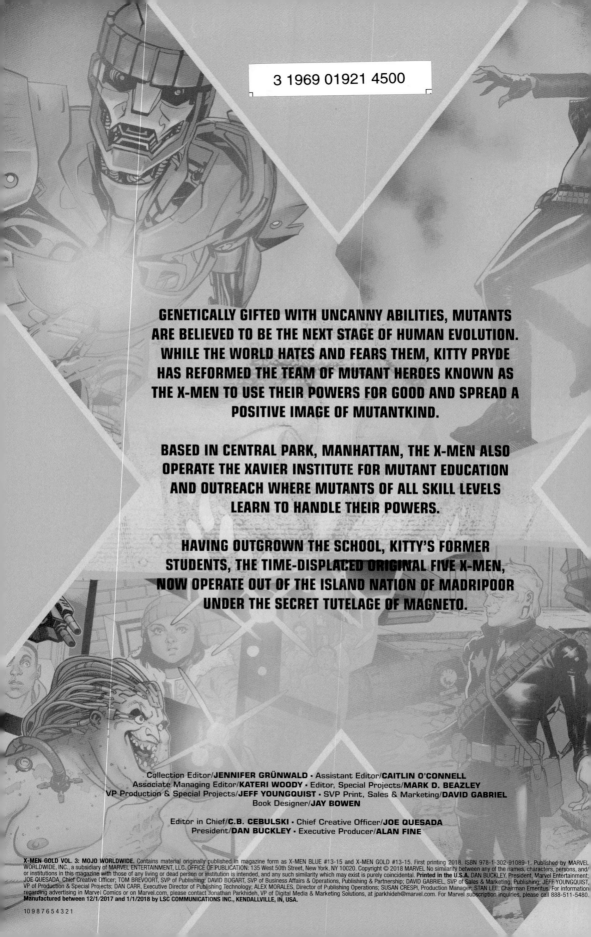

3 1969 01921 4500

GENETICALLY GIFTED WITH UNCANNY ABILITIES, MUTANTS
ARE BELIEVED TO BE THE NEXT STAGE OF HUMAN EVOLUTION.
WHILE THE WORLD HATES AND FEARS THEM, KITTY PRYDE
HAS REFORMED THE TEAM OF MUTANT HEROES KNOWN AS
THE X-MEN TO USE THEIR POWERS FOR GOOD AND SPREAD A
POSITIVE IMAGE OF MUTANTKIND.

BASED IN CENTRAL PARK, MANHATTAN, THE X-MEN ALSO
OPERATE THE XAVIER INSTITUTE FOR MUTANT EDUCATION
AND OUTREACH WHERE MUTANTS OF ALL SKILL LEVELS
LEARN TO HANDLE THEIR POWERS.

HAVING OUTGROWN THE SCHOOL, KITTY'S FORMER
STUDENTS, THE TIME-DISPLACED ORIGINAL FIVE X-MEN,
NOW OPERATE OUT OF THE ISLAND NATION OF MADRIPOOR
UNDER THE SECRET TUTELAGE OF MAGNETO.

Collection Editor/**JENNIFER GRÜNWALD** · Assistant Editor/**CAITLIN O'CONNELL**
Associate Managing Editor/**KATERI WOODY** · Editor, Special Projects/**MARK D. BEAZLEY**
VP Production & Special Projects/**JEFF YOUNGQUIST** · SVP Print, Sales & Marketing/**DAVID GABRIEL**
Book Designer/**JAY BOWEN**

Editor in Chief/**C.B. CEBULSKI** · Chief Creative Officer/**JOE QUESADA**
President/**DAN BUCKLEY** · Executive Producer/**ALAN FINE**

X-MEN GOLD VOL. 3: MOJO WORLDWIDE. Contains material originally published in magazine form as X-MEN BLUE #13-15 and X-MEN GOLD #13-15. First printing 2018. ISBN 978-1-302-91089-1. Published by MARVEL WORLDWIDE, INC., a subsidiary of MARVEL ENTERTAINMENT, LLC. OFFICE OF PUBLICATION: 135 West 50th Street, New York, NY 10020. Copyright © 2018 MARVEL No similarity between any of the names, characters, persons, and/ or institutions in this magazine with those of any living or dead person or institution is intended, and any such similarity which may exist is purely coincidental. **Printed in the U.S.A.** DAN BUCKLEY, President, Marvel Entertainment; JOE QUESADA, Chief Creative Officer; TOM BREVOORT, SVP of Publishing; DAVID BOGART, SVP of Business Affairs & Operations, Publishing & Partnership; DAVID GABRIEL, SVP of Sales & Marketing, Publishing; JEFF YOUNGQUIST, VP of Production & Special Projects; DAN CARR, Executive Director of Publishing Technology; ALEX MORALES, Director of Publishing Operations; SUSAN CRESPI, Production Manager; STAN LEE, Chairman Emeritus. For information regarding advertising in Marvel Comics or on Marvel.com, please contact Jonathan Parkhideh, VP of Digital Media & Communications Solutions, at jparkhideh@marvel.com. For Marvel subscription inquiries, please call 888-511-5480. **Manufactured between 12/1/2017 and 1/1/2018 by LSC COMMUNICATIONS INC., KENDALLVILLE, IN, USA.**

10 9 8 7 6 5 4 3 2 1

X-MEN GOLD

MOJO WORLDWIDE

X-MEN GOLD #13-14
Writer/**MARC GUGGENHEIM**
Artists/**MIKE MAYHEW** (#13) & **MARC LAMING** (#14)
Color Artist/**RAIN BEREDO**
Letterer/**VC'S CORY PETIT**
Cover Art/**ARTHUR ADAMS** & **PETER STEIGERWALD** (#13)
and **DAN MORA** & **CARLOS CABRERA** (#14)

X-MEN GOLD #15
Writer/**MARC GUGGENHEIM**
Penciler/**DIEGO BERNARD**
Inker/**JP MAYER**
Color Artist/**RAIN BEREDO**
Letterer/**VC'S CORY PETIT**
Cover Art/**DAN MORA** & **JUAN FERNANDEZ**

X-MEN BLUE #13-15
Writer/**CULLEN BUNN**
Artist/**JORGE MOLINA**
Color Artists/**MATT MILLA** with **GURU-eFX** (#14)
Letterer/**VC'S JOE CARAMAGNA**
Cover Art/**ARTHUR ADAMS** with **PETER STEIGERWALD** (#13-14)
& **FEDERICO BLEE** (#15)

Assistant Editors/**CHRIS ROBINSON** & **CHRISTINA HARRINGTON**
Editor/**MARK PANICCIA**

X-MEN CREATED BY **STAN LEE** & **JACK KIRBY**

X-MEN GOLD #13

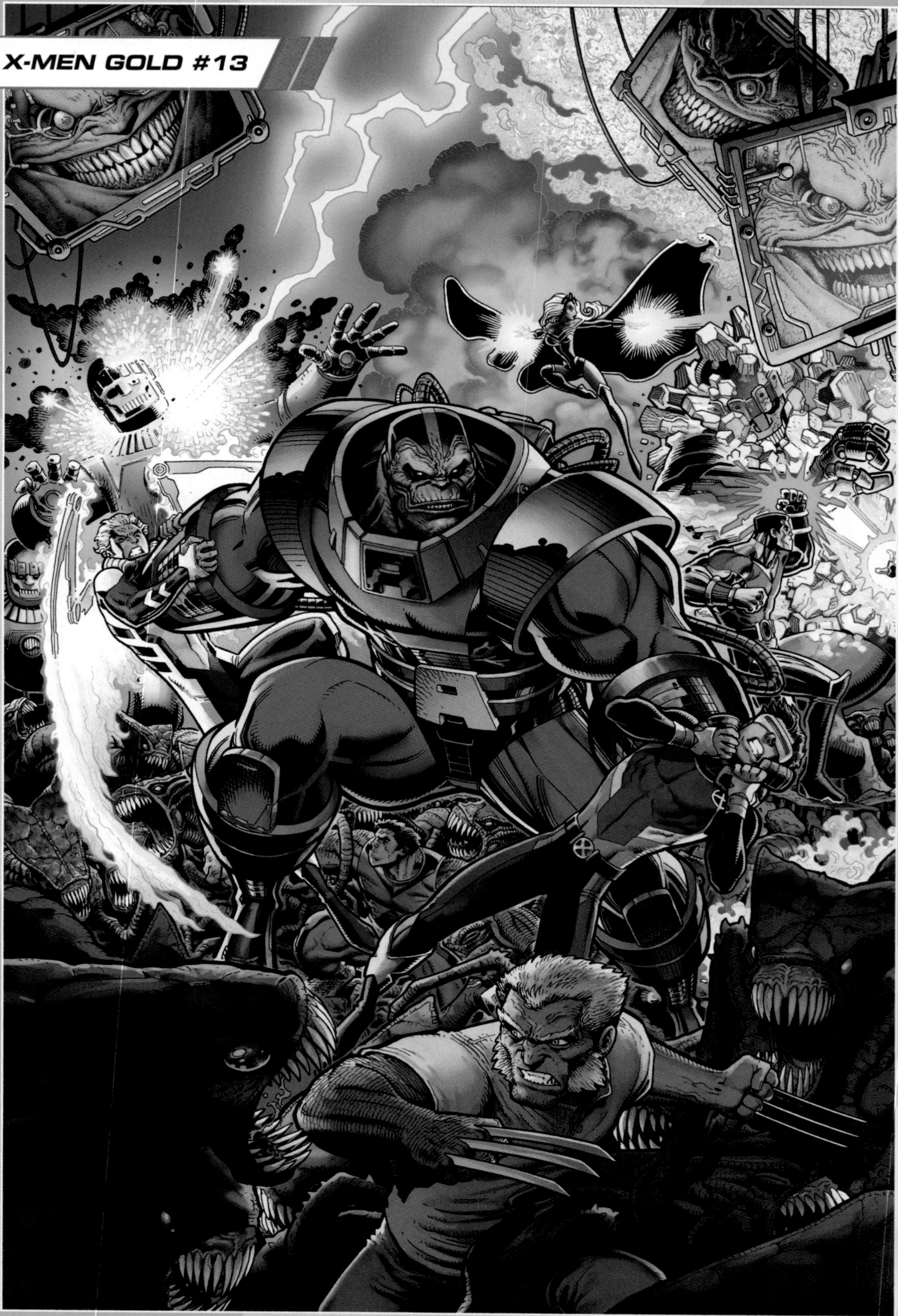

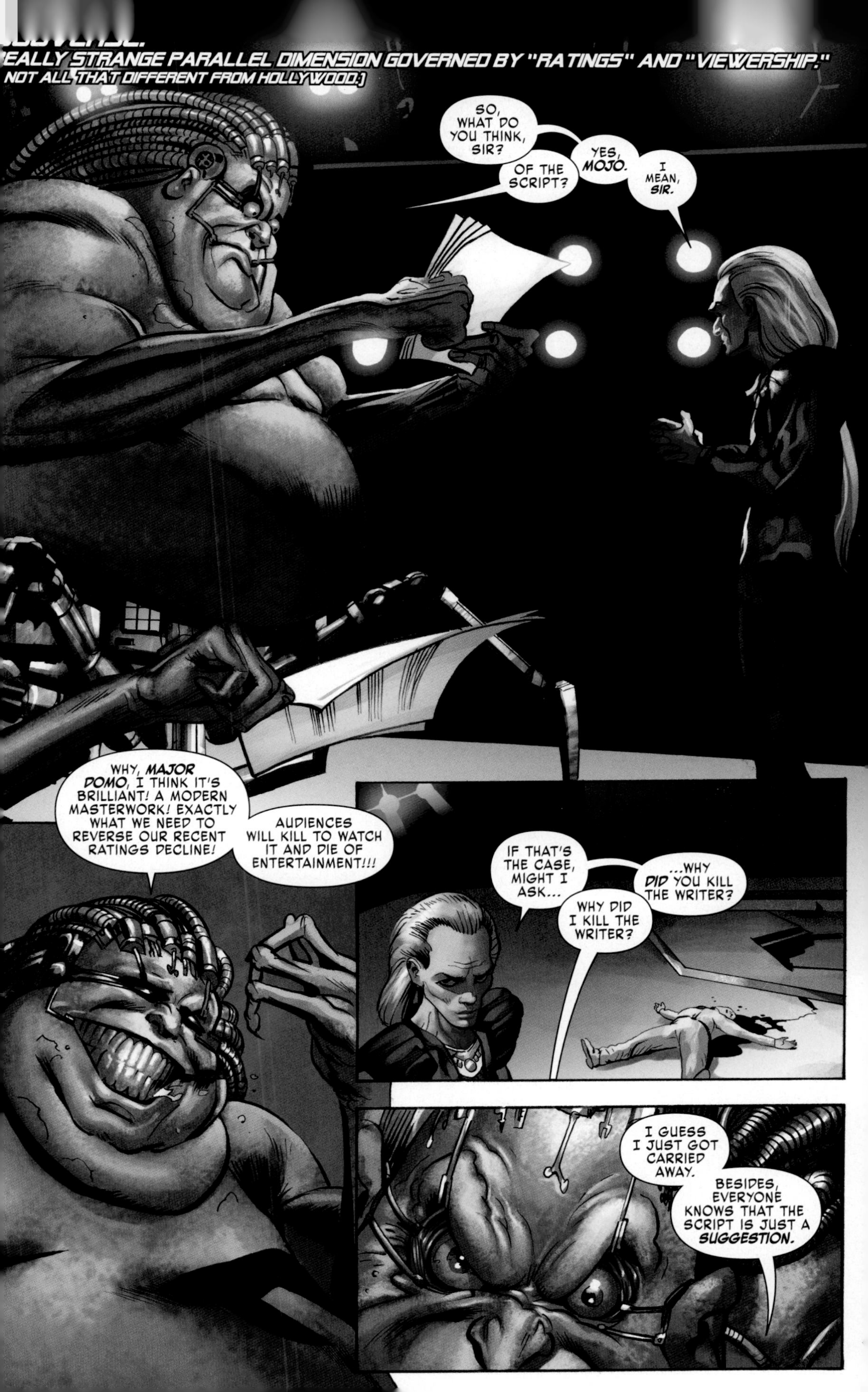
EALLY STRANGE PARALLEL DIMENSION GOVERNED BY "RATINGS" AND "VIEWERSHIP."
NOT ALL THAT DIFFERENT FROM HOLLYWOOD.)
SO, WHAT DO YOU THINK, SIR?
OF THE SCRIPT?
YES, MOJO.
I MEAN, SIR.
WHY, MAJOR DOMO, I THINK IT'S BRILLIANT! A MODERN MASTERWORK! EXACTLY WHAT WE NEED TO REVERSE OUR RECENT RATINGS DECLINE!
AUDIENCES WILL KILL TO WATCH IT AND DIE OF ENTERTAINMENT!!!
IF THAT'S THE CASE, MIGHT I ASK...
...WHY DID YOU KILL THE WRITER?
WHY DID I KILL THE WRITER?
I GUESS I JUST GOT CARRIED AWAY.
BESIDES, EVERYONE KNOWS THAT THE SCRIPT IS JUST A SUGGESTION.

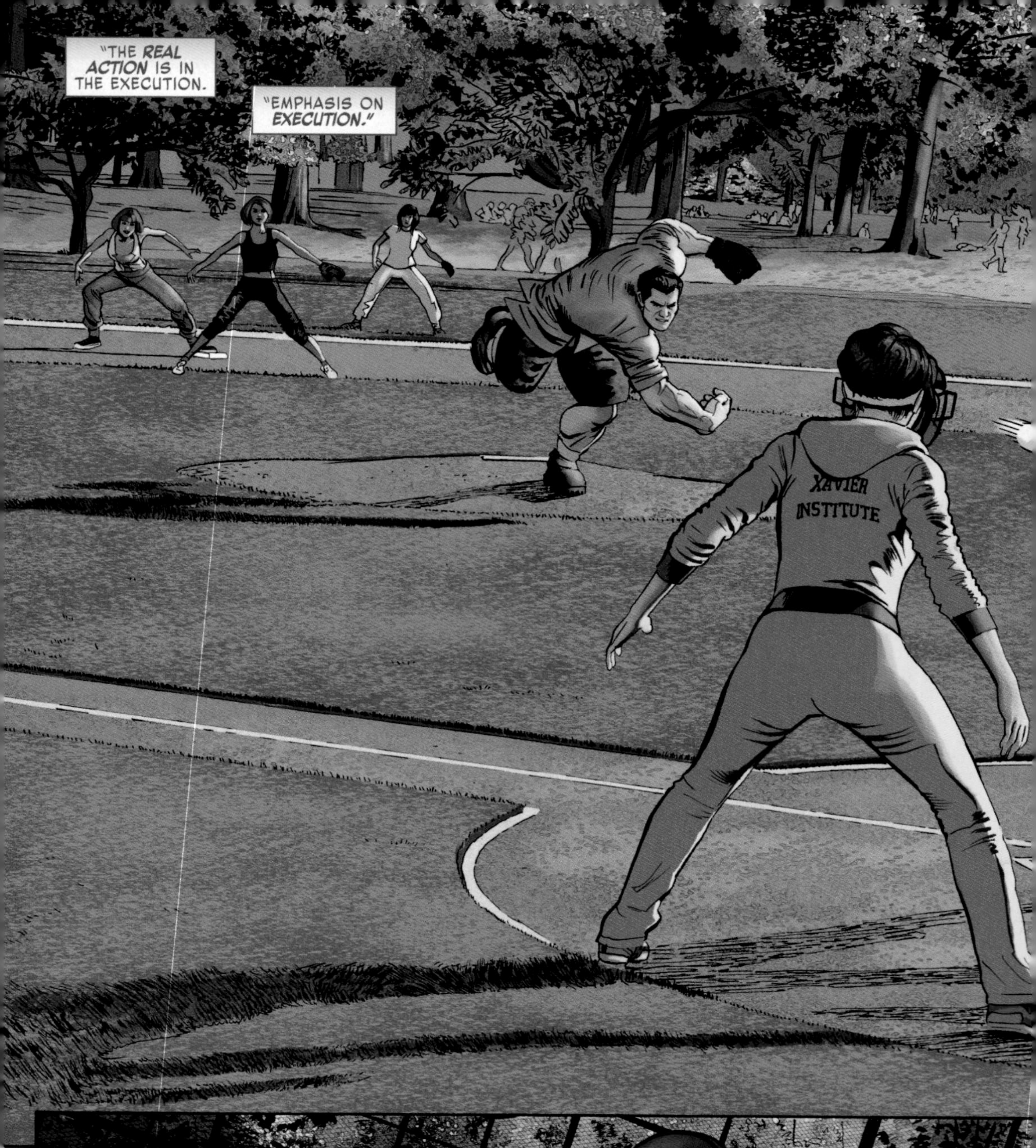
"THE *REAL ACTION* IS IN THE EXECUTION.
"EMPHASIS ON *EXECUTION*."
XAVIER INSTITUTE

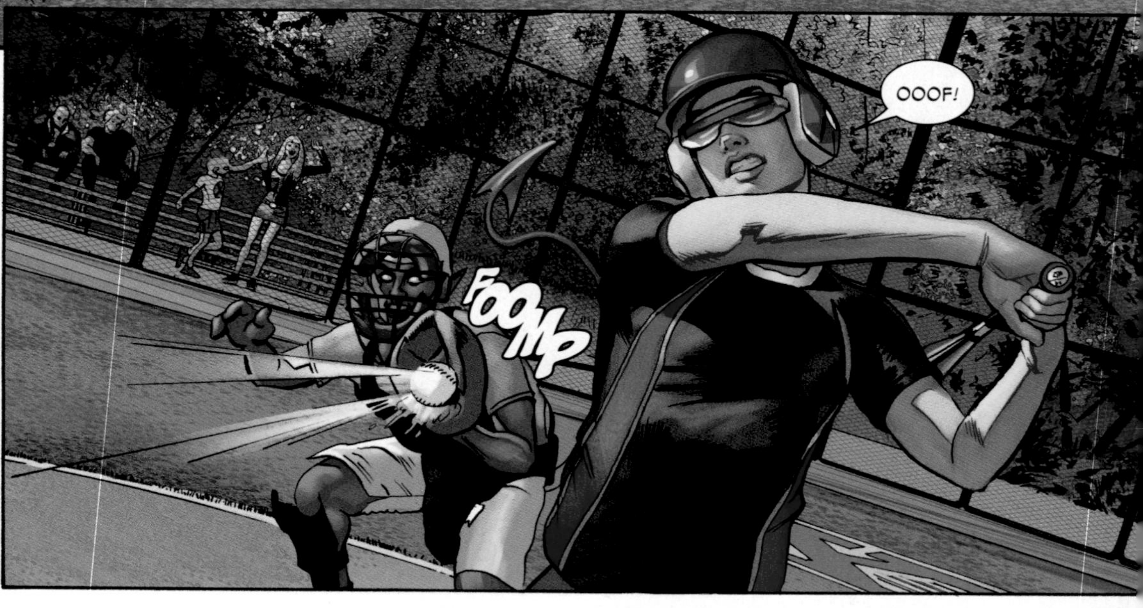
OOOF!
FOOMP

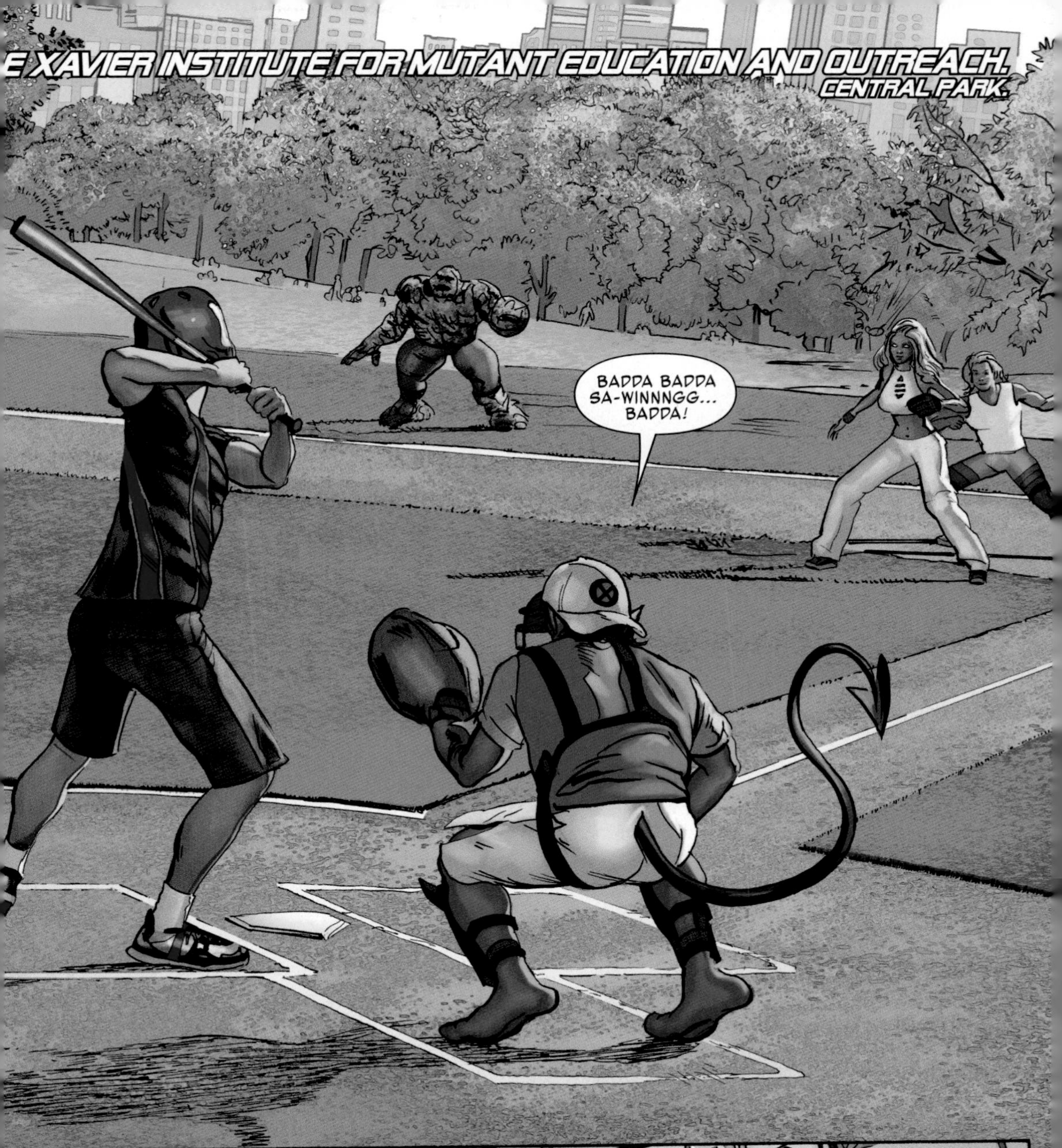
E XAVIER INSTITUTE FOR MUTANT EDUCATION AND OUTREACH.
CENTRAL PARK.
BADDA BADDA SA-WINNNGG... BADDA!

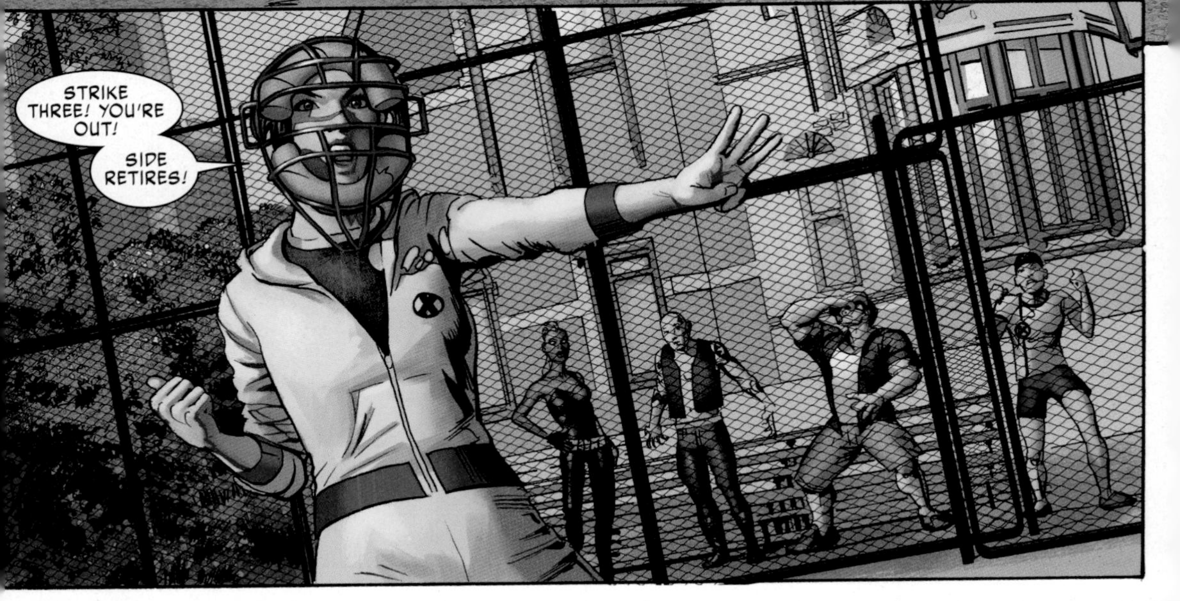
STRIKE THREE! YOU'RE OUT!
SIDE RETIRES!

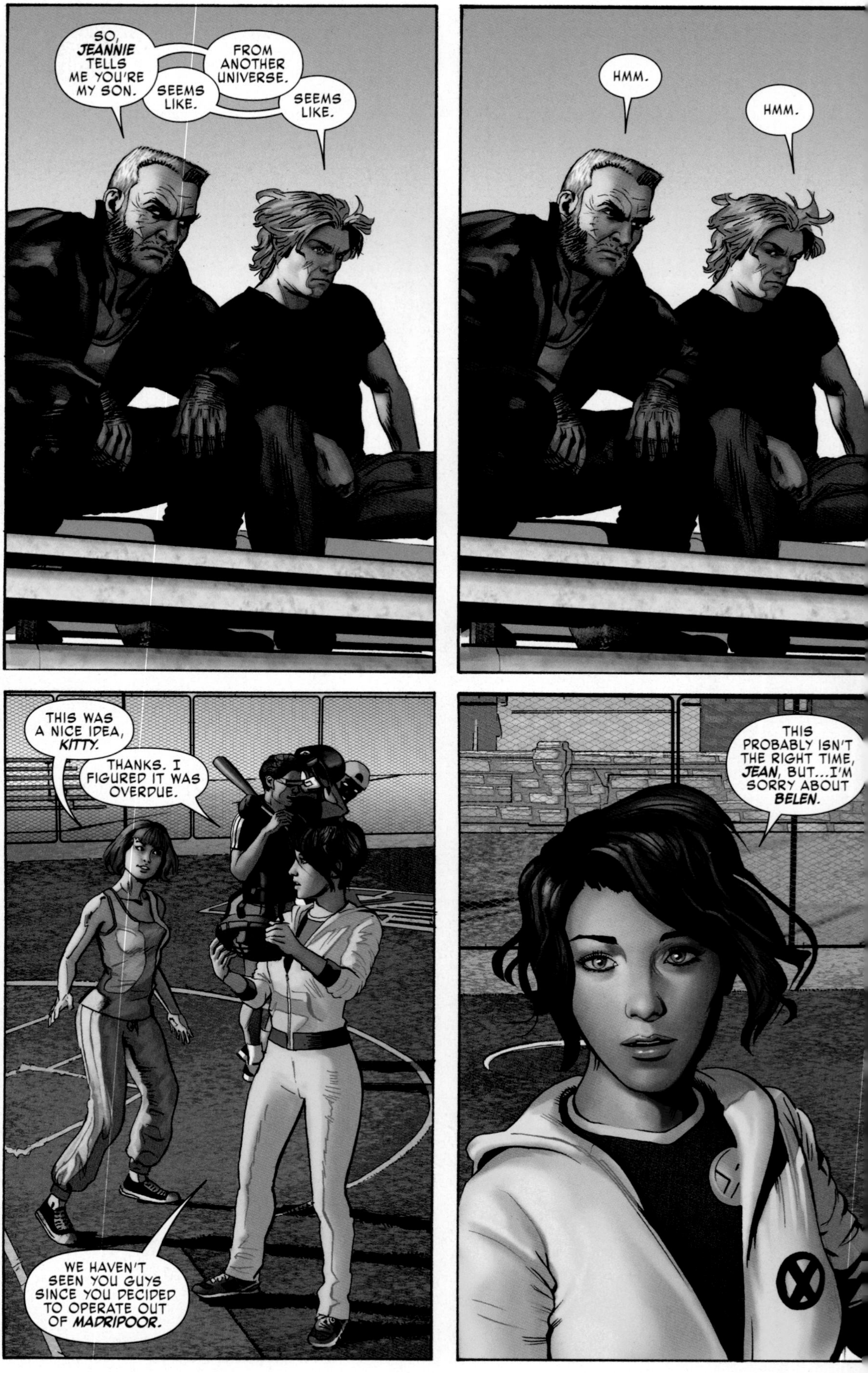
SO, JEANNIE TELLS ME YOU'RE MY SON.
FROM ANOTHER UNIVERSE.
SEEMS LIKE.
SEEMS LIKE.
HMM.
HMM.
THIS WAS A NICE IDEA, KITTY.
THANKS. I FIGURED IT WAS OVERDUE.
WE HAVEN'T SEEN YOU GUYS SINCE YOU DECIDED TO OPERATE OUT OF MADRIPOOR.
THIS PROBABLY ISN'T THE RIGHT TIME, JEAN, BUT...I'M SORRY ABOUT BELEN.

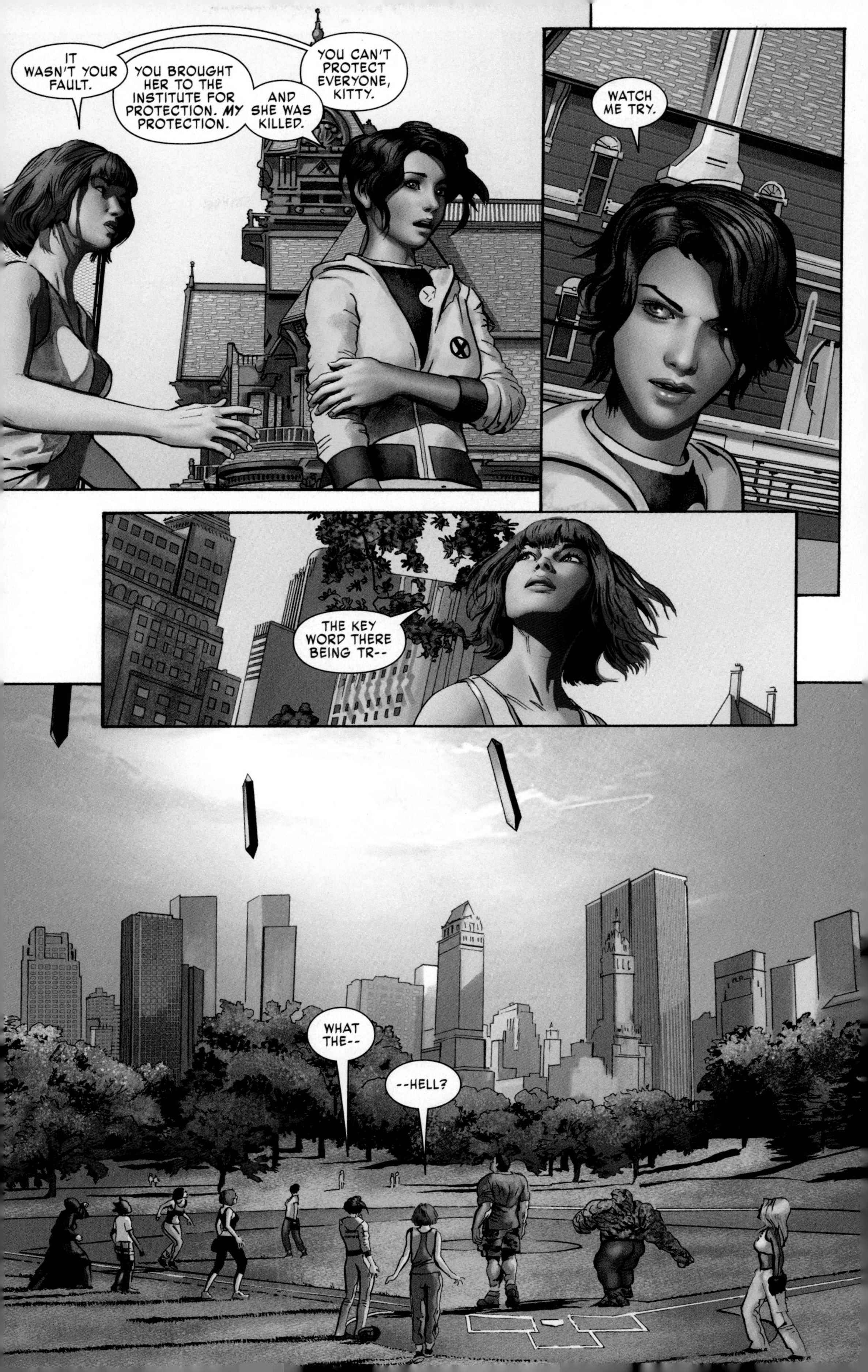
IT WASN'T YOUR FAULT.
YOU BROUGHT HER TO THE INSTITUTE FOR PROTECTION. MY PROTECTION.
AND SHE WAS KILLED.
YOU CAN'T PROTECT EVERYONE, KITTY.
WATCH ME TRY.
THE KEY WORD THERE BEING TR--
WHAT THE--
--HELL?

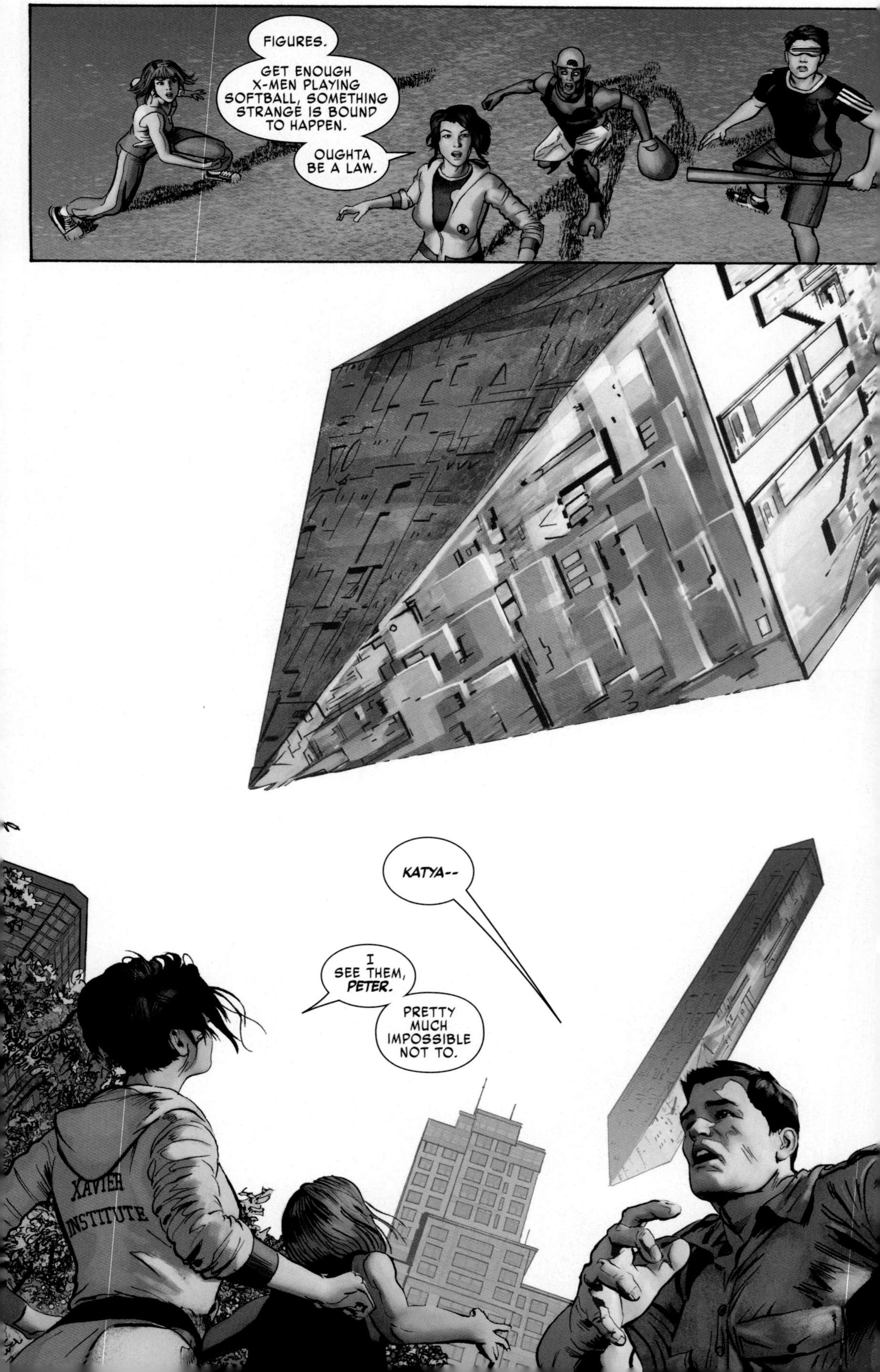
FIGURES.
GET ENOUGH X-MEN PLAYING SOFTBALL, SOMETHING STRANGE IS BOUND TO HAPPEN.
OUGHTA BE A LAW.
KATYA--
I SEE THEM, PETER.
PRETTY MUCH IMPOSSIBLE NOT TO.
XAVIER INSTITUTE

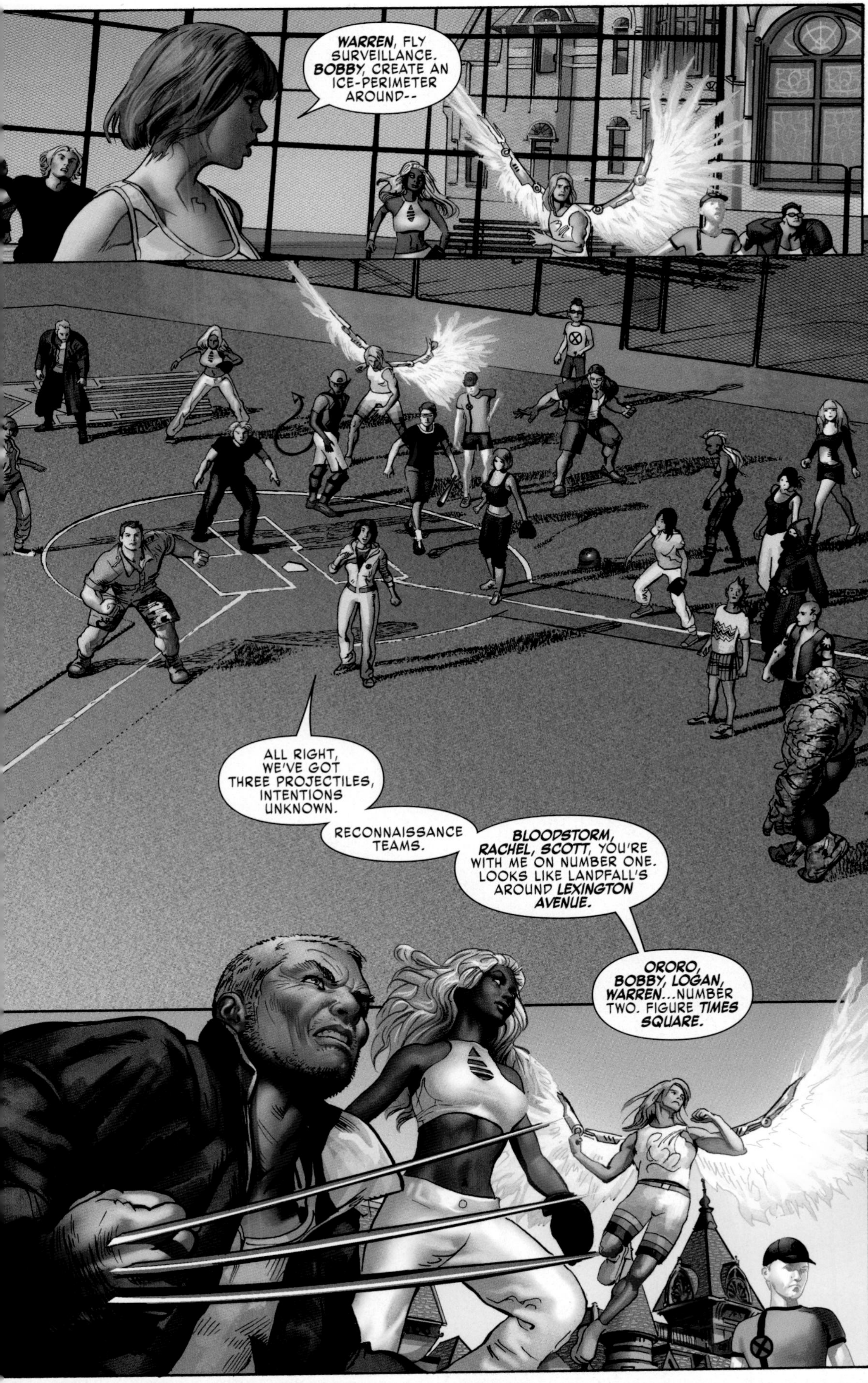
WARREN, FLY SURVEILLANCE. BOBBY, CREATE AN ICE-PERIMETER AROUND--
ALL RIGHT, WE'VE GOT THREE PROJECTILES, INTENTIONS UNKNOWN.
RECONNAISSANCE TEAMS.
BLOODSTORM, RACHEL, SCOTT, YOU'RE WITH ME ON NUMBER ONE. LOOKS LIKE LANDFALL'S AROUND LEXINGTON AVENUE.
ORORO, BOBBY, LOGAN, WARREN...NUMBER TWO. FIGURE TIMES SQUARE.

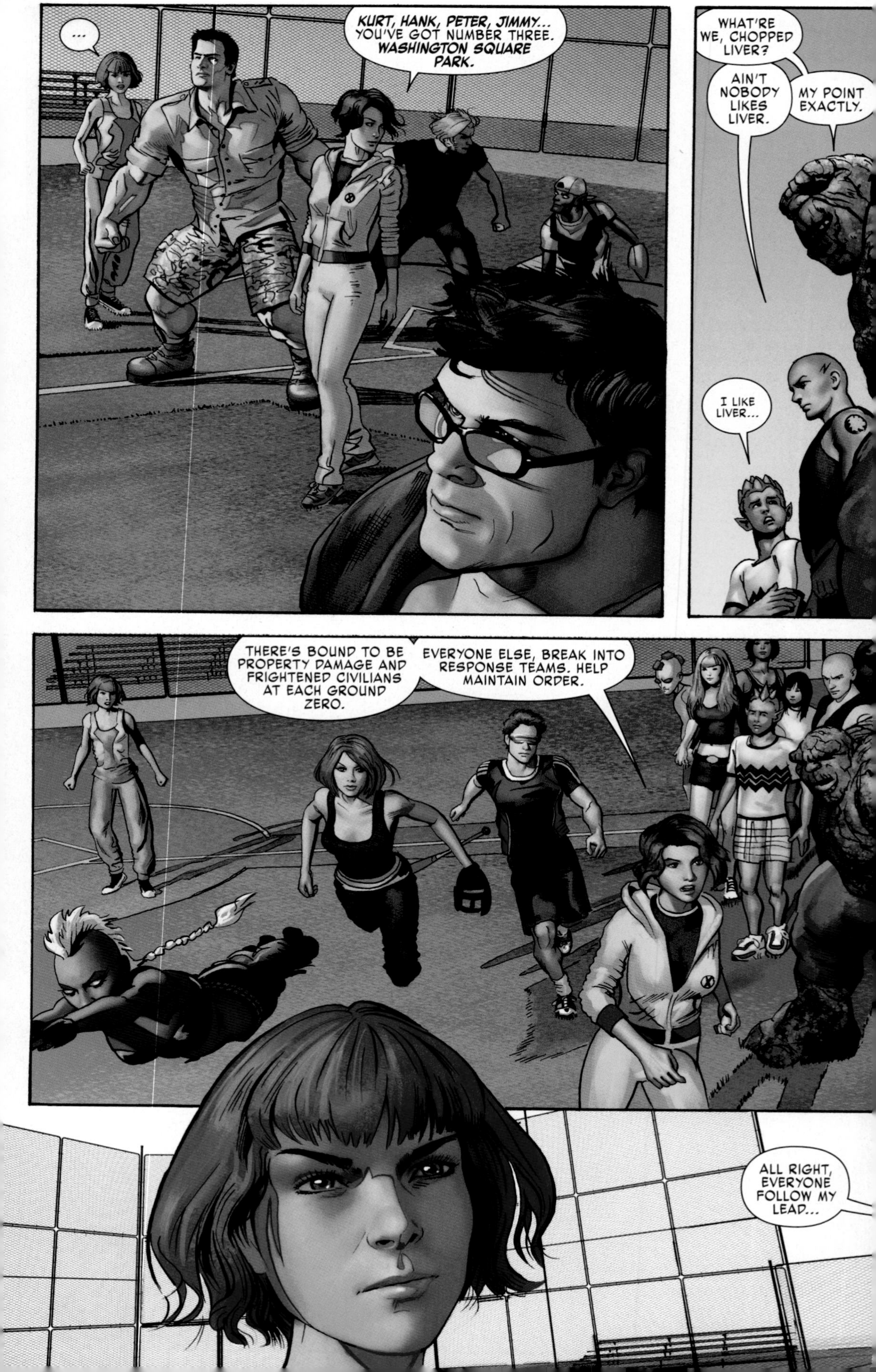
...
KURT, HANK, PETER, JIMMY... YOU'VE GOT NUMBER THREE. WASHINGTON SQUARE PARK.
WHAT'RE WE, CHOPPED LIVER?
AIN'T NOBODY LIKES LIVER.
MY POINT EXACTLY.
I LIKE LIVER...
THERE'S BOUND TO BE PROPERTY DAMAGE AND FRIGHTENED CIVILIANS AT EACH GROUND ZERO.
EVERYONE ELSE, BREAK INTO RESPONSE TEAMS. HELP MAINTAIN ORDER.
ALL RIGHT, EVERYONE FOLLOW MY LEAD...

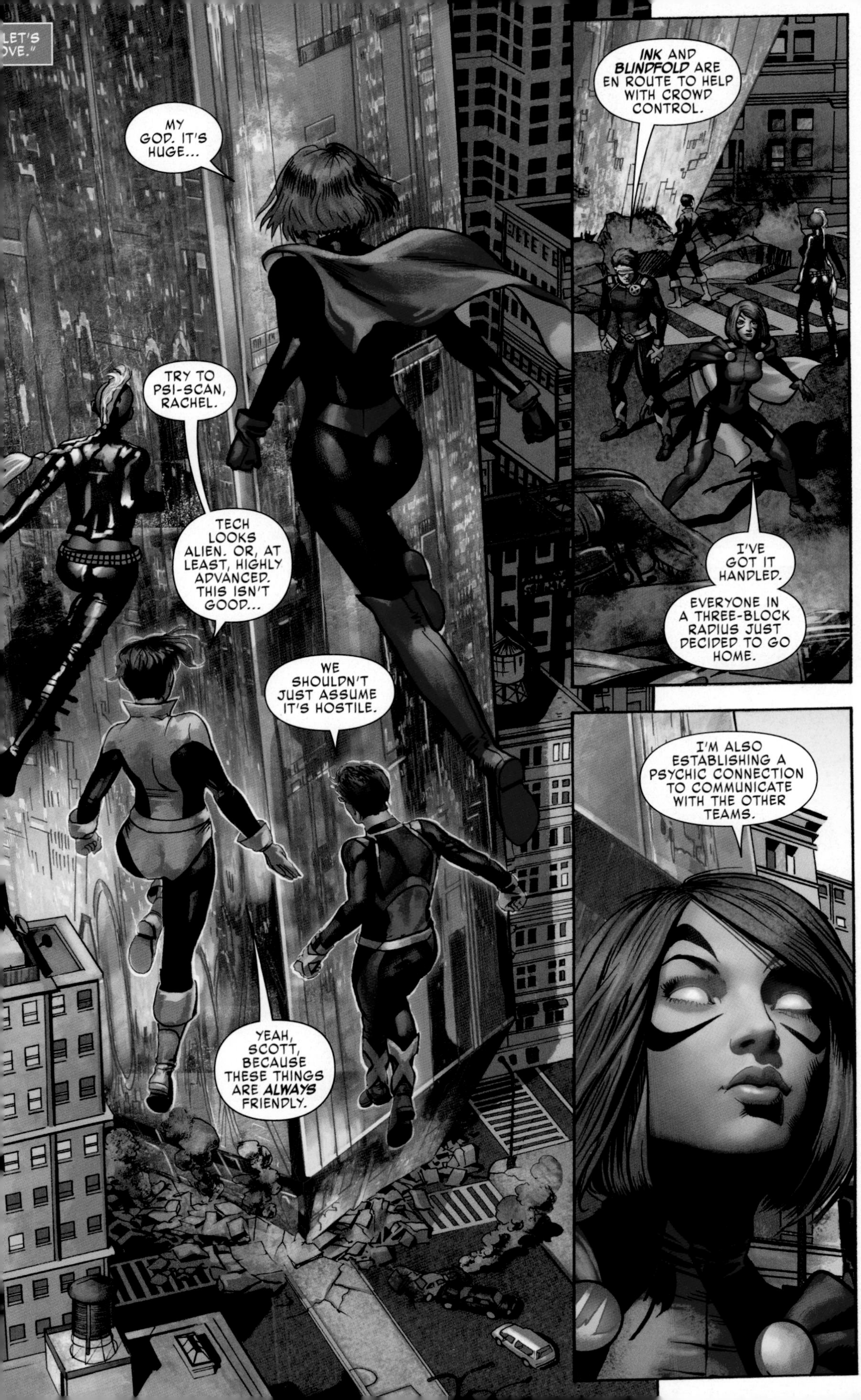
LET'S
...OVE."
MY GOD. IT'S HUGE...
TRY TO PSI-SCAN, RACHEL.
TECH LOOKS ALIEN. OR, AT LEAST, HIGHLY ADVANCED. THIS ISN'T GOOD...
WE SHOULDN'T JUST ASSUME IT'S HOSTILE.
YEAH, SCOTT, BECAUSE THESE THINGS ARE ALWAYS FRIENDLY.
INK AND BLINDFOLD ARE EN ROUTE TO HELP WITH CROWD CONTROL.
I'VE GOT IT HANDLED.
EVERYONE IN A THREE-BLOCK RADIUS JUST DECIDED TO GO HOME.
I'M ALSO ESTABLISHING A PSYCHIC CONNECTION TO COMMUNICATE WITH THE OTHER TEAMS.

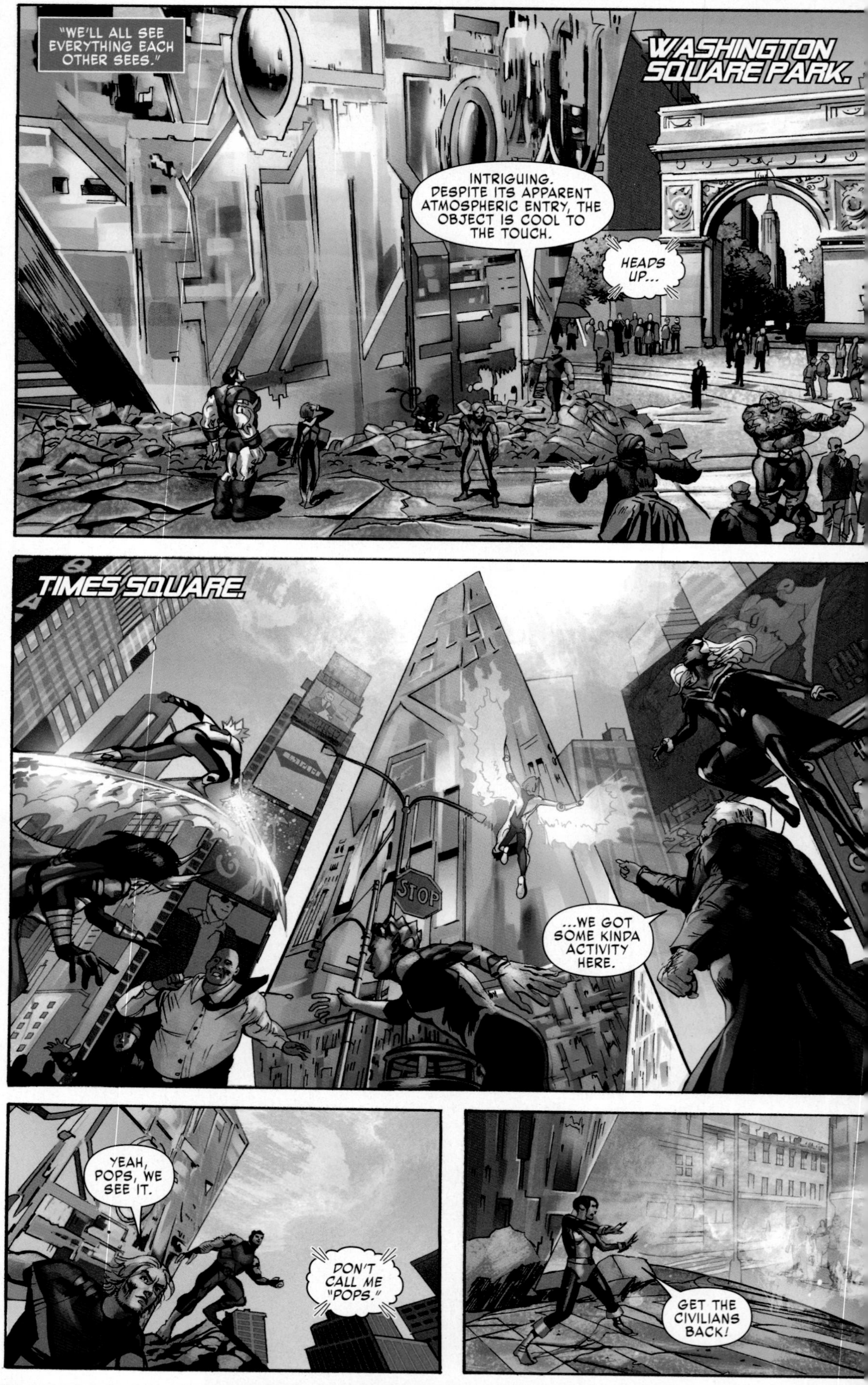
"WE'LL ALL SEE EVERYTHING EACH OTHER SEES."
WASHINGTON SQUARE PARK.
INTRIGUING. DESPITE ITS APPARENT ATMOSPHERIC ENTRY, THE OBJECT IS COOL TO THE TOUCH.
HEADS UP...
TIMES SQUARE.
...WE GOT SOME KINDA ACTIVITY HERE.
STOP
YEAH, POPS, WE SEE IT.
DON'T CALL ME "POPS."
GET THE CIVILIANS BACK!

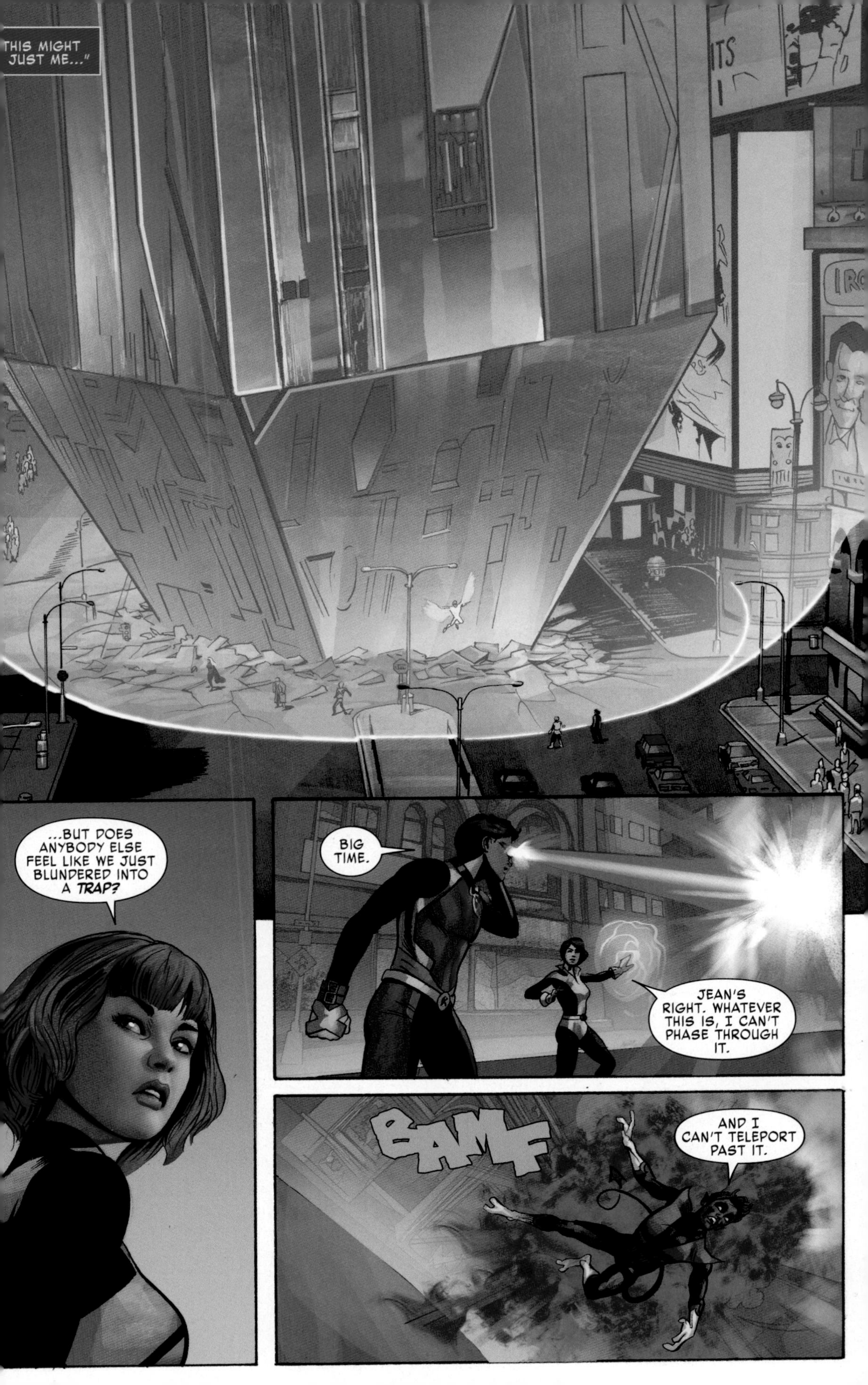
THIS MIGHT JUST ME..."
...BUT DOES ANYBODY ELSE FEEL LIKE WE JUST BLUNDERED INTO A *TRAP?*
BIG TIME.
JEAN'S RIGHT. WHATEVER THIS IS, I CAN'T PHASE THROUGH IT.
BAMF
AND I CAN'T TELEPORT PAST IT.

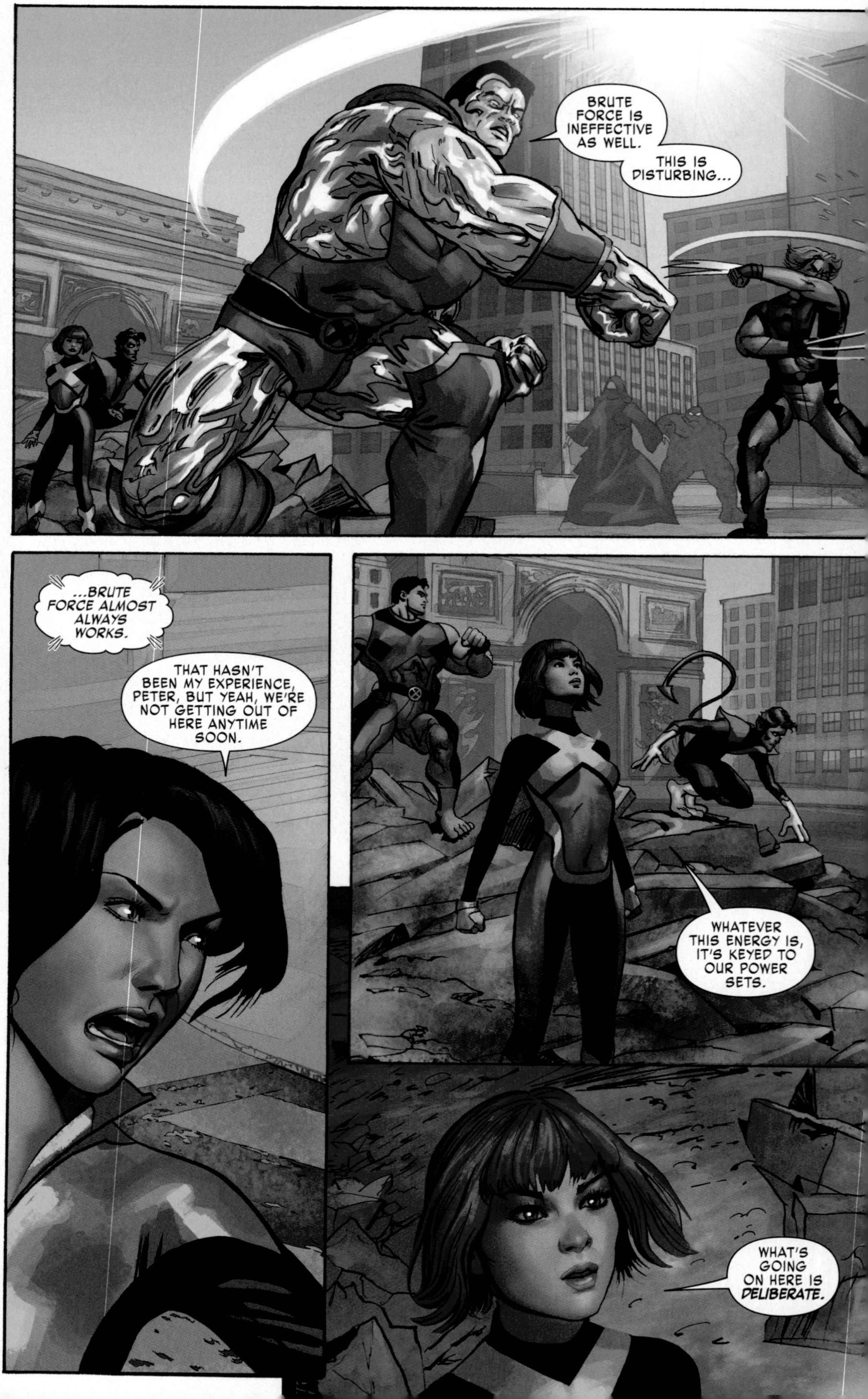
BRUTE FORCE IS INEFFECTIVE AS WELL.
THIS IS DISTURBING...
...BRUTE FORCE ALMOST ALWAYS WORKS.
THAT HASN'T BEEN MY EXPERIENCE, PETER, BUT YEAH, WE'RE NOT GETTING OUT OF HERE ANYTIME SOON.
WHATEVER THIS ENERGY IS, IT'S KEYED TO OUR POWER SETS.
WHAT'S GOING ON HERE IS *DELIBERATE.*

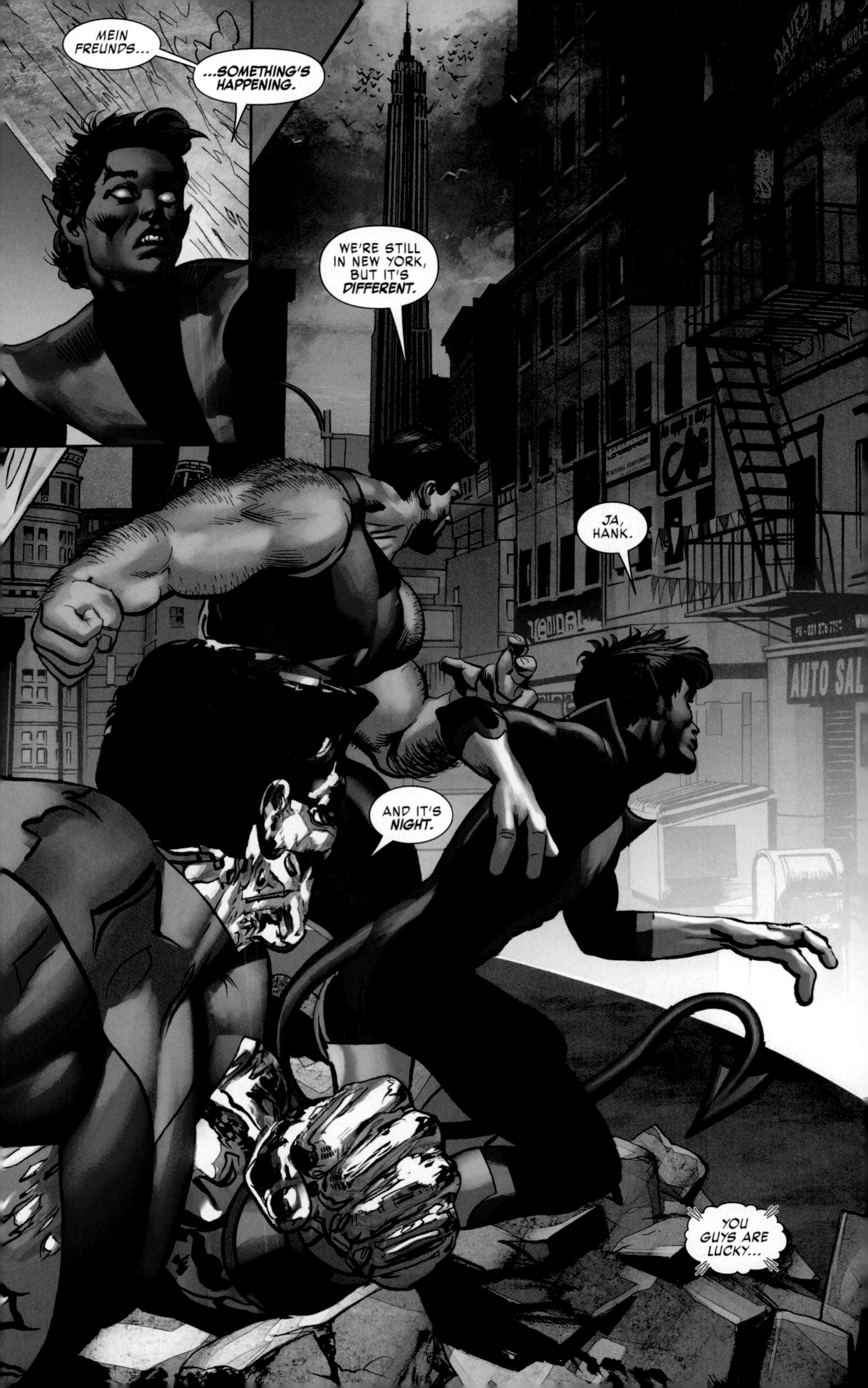
MEIN FREUNDS...
...SOMETHING'S HAPPENING.
WE'RE STILL IN NEW YORK, BUT IT'S *DIFFERENT.*
JA, HANK.
AND IT'S *NIGHT.*
YOU GUYS ARE LUCKY...
AUTO SAL

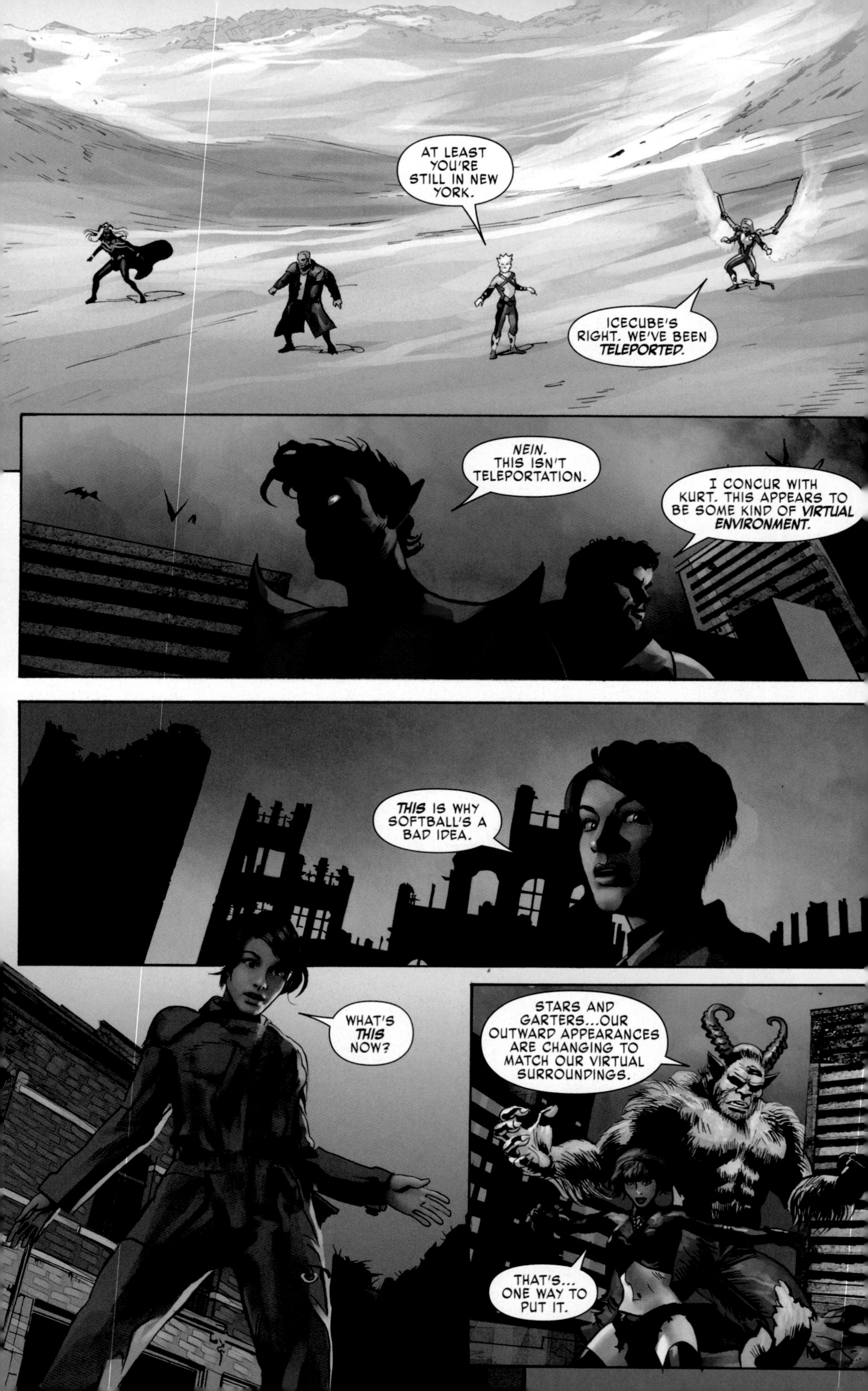
AT LEAST YOU'RE STILL IN NEW YORK.
ICECUBE'S RIGHT. WE'VE BEEN TELEPORTED.
NEIN. THIS ISN'T TELEPORTATION.
I CONCUR WITH KURT. THIS APPEARS TO BE SOME KIND OF VIRTUAL ENVIRONMENT.
THIS IS WHY SOFTBALL'S A BAD IDEA.
WHAT'S THIS NOW?
STARS AND GARTERS...OUR OUTWARD APPEARANCES ARE CHANGING TO MATCH OUR VIRTUAL SURROUNDINGS.
THAT'S... ONE WAY TO PUT IT.

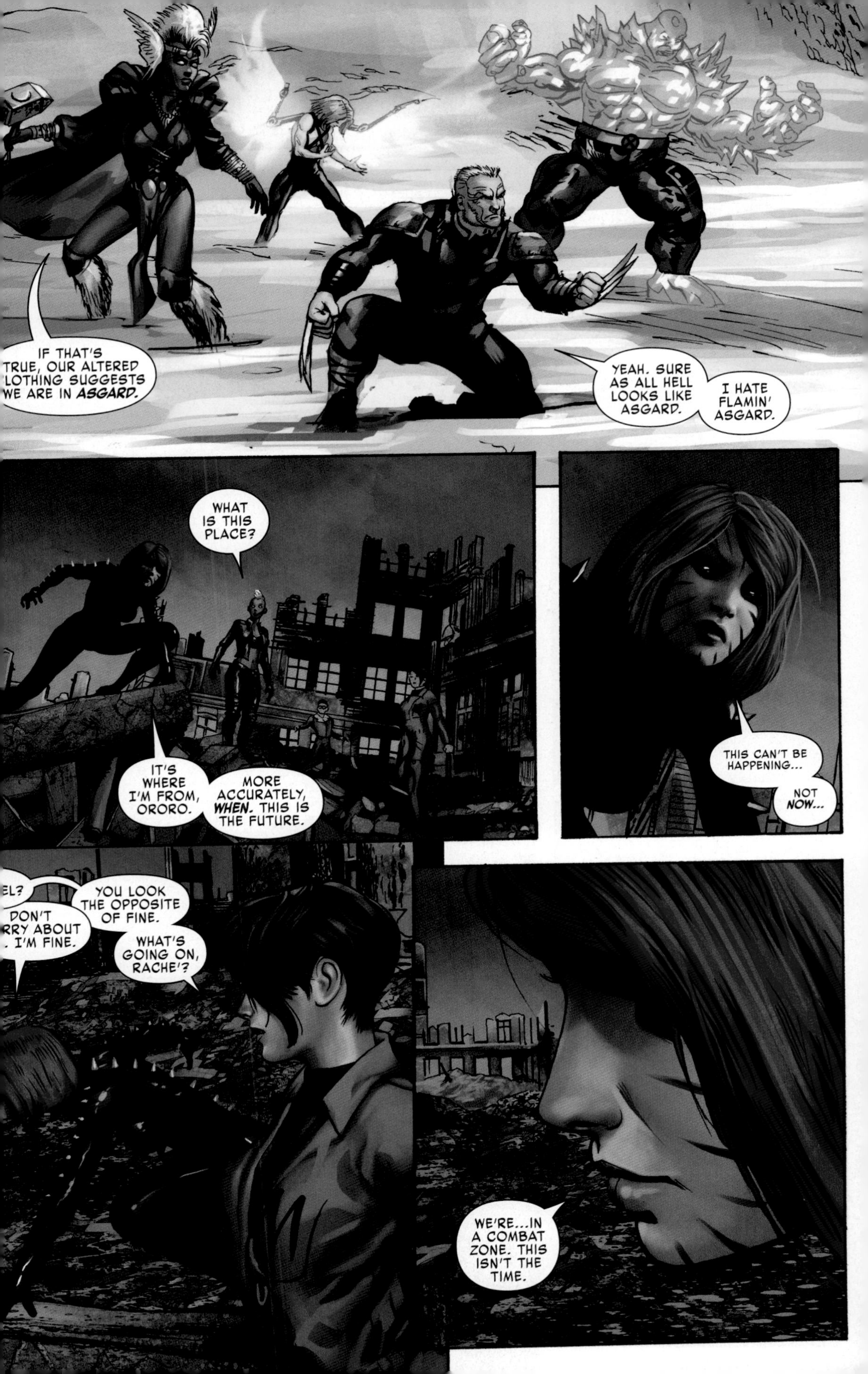
IF THAT'S TRUE, OUR ALTERED LOTHING SUGGESTS WE ARE IN ASGARD.
YEAH. SURE AS ALL HELL LOOKS LIKE ASGARD.
I HATE FLAMIN' ASGARD.
WHAT IS THIS PLACE?
IT'S WHERE I'M FROM, ORORO.
MORE ACCURATELY, WHEN. THIS IS THE FUTURE.
THIS CAN'T BE HAPPENING...
NOT NOW...
EL?
YOU LOOK THE OPPOSITE OF FINE.
DON'T RRY ABOUT . I'M FINE.
WHAT'S GOING ON, RACHE'?
WE'RE...IN A COMBAT ZONE. THIS ISN'T THE TIME.

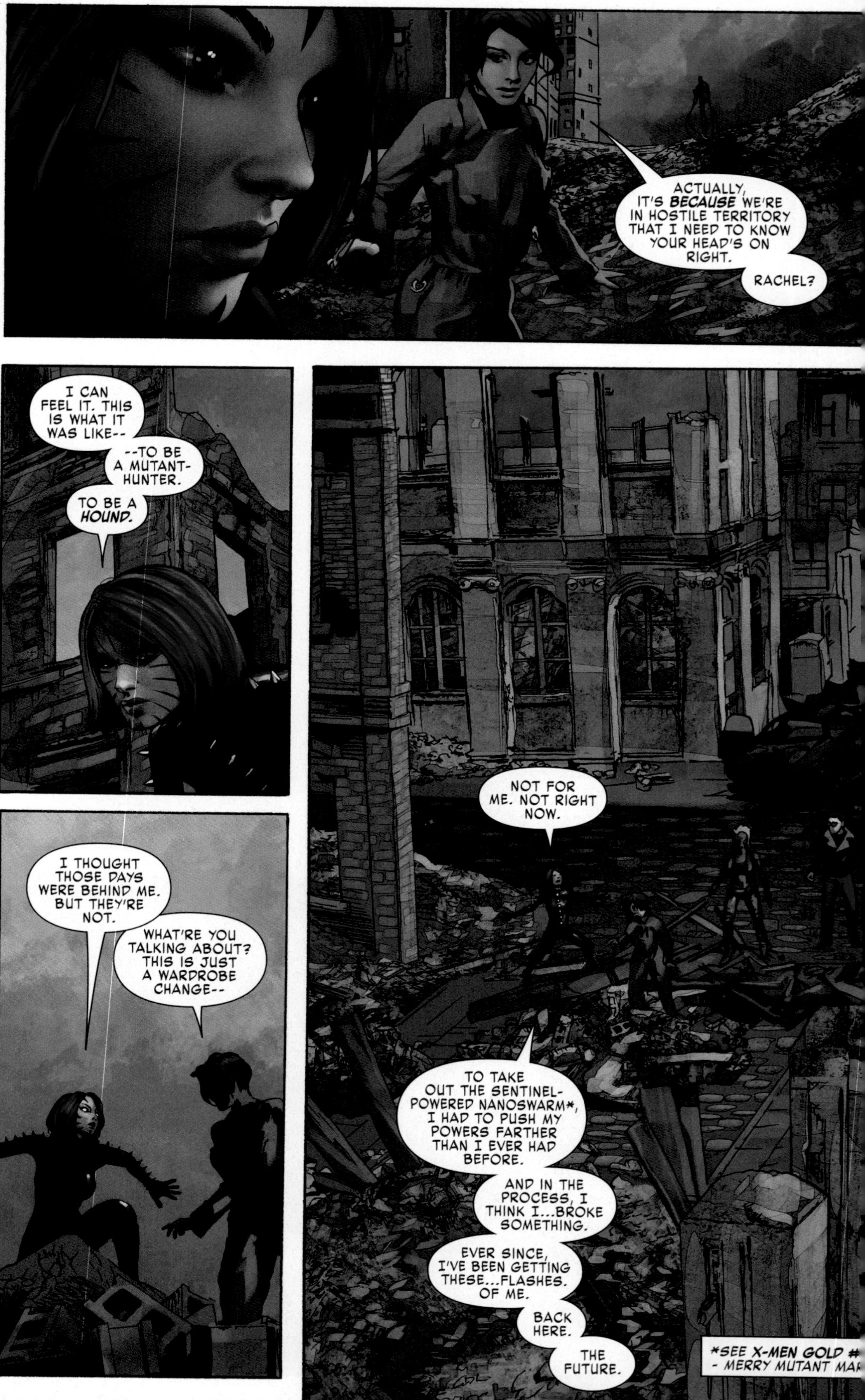
ACTUALLY, IT'S BECAUSE WE'RE IN HOSTILE TERRITORY THAT I NEED TO KNOW YOUR HEAD'S ON RIGHT.
RACHEL?
I CAN FEEL IT. THIS IS WHAT IT WAS LIKE--
--TO BE A MUTANT-HUNTER.
TO BE A HOUND.
I THOUGHT THOSE DAYS WERE BEHIND ME. BUT THEY'RE NOT.
WHAT'RE YOU TALKING ABOUT? THIS IS JUST A WARDROBE CHANGE--
NOT FOR ME. NOT RIGHT NOW.
TO TAKE OUT THE SENTINEL-POWERED NANOSWARM*, I HAD TO PUSH MY POWERS FARTHER THAN I EVER HAD BEFORE.
AND IN THE PROCESS, I THINK I...BROKE SOMETHING.
EVER SINCE, I'VE BEEN GETTING THESE...FLASHES. OF ME.
BACK HERE.
THE FUTURE.
*SEE X-MEN GOLD #
- MERRY MUTANT MA

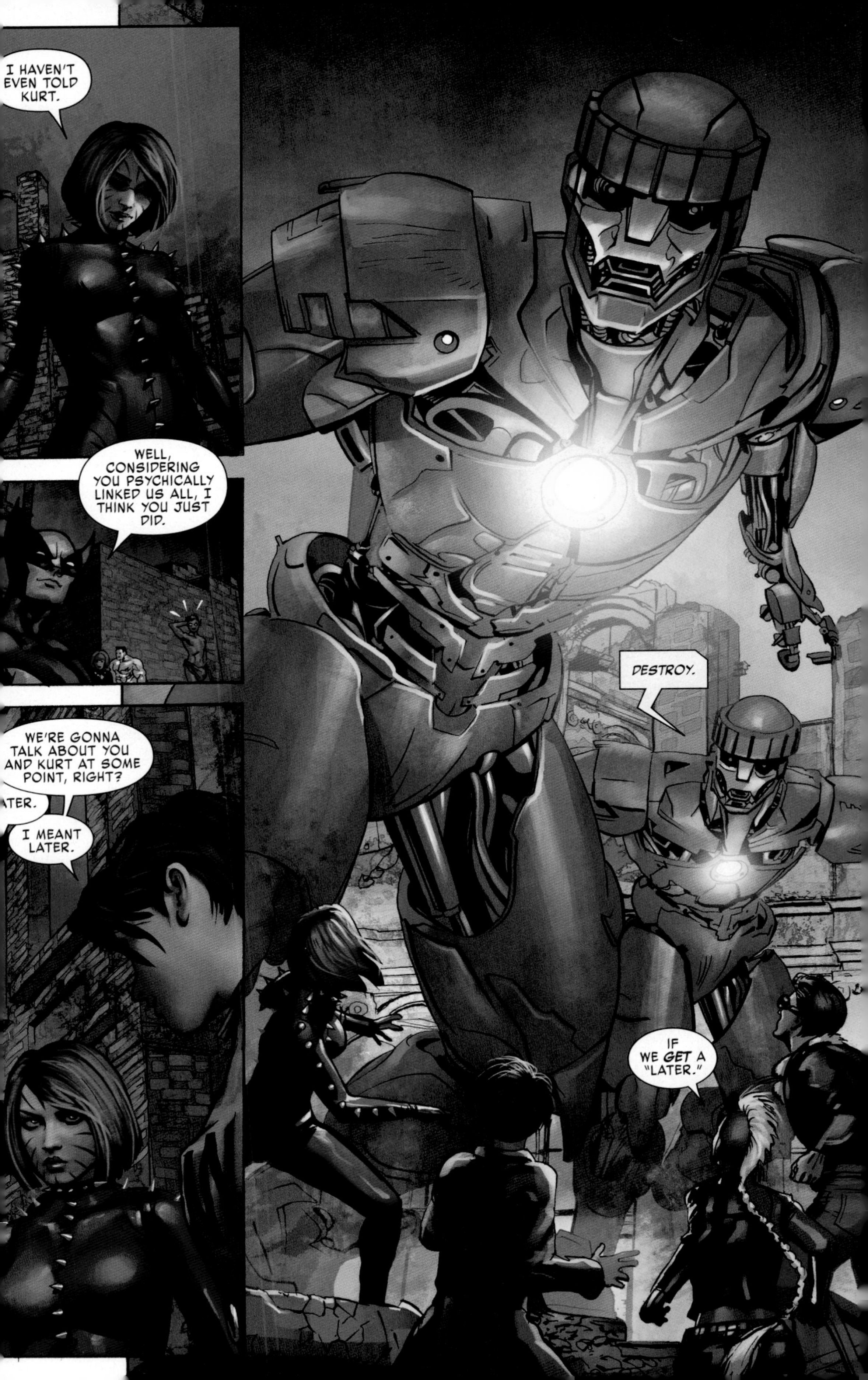
I HAVEN'T EVEN TOLD KURT.
WELL, CONSIDERING YOU PSYCHICALLY LINKED US ALL, I THINK YOU JUST DID.
WE'RE GONNA TALK ABOUT YOU AND KURT AT SOME POINT, RIGHT?
LATER.
I MEANT LATER.
DESTROY.
IF WE GET A "LATER."

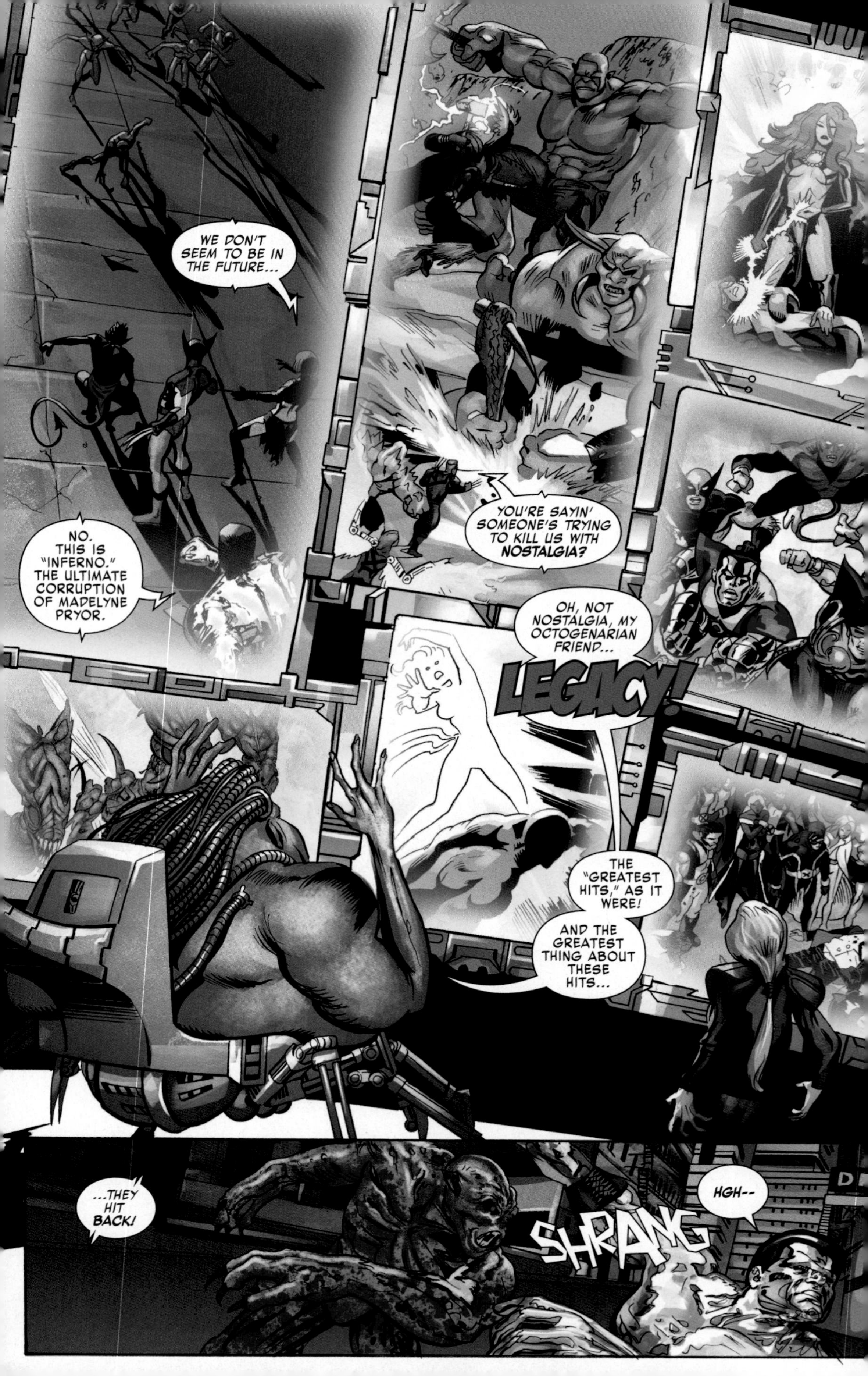
WE DON'T SEEM TO BE IN THE FUTURE...
YOU'RE SAYIN' SOMEONE'S TRYING TO KILL US WITH NOSTALGIA?
NO. THIS IS "INFERNO." THE ULTIMATE CORRUPTION OF MADELYNE PRYOR.
OH, NOT NOSTALGIA, MY OCTOGENARIAN FRIEND...
LEGACY!
THE "GREATEST HITS," AS IT WERE!
AND THE GREATEST THING ABOUT THESE HITS...
...THEY HIT BACK!
HGH--
SHRANG

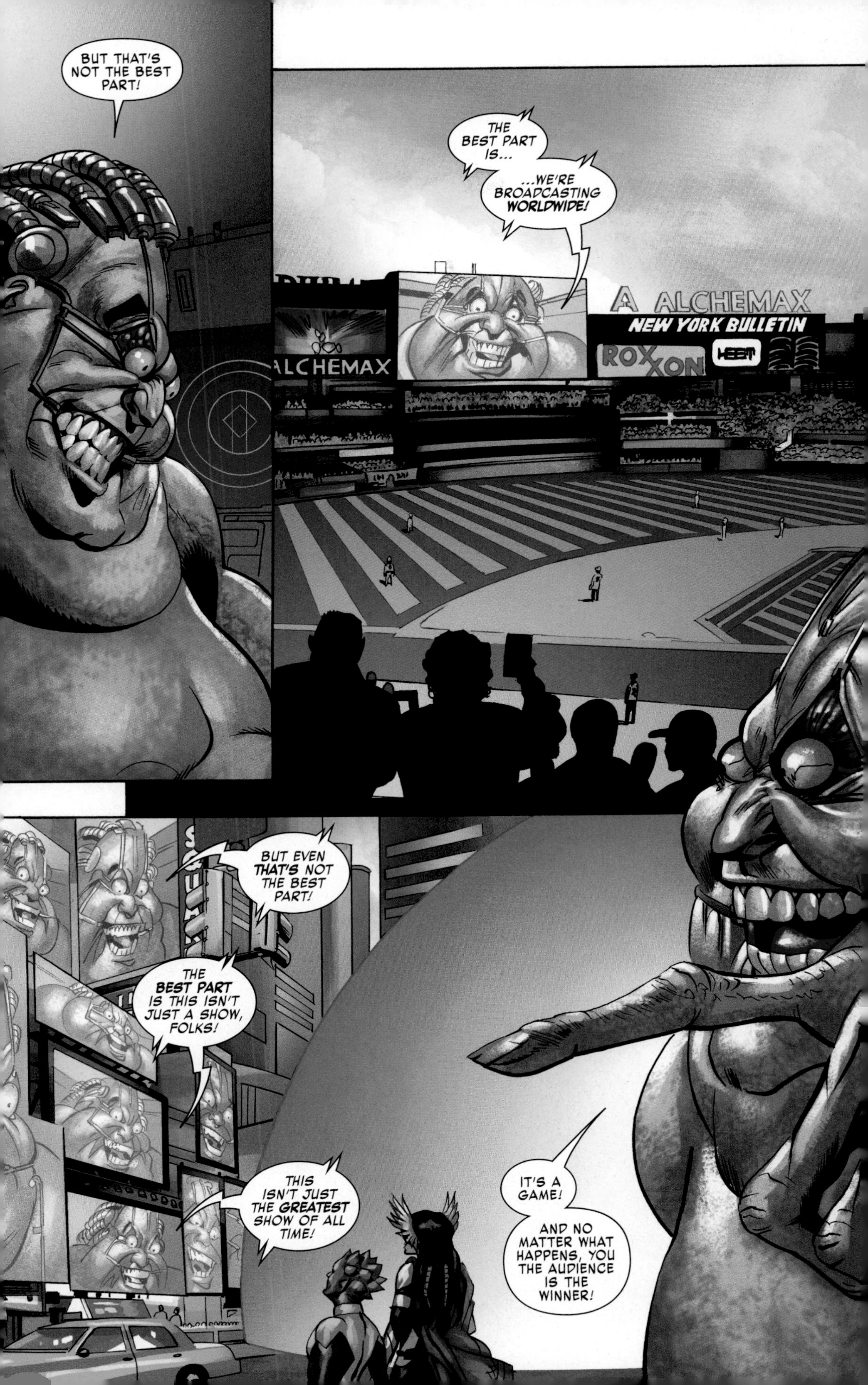
BUT THAT'S NOT THE BEST PART!
THE BEST PART IS...
...WE'RE BROADCASTING WORLDWIDE!
A ALCHEMAX
NEW YORK BULLETIN
ROXXON
ALCHEMAX
BUT EVEN THAT'S NOT THE BEST PART!
THE BEST PART IS THIS ISN'T JUST A SHOW, FOLKS!
THIS ISN'T JUST THE GREATEST SHOW OF ALL TIME!
IT'S A GAME!
AND NO MATTER WHAT HAPPENS, YOU THE AUDIENCE IS THE WINNER!

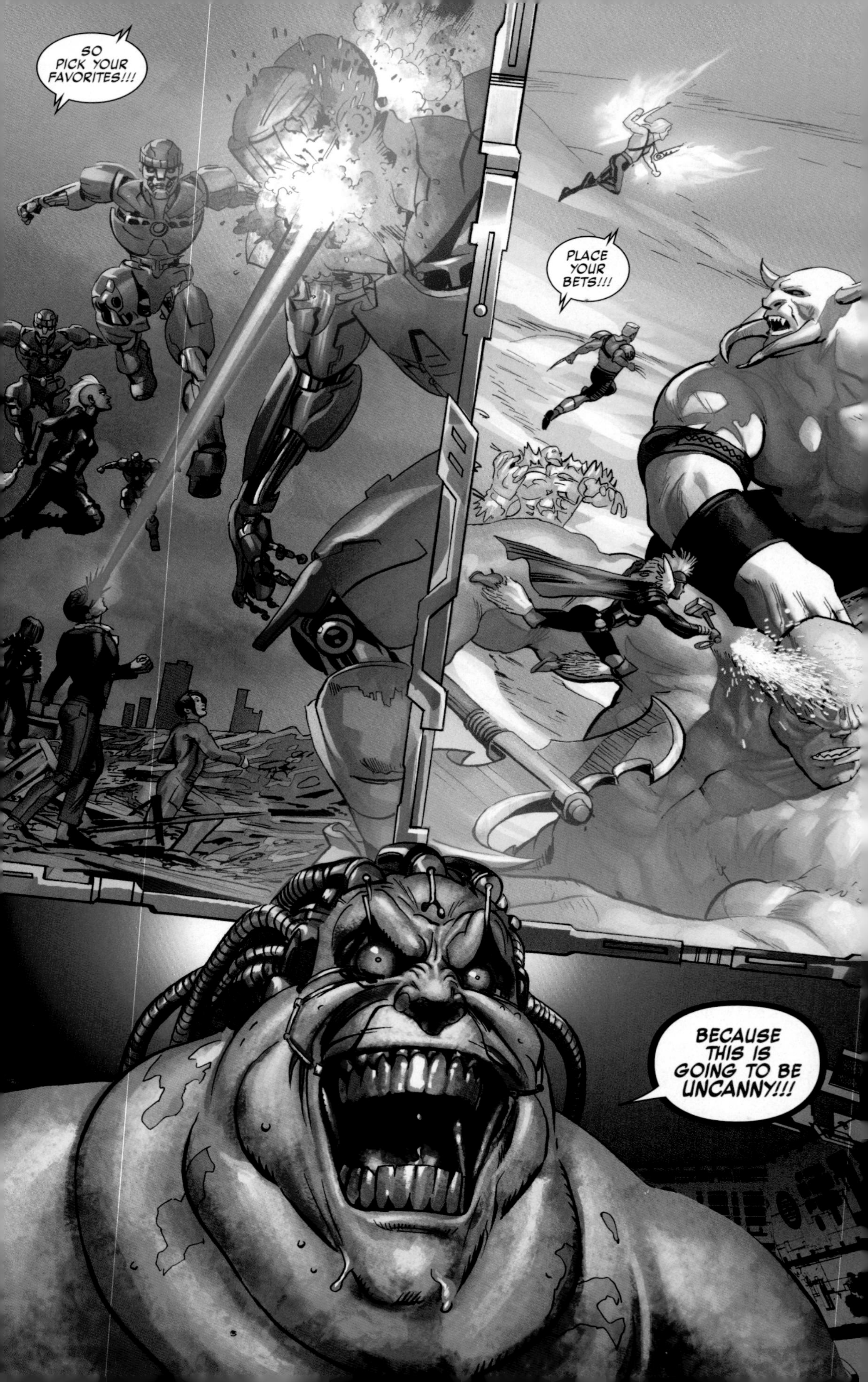
SO PICK YOUR FAVORITES!!!
PLACE YOUR BETS!!!
BECAUSE THIS IS GOING TO BE UNCANNY!!!

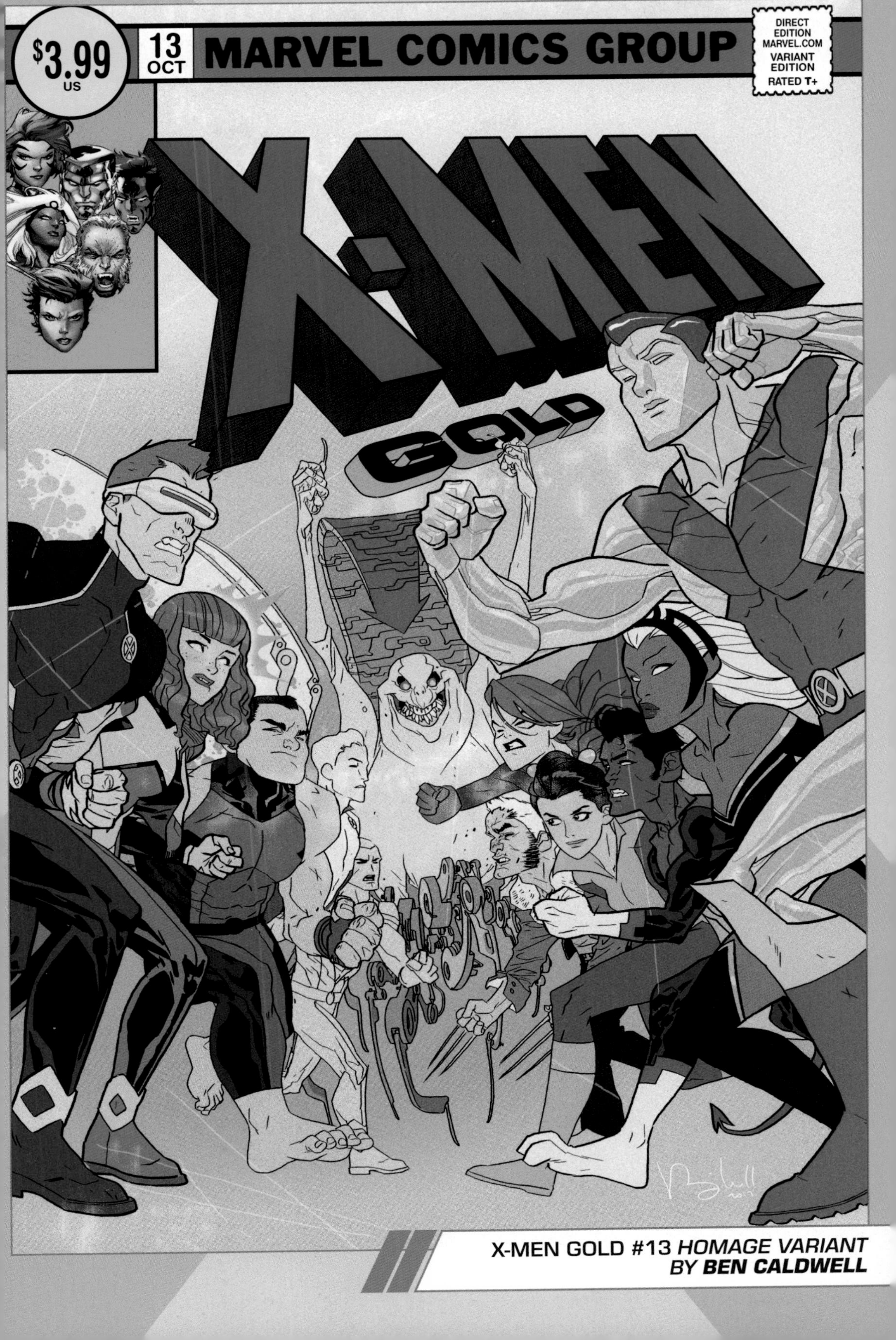
$3.99
US
13
OCT
MARVEL COMICS GROUP
DIRECT EDITION
MARVEL.COM
VARIANT EDITION
RATED T+
X-MEN
GOLD

X-MEN GOLD #13 *HOMAGE VARIANT*
BY ***BEN CALDWELL***

X-MEN BLUE #13

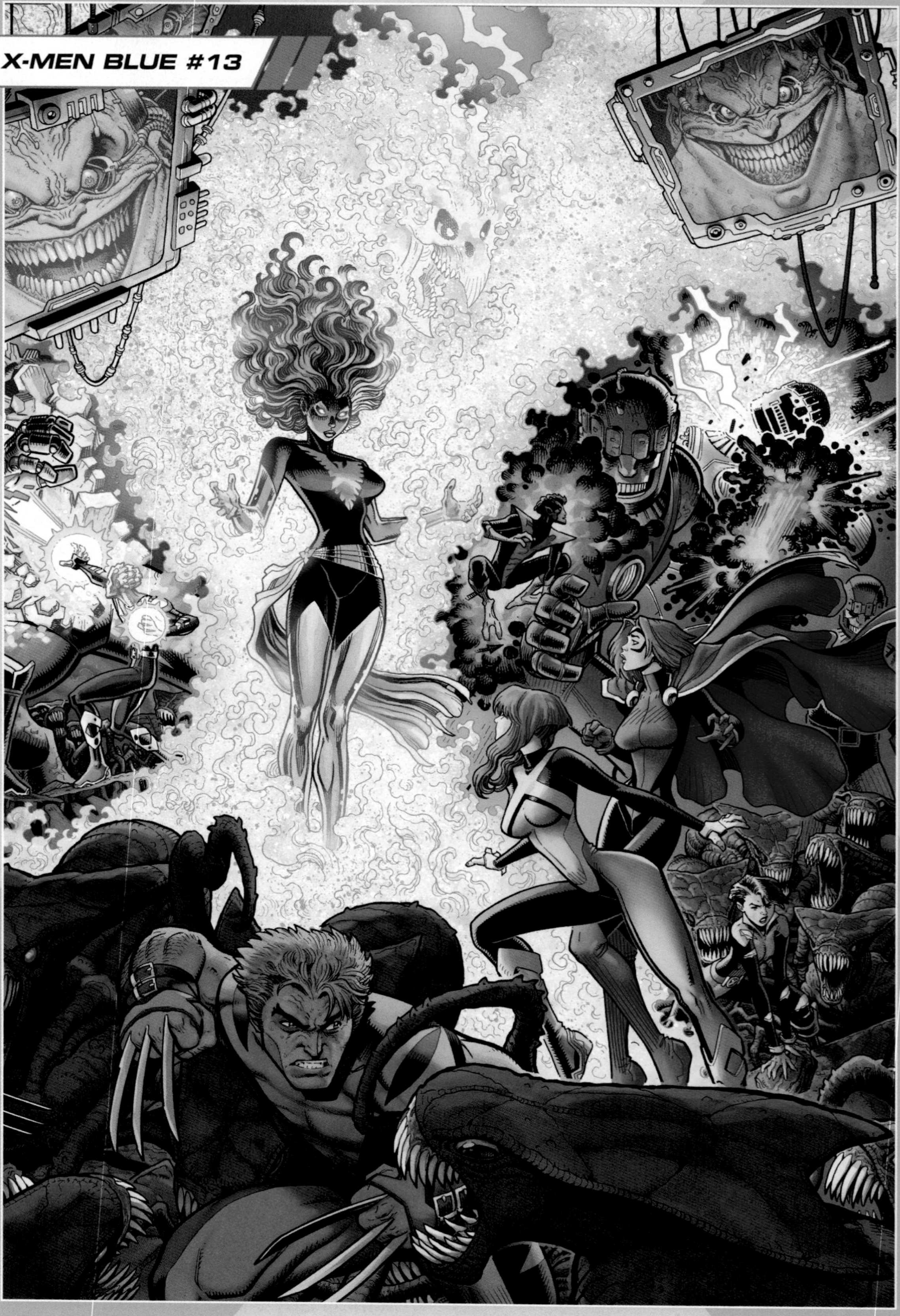

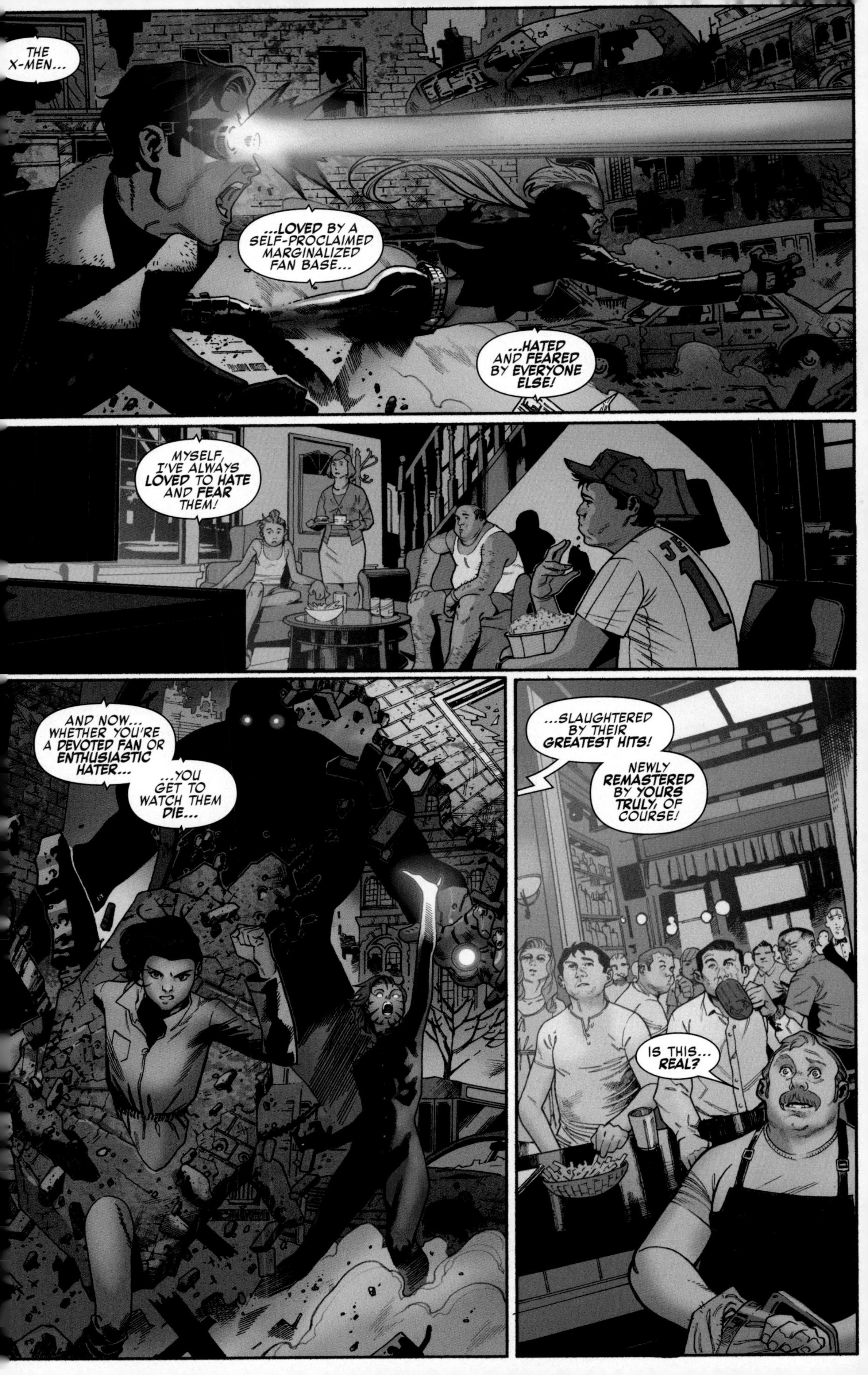
THE X-MEN...
...LOVED BY A SELF-PROCLAIMED MARGINALIZED FAN BASE...
...HATED AND FEARED BY EVERYONE ELSE!
MYSELF, I'VE ALWAYS LOVED TO HATE AND FEAR THEM!
AND NOW... WHETHER YOU'RE A DEVOTED FAN OR ENTHUSIASTIC HATER...
...YOU GET TO WATCH THEM DIE...
...SLAUGHTERED BY THEIR GREATEST HITS!
NEWLY REMASTERED BY YOURS TRULY, OF COURSE!
IS THIS... REAL?

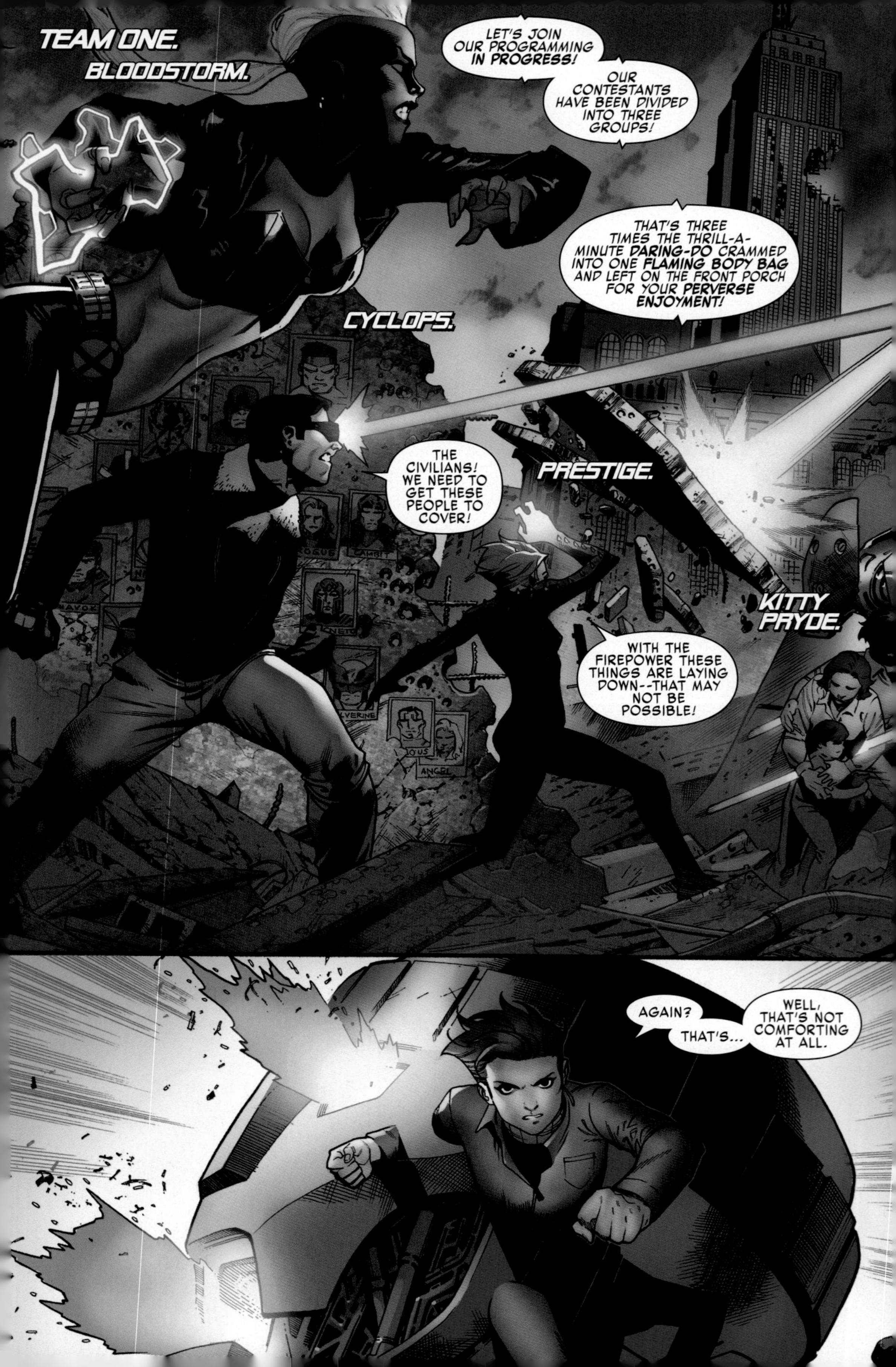
TEAM ONE.
BLOODSTORM.
LET'S JOIN OUR PROGRAMMING IN PROGRESS!
OUR CONTESTANTS HAVE BEEN DIVIDED INTO THREE GROUPS!
THAT'S THREE TIMES THE THRILL-A-MINUTE DARING-DO CRAMMED INTO ONE FLAMING BODY BAG AND LEFT ON THE FRONT PORCH FOR YOUR PERVERSE ENJOYMENT!
CYCLOPS.
THE CIVILIANS! WE NEED TO GET THESE PEOPLE TO COVER!
PRESTIGE.
KITTY PRYDE.
WITH THE FIREPOWER THESE THINGS ARE LAYING DOWN--THAT MAY NOT BE POSSIBLE!
AGAIN?
THAT'S...
WELL, THAT'S NOT COMFORTING AT ALL.

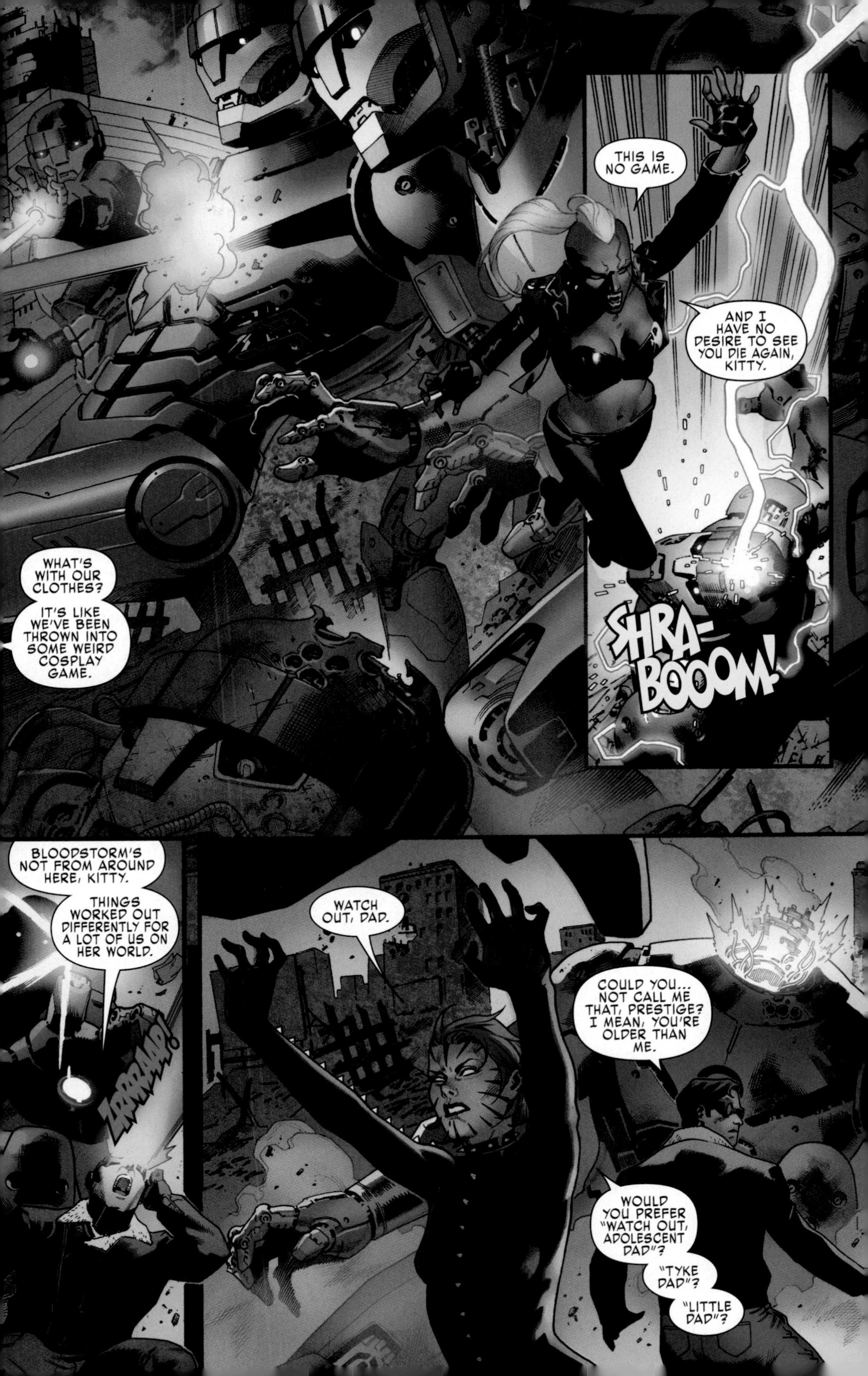
THIS IS NO GAME.
AND I HAVE NO DESIRE TO SEE YOU DIE AGAIN, KITTY.
WHAT'S WITH OUR CLOTHES?
IT'S LIKE WE'VE BEEN THROWN INTO SOME WEIRD COSPLAY GAME.
SHRA-BOOOM!
BLOODSTORM'S NOT FROM AROUND HERE, KITTY.
THINGS WORKED OUT DIFFERENTLY FOR A LOT OF US ON HER WORLD.
ZRRRAAP!
WATCH OUT, DAD.
COULD YOU... NOT CALL ME THAT, PRESTIGE? I MEAN, YOU'RE OLDER THAN ME.
WOULD YOU PREFER "WATCH OUT, ADOLESCENT DAD"?
"TYKE DAD"?
"LITTLE DAD"?

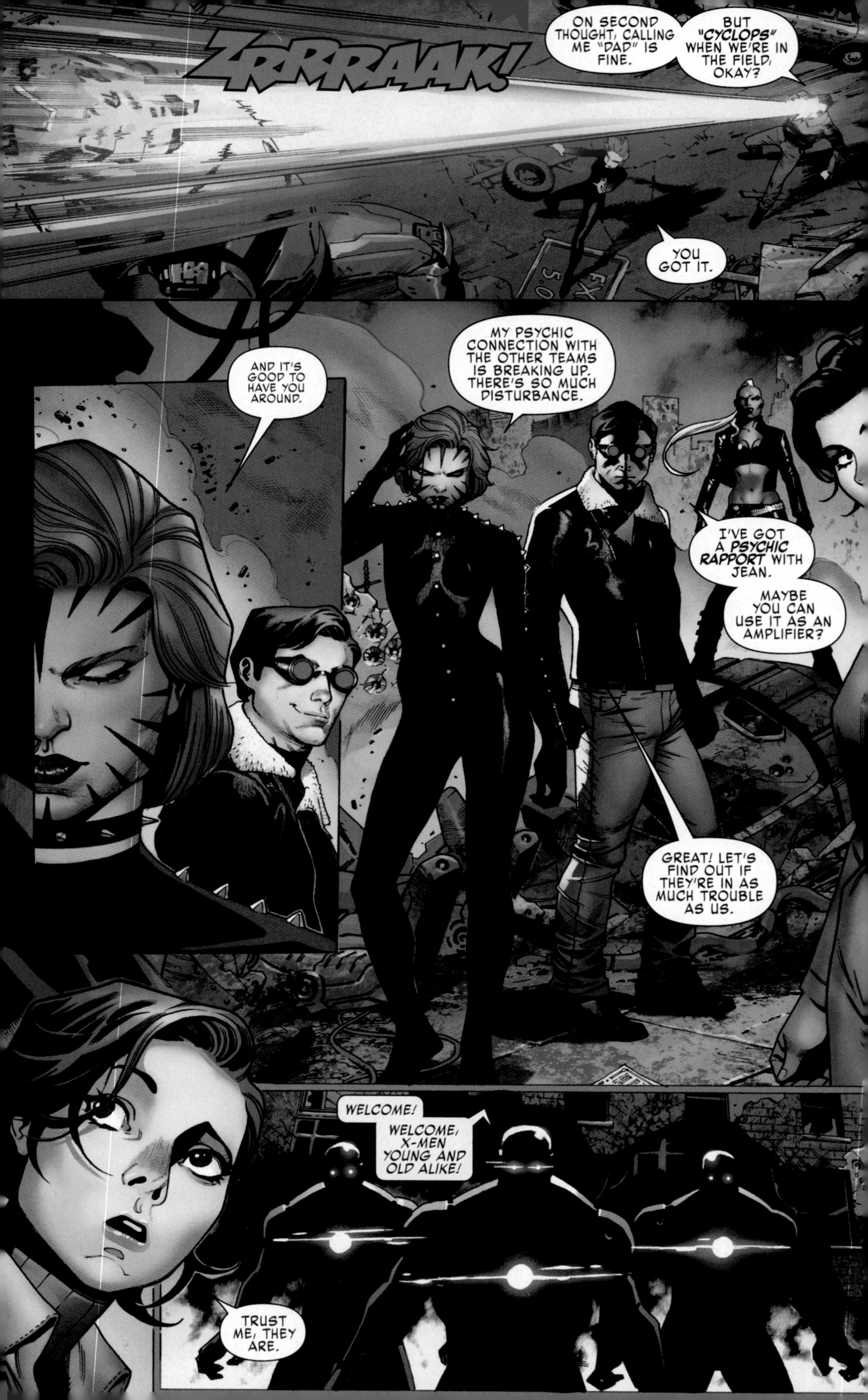
ZRRRAAK!
ON SECOND THOUGHT, CALLING ME "DAD" IS FINE.
BUT "CYCLOPS" WHEN WE'RE IN THE FIELD, OKAY?
YOU GOT IT.
AND IT'S GOOD TO HAVE YOU AROUND.
MY PSYCHIC CONNECTION WITH THE OTHER TEAMS IS BREAKING UP. THERE'S SO MUCH DISTURBANCE.
I'VE GOT A PSYCHIC RAPPORT WITH JEAN.
MAYBE YOU CAN USE IT AS AN AMPLIFIER?
GREAT! LET'S FIND OUT IF THEY'RE IN AS MUCH TROUBLE AS US.
WELCOME!
WELCOME, X-MEN YOUNG AND OLD ALIKE!
TRUST ME, THEY ARE.

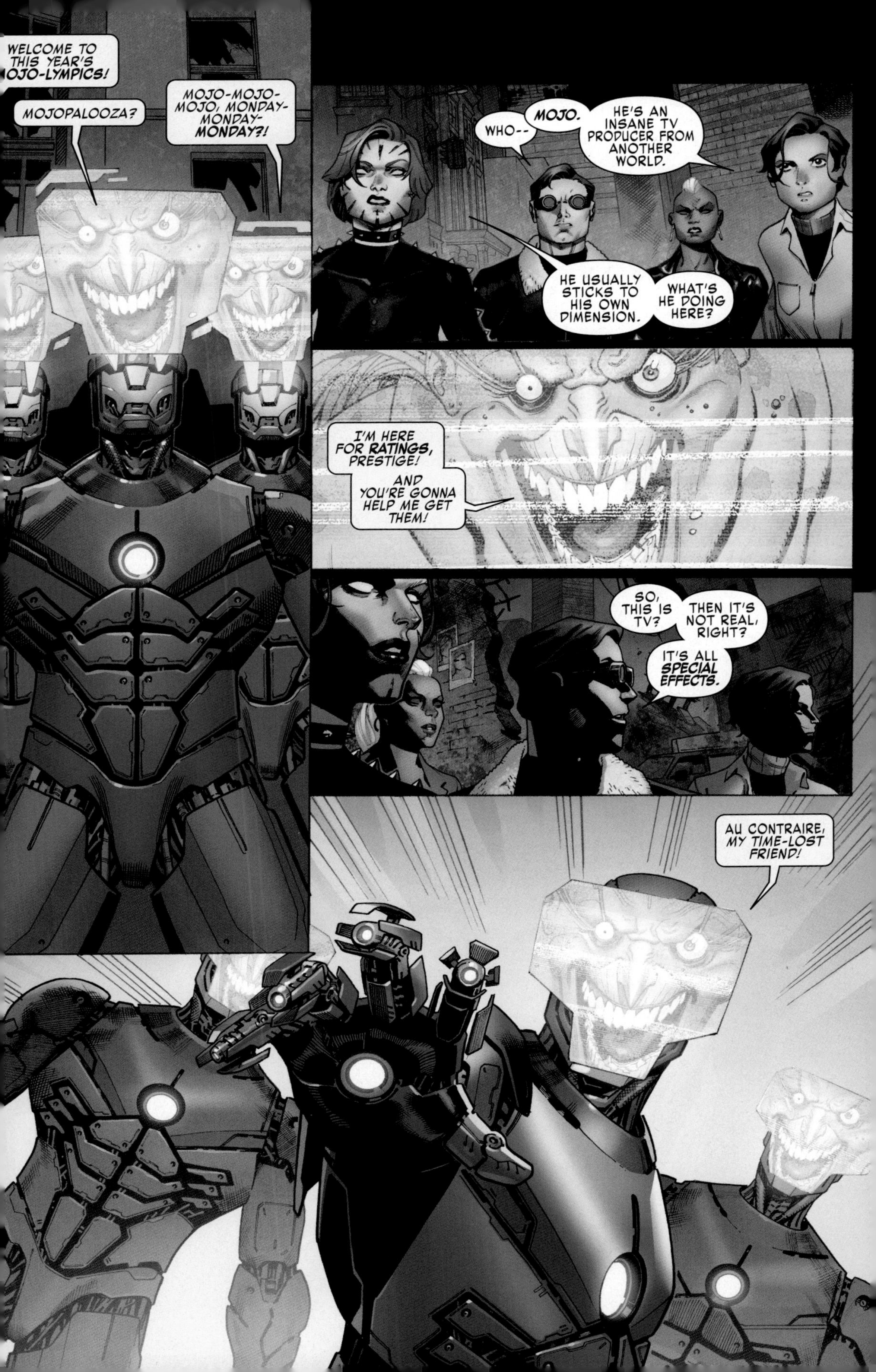
WELCOME TO THIS YEAR'S MOJO-LYMPICS!
MOJOPALOOZA?
MOJO-MOJO-MOJO, MONDAY-MONDAY-MONDAY?!
WHO--
MOJO.
HE'S AN INSANE TV PRODUCER FROM ANOTHER WORLD.
HE USUALLY STICKS TO HIS OWN DIMENSION.
WHAT'S HE DOING HERE?
I'M HERE FOR RATINGS, PRESTIGE!
AND YOU'RE GONNA HELP ME GET THEM!
SO, THIS IS TV?
THEN IT'S NOT REAL, RIGHT?
IT'S ALL SPECIAL EFFECTS.
AU CONTRAIRE, MY TIME-LOST FRIEND!

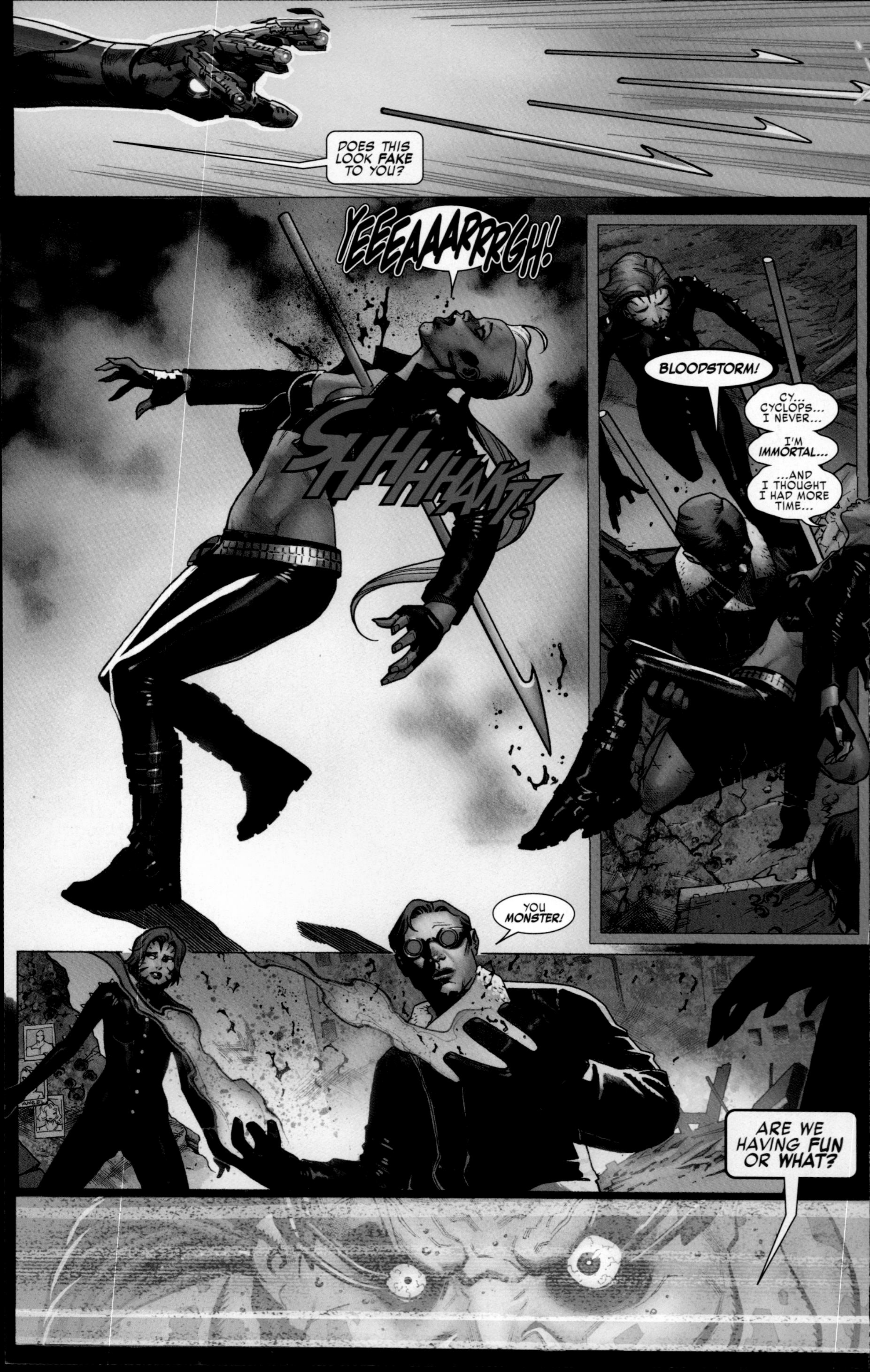
DOES THIS LOOK FAKE TO YOU?
YEEEAAARRRGH!
SHHHHAKT!
BLOODSTORM!
CY... CYCLOPS... I NEVER...
I'M IMMORTAL...
...AND I THOUGHT I HAD MORE TIME...
YOU MONSTER!
ARE WE HAVING FUN OR WHAT?

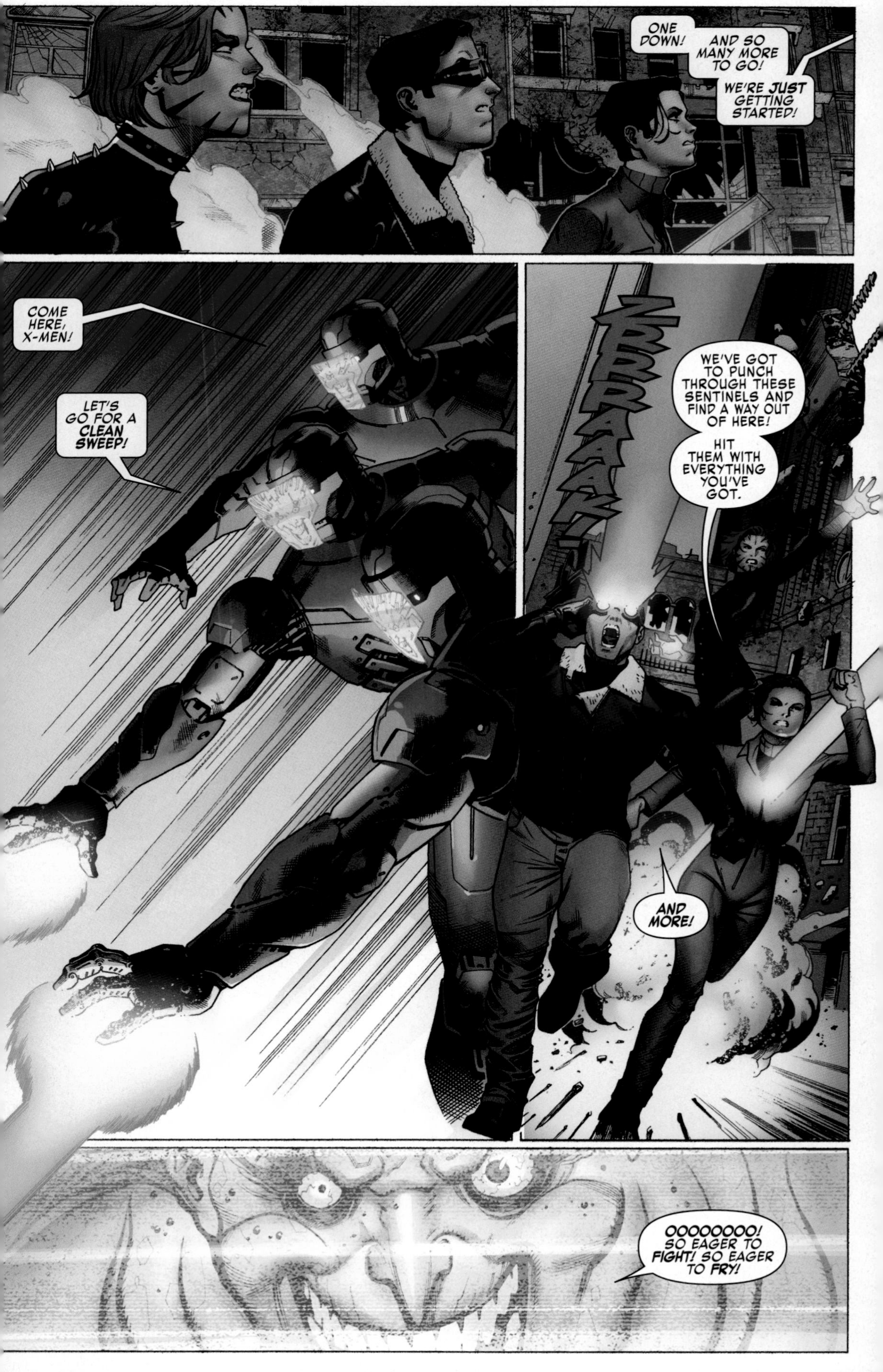
ONE DOWN!
AND SO MANY MORE TO GO!
WE'RE JUST GETTING STARTED!
COME HERE, X-MEN!
LET'S GO FOR A CLEAN SWEEP!
ZZRRAAAAK!!
WE'VE GOT TO PUNCH THROUGH THESE SENTINELS AND FIND A WAY OUT OF HERE!
HIT THEM WITH EVERYTHING YOU'VE GOT.
AND MORE!
OOOOOOOO! SO EAGER TO FIGHT! SO EAGER TO FRY!

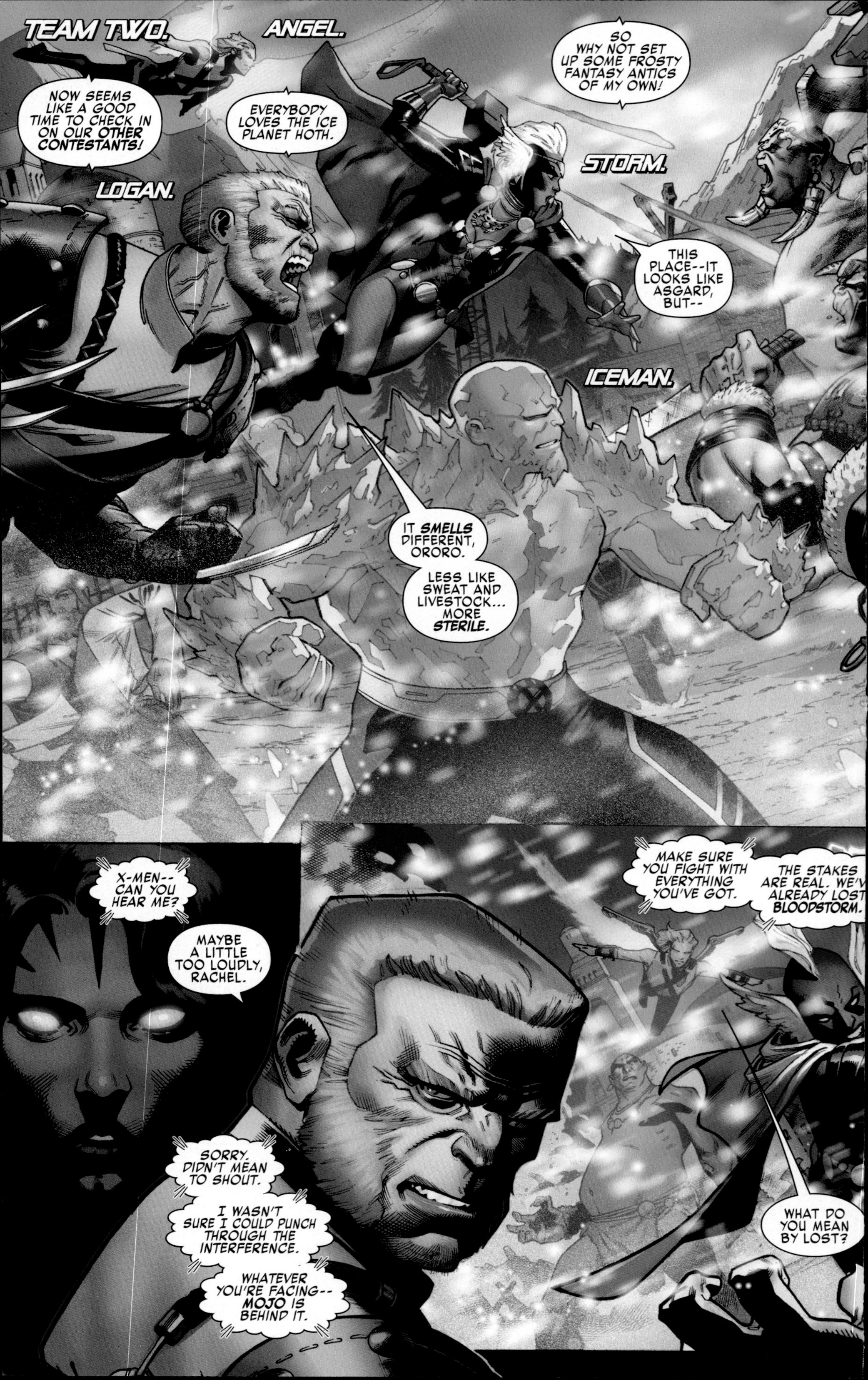
TEAM TWO.
ANGEL.
NOW SEEMS LIKE A GOOD TIME TO CHECK IN ON OUR OTHER CONTESTANTS!
EVERYBODY LOVES THE ICE PLANET HOTH.
SO WHY NOT SET UP SOME FROSTY FANTASY ANTICS OF MY OWN!
LOGAN.
STORM.
THIS PLACE--IT LOOKS LIKE ASGARD, BUT--
ICEMAN.
IT SMELLS DIFFERENT, ORORO.
LESS LIKE SWEAT AND LIVESTOCK... MORE STERILE.
X-MEN--CAN YOU HEAR ME?
MAYBE A LITTLE TOO LOUDLY, RACHEL.
MAKE SURE YOU FIGHT WITH EVERYTHING YOU'VE GOT.
THE STAKES ARE REAL. WE'VE ALREADY LOST BLOODSTORM.
SORRY. DIDN'T MEAN TO SHOUT.
I WASN'T SURE I COULD PUNCH THROUGH THE INTERFERENCE.
WHATEVER YOU'RE FACING--MOJO IS BEHIND IT.
WHAT DO YOU MEAN BY LOST?

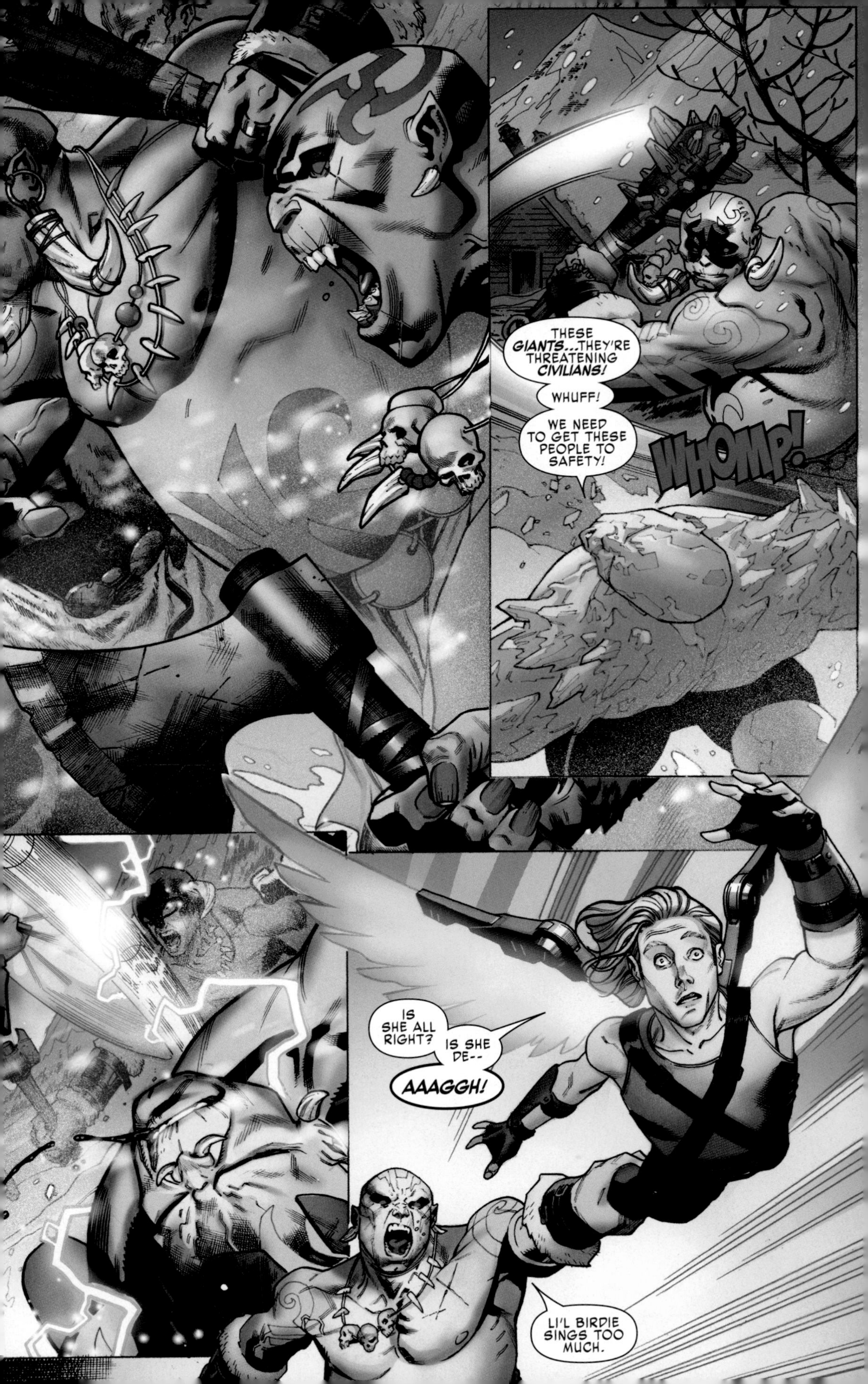
THESE GIANTS...THEY'RE THREATENING CIVILIANS!
WHUFF!
WE NEED TO GET THESE PEOPLE TO SAFETY!
WHOMP!
IS SHE ALL RIGHT?
IS SHE DE--
AAAGGH!
LI'L BIRDIE SINGS TOO MUCH.

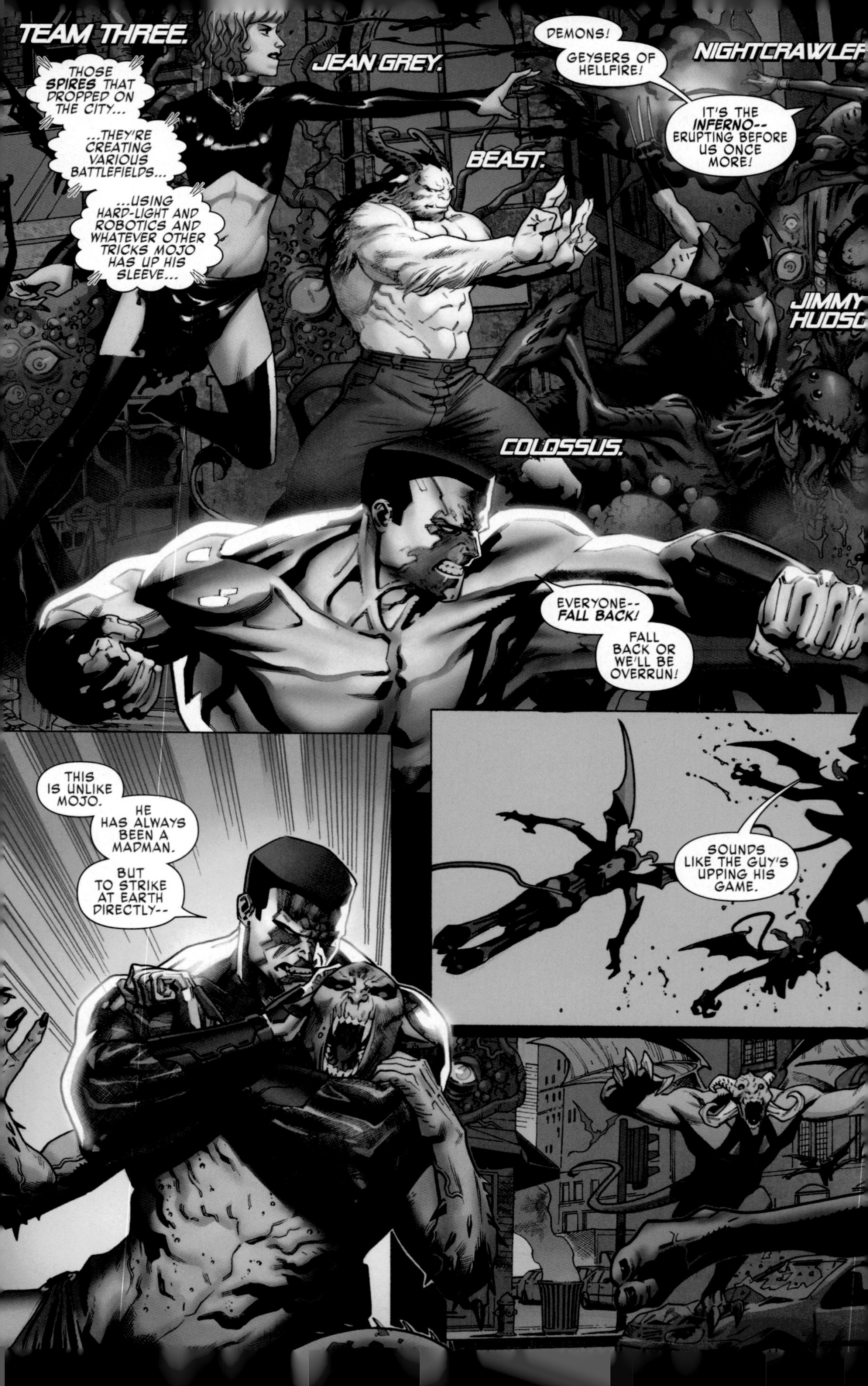
TEAM THREE.
JEAN GREY.
THOSE SPIRES THAT DROPPED ON THE CITY...
...THEY'RE CREATING VARIOUS BATTLEFIELDS...
...USING HARD-LIGHT AND ROBOTICS AND WHATEVER OTHER TRICKS MOJO HAS UP HIS SLEEVE...
BEAST.
NIGHTCRAWLER
DEMONS!
GEYSERS OF HELLFIRE!
IT'S THE INFERNO-- ERUPTING BEFORE US ONCE MORE!
JIMMY HUDSO
COLOSSUS.
EVERYONE-- FALL BACK!
FALL BACK OR WE'LL BE OVERRUN!
THIS IS UNLIKE MOJO.
HE HAS ALWAYS BEEN A MADMAN.
BUT TO STRIKE AT EARTH DIRECTLY--
SOUNDS LIKE THE GUY'S UPPING HIS GAME.

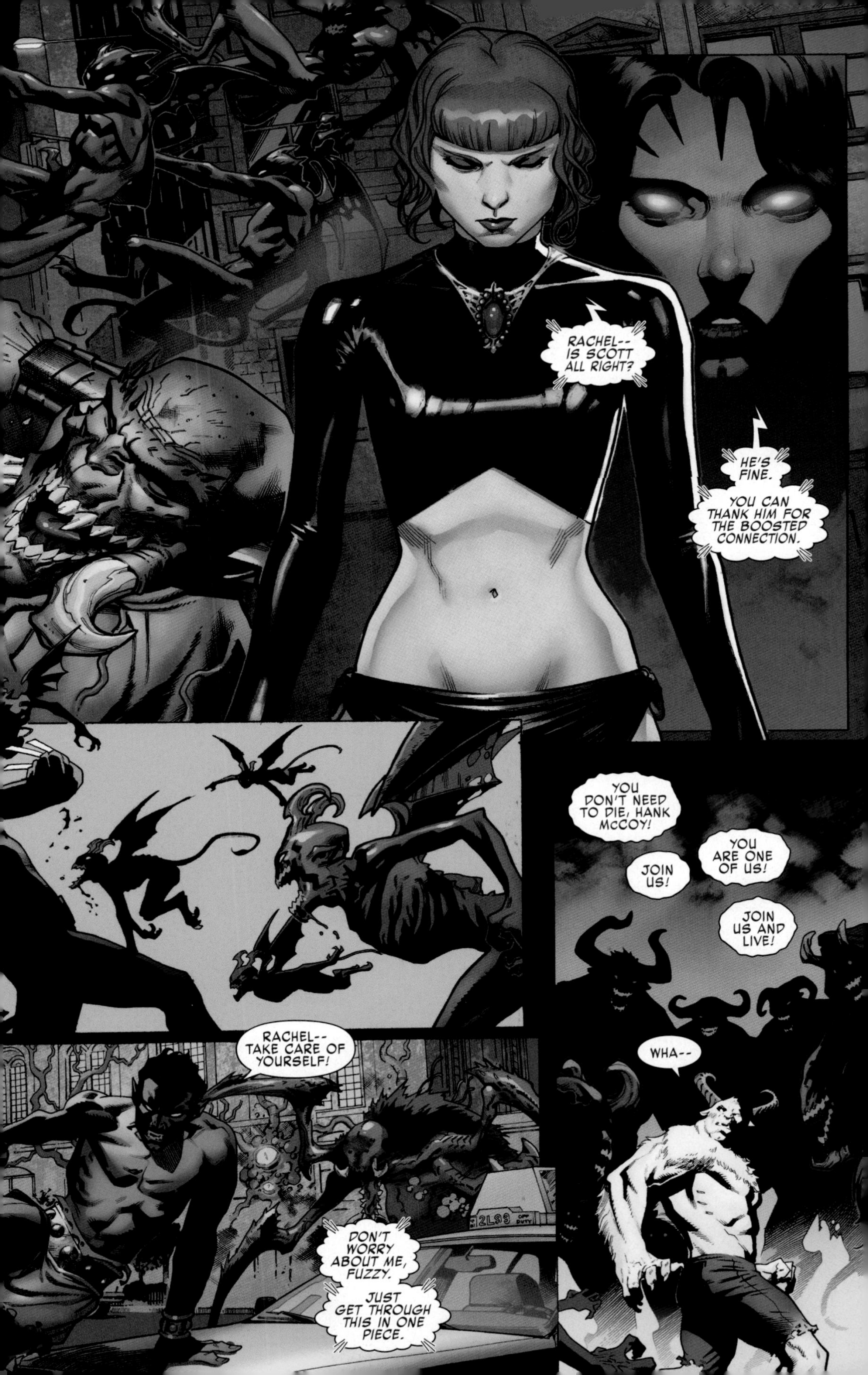
RACHEL-- IS SCOTT ALL RIGHT?
HE'S FINE.
YOU CAN THANK HIM FOR THE BOOSTED CONNECTION.
YOU DON'T NEED TO DIE, HANK McCOY!
JOIN US!
YOU ARE ONE OF US!
JOIN US AND LIVE!
RACHEL-- TAKE CARE OF YOURSELF!
DON'T WORRY ABOUT ME, FUZZY.
JUST GET THROUGH THIS IN ONE PIECE.
WHA--

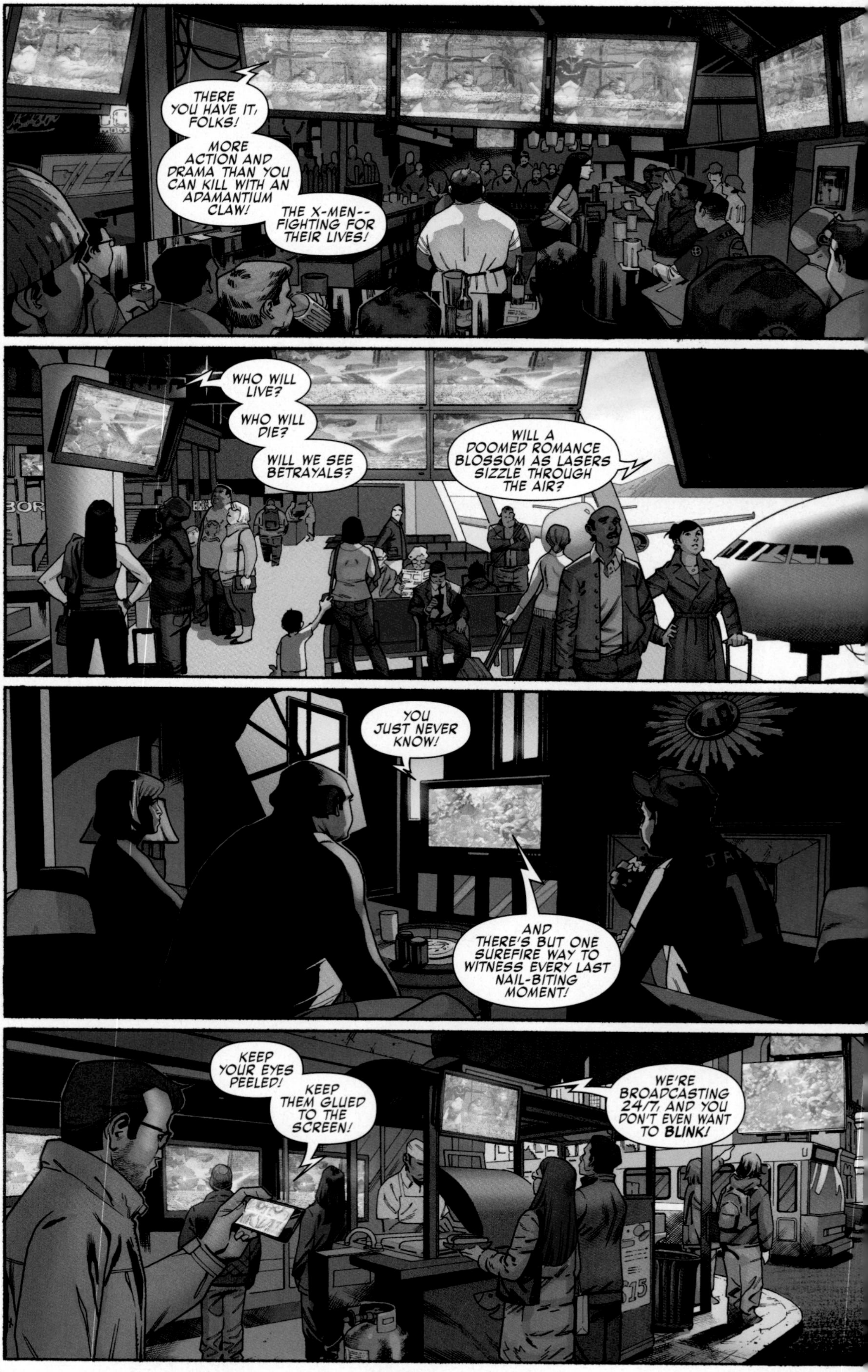
THERE YOU HAVE IT, FOLKS!
MORE ACTION AND DRAMA THAN YOU CAN KILL WITH AN ADAMANTIUM CLAW!
THE X-MEN-- FIGHTING FOR THEIR LIVES!
WHO WILL LIVE?
WHO WILL DIE?
WILL WE SEE BETRAYALS?
WILL A DOOMED ROMANCE BLOSSOM AS LASERS SIZZLE THROUGH THE AIR?
YOU JUST NEVER KNOW!
AND THERE'S BUT ONE SUREFIRE WAY TO WITNESS EVERY LAST NAIL-BITING MOMENT!
KEEP YOUR EYES PEELED!
KEEP THEM GLUED TO THE SCREEN!
WE'RE BROADCASTING 24/7, AND YOU DON'T EVEN WANT TO **BLINK!**

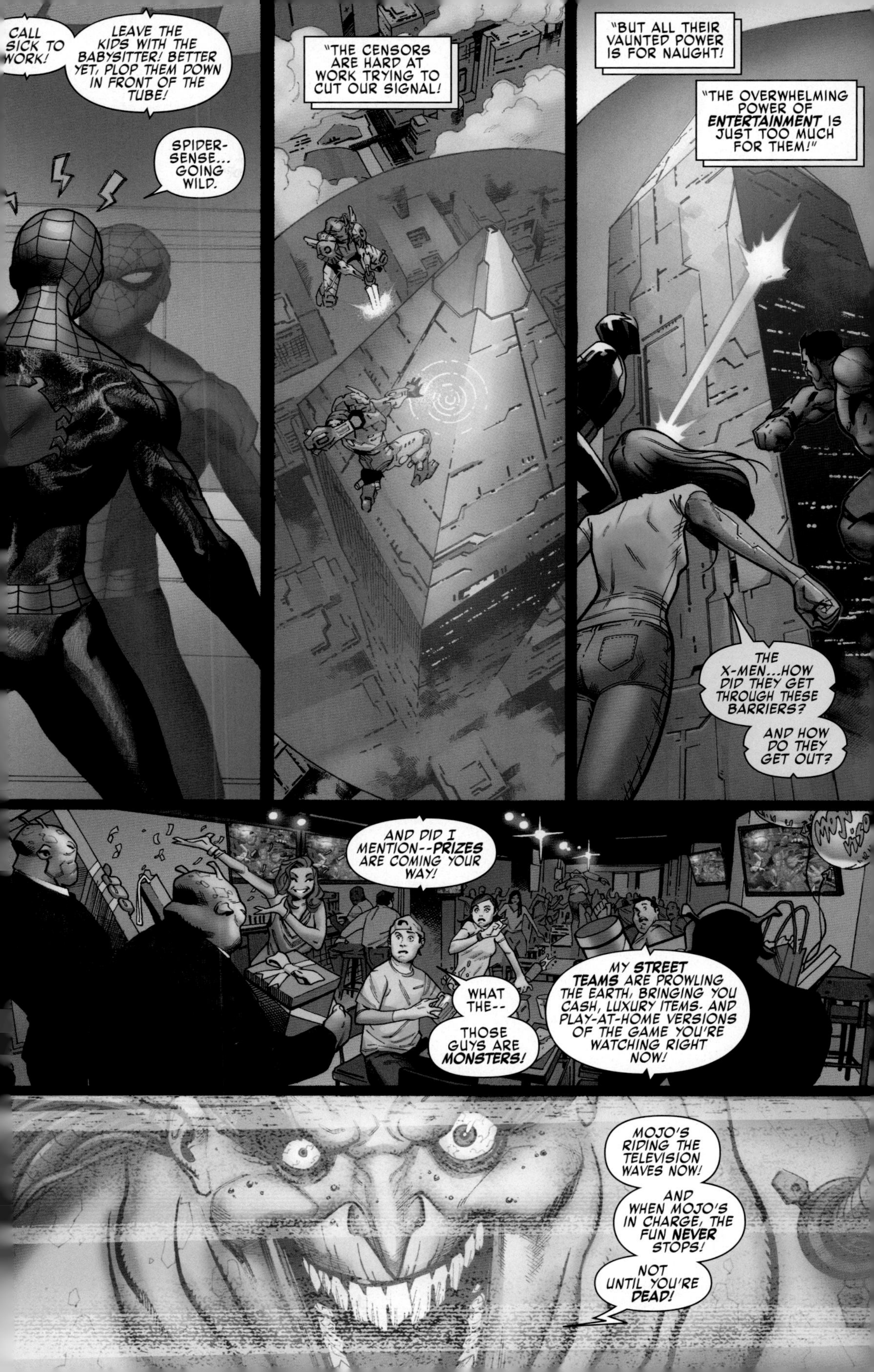
CALL SICK TO WORK!
LEAVE THE KIDS WITH THE BABYSITTER! BETTER YET, PLOP THEM DOWN IN FRONT OF THE TUBE!
SPIDER-SENSE... GOING WILD.
"THE CENSORS ARE HARD AT WORK TRYING TO CUT OUR SIGNAL!
"BUT ALL THEIR VAUNTED POWER IS FOR NAUGHT!
"THE OVERWHELMING POWER OF ENTERTAINMENT IS JUST TOO MUCH FOR THEM!"
THE X-MEN...HOW DID THEY GET THROUGH THESE BARRIERS?
AND HOW DO THEY GET OUT?
AND DID I MENTION--PRIZES ARE COMING YOUR WAY!
WHAT THE--
THOSE GUYS ARE MONSTERS!
MY STREET TEAMS ARE PROWLING THE EARTH, BRINGING YOU CASH, LUXURY ITEMS, AND PLAY-AT-HOME VERSIONS OF THE GAME YOU'RE WATCHING RIGHT NOW!
MOJO'S RIDING THE TELEVISION WAVES NOW!
AND WHEN MOJO'S IN CHARGE, THE FUN NEVER STOPS!
NOT UNTIL YOU'RE DEAD!

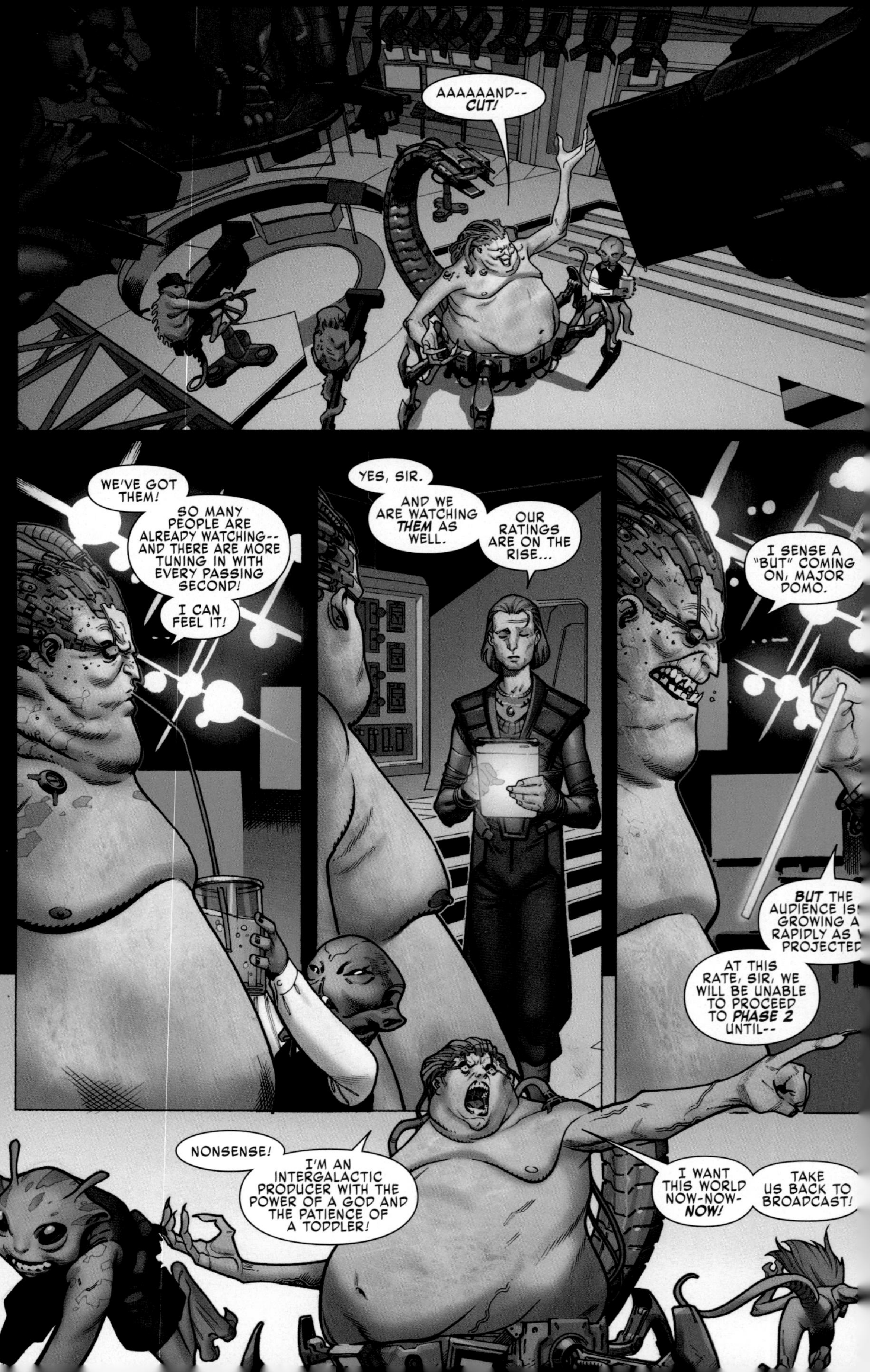
AAAAAAND--
CUT!
WE'VE GOT THEM!
SO MANY PEOPLE ARE ALREADY WATCHING-- AND THERE ARE MORE TUNING IN WITH EVERY PASSING SECOND!
I CAN FEEL IT!
YES, SIR.
AND WE ARE WATCHING THEM AS WELL.
OUR RATINGS ARE ON THE RISE...
I SENSE A "BUT" COMING ON, MAJOR DOMO.
BUT THE AUDIENCE IS GROWING A RAPIDLY AS PROJECTED
AT THIS RATE, SIR, WE WILL BE UNABLE TO PROCEED TO PHASE 2 UNTIL--
NONSENSE!
I'M AN INTERGALACTIC PRODUCER WITH THE POWER OF A GOD AND THE PATIENCE OF A TODDLER!
I WANT THIS WORLD NOW-NOW-NOW!
TAKE US BACK TO BROADCAST!

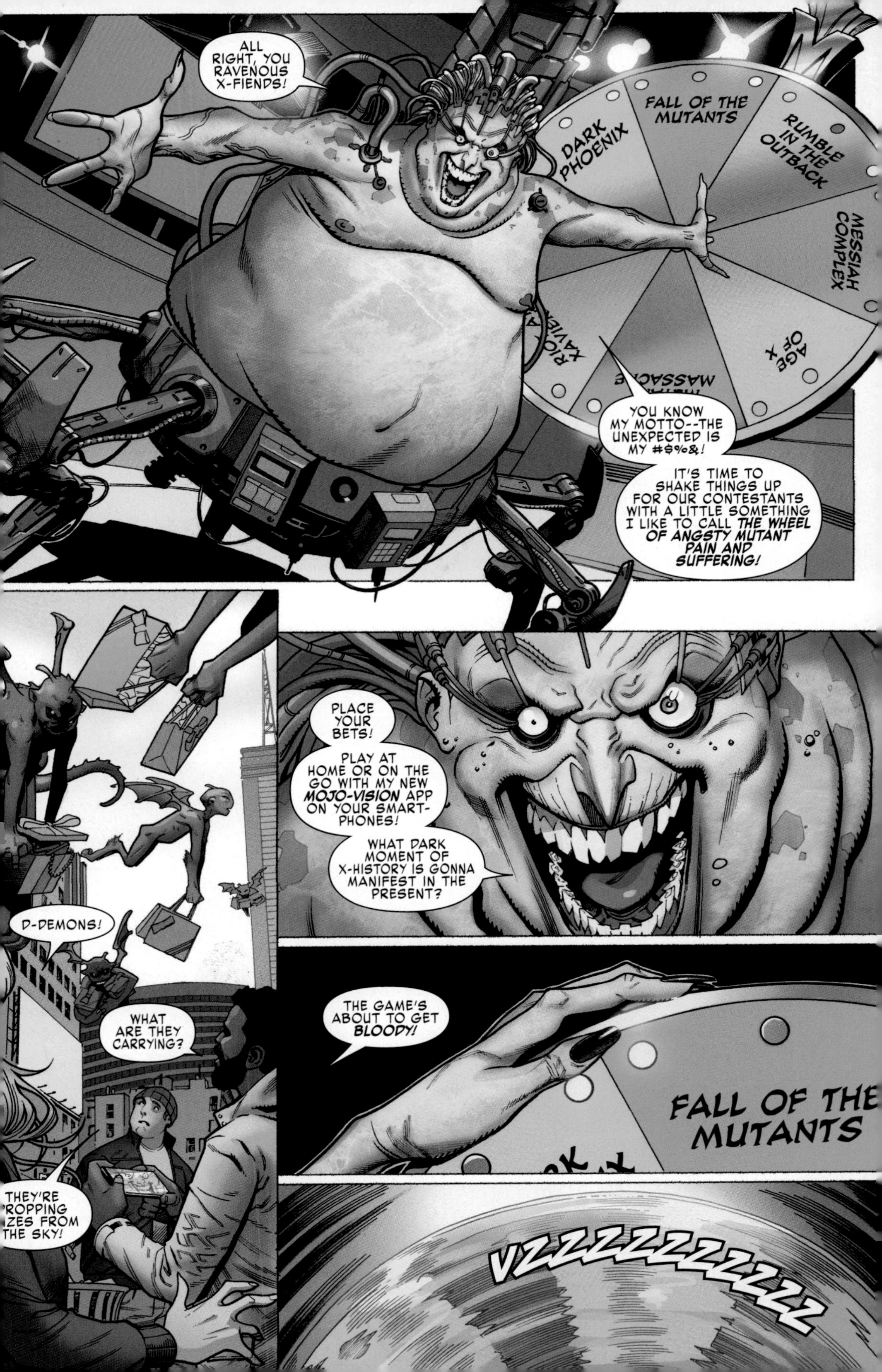

ALL RIGHT, YOU RAVENOUS X-FIENDS!
DARK PHOENIX
FALL OF THE MUTANTS
RUMBLE IN THE OUTBACK
MESSIAH COMPLEX
AGE OF X
MASSACRE
XAVIER
YOU KNOW MY MOTTO--THE UNEXPECTED IS MY #$%&!
IT'S TIME TO SHAKE THINGS UP FOR OUR CONTESTANTS WITH A LITTLE SOMETHING I LIKE TO CALL THE WHEEL OF ANGSTY MUTANT PAIN AND SUFFERING!
PLACE YOUR BETS!
PLAY AT HOME OR ON THE GO WITH MY NEW MOJO-VISION APP ON YOUR SMART-PHONES!
WHAT DARK MOMENT OF X-HISTORY IS GONNA MANIFEST IN THE PRESENT?
D-DEMONS!
WHAT ARE THEY CARRYING?
THEY'RE 'ROPPING IZES FROM THE SKY!
THE GAME'S ABOUT TO GET BLOODY!
FALL OF THE MUTANTS
VZZZZZZZZZZZ

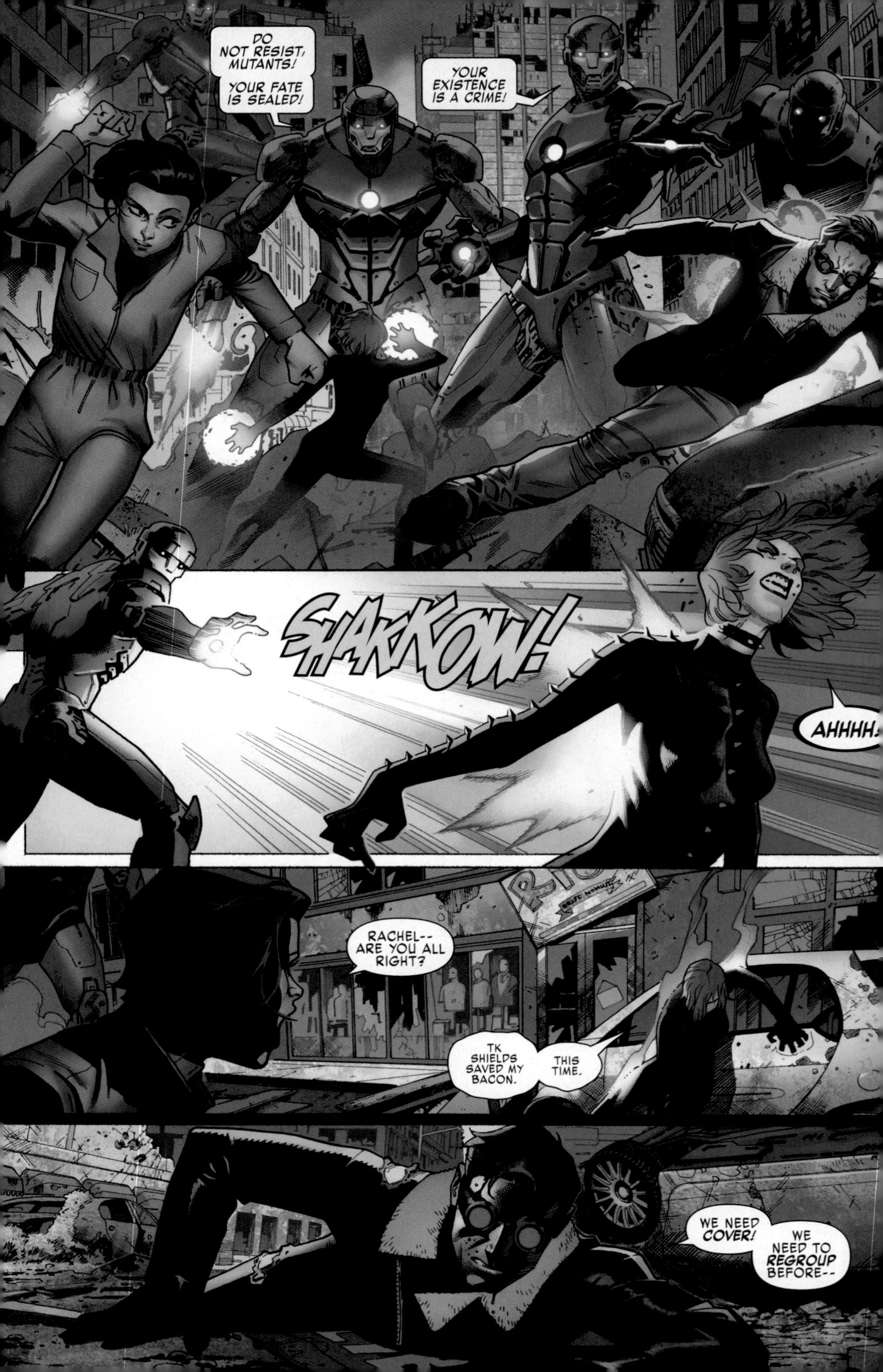
DO NOT RESIST, MUTANTS!
YOUR FATE IS SEALED!
YOUR EXISTENCE IS A CRIME!
SHAKOW!
AHHHH
RACHEL-- ARE YOU ALL RIGHT?
TK SHIELDS SAVED MY BACON.
THIS TIME.
WE NEED COVER!
WE NEED TO REGROUP BEFORE--

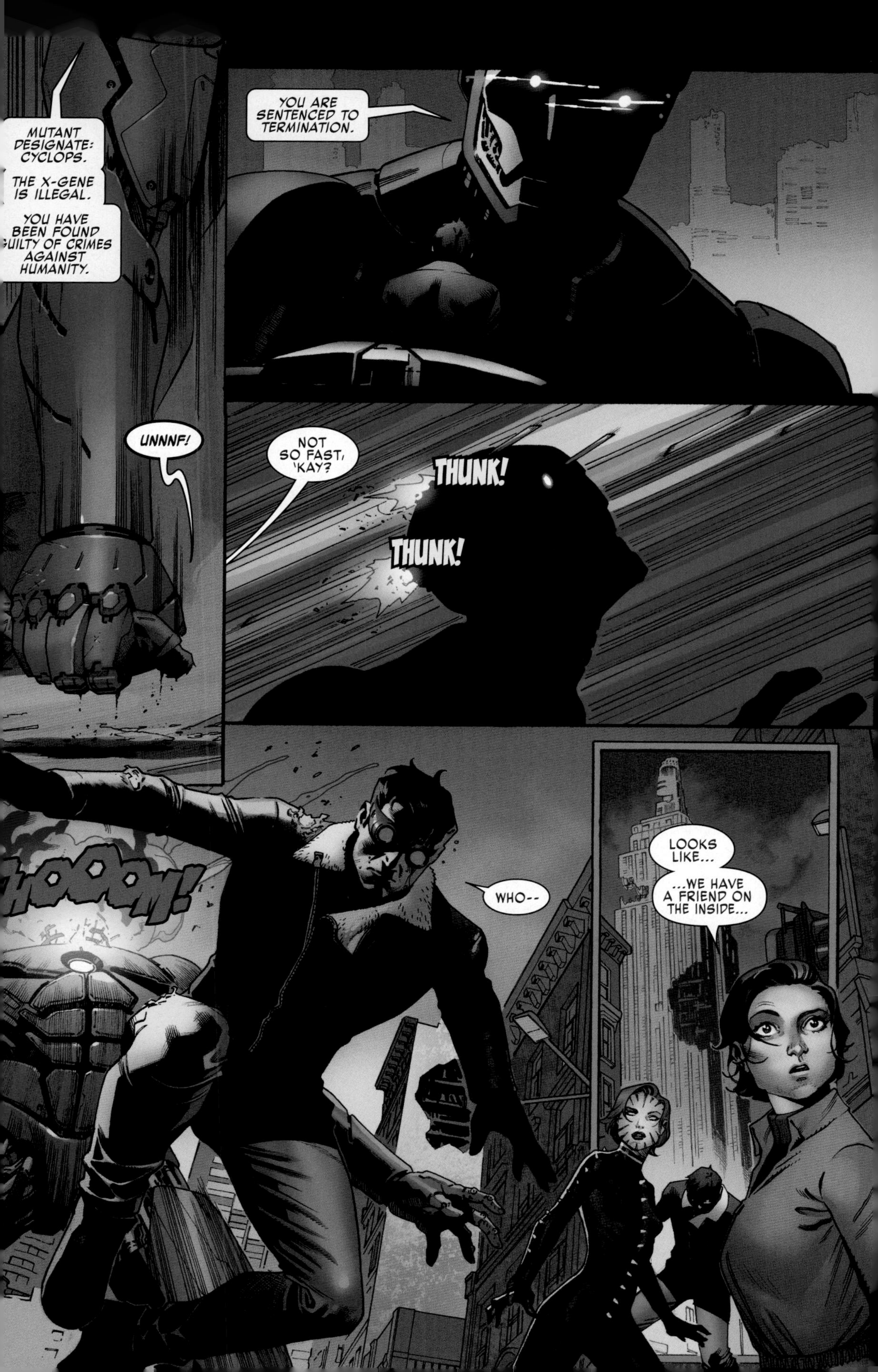
MUTANT DESIGNATE: CYCLOPS.
THE X-GENE IS ILLEGAL.
YOU HAVE BEEN FOUND GUILTY OF CRIMES AGAINST HUMANITY.
YOU ARE SENTENCED TO TERMINATION.
UNNNF!
NOT SO FAST, 'KAY?
THUNK!
THUNK!
WHO--
LOOKS LIKE...
...WE HAVE A FRIEND ON THE INSIDE...

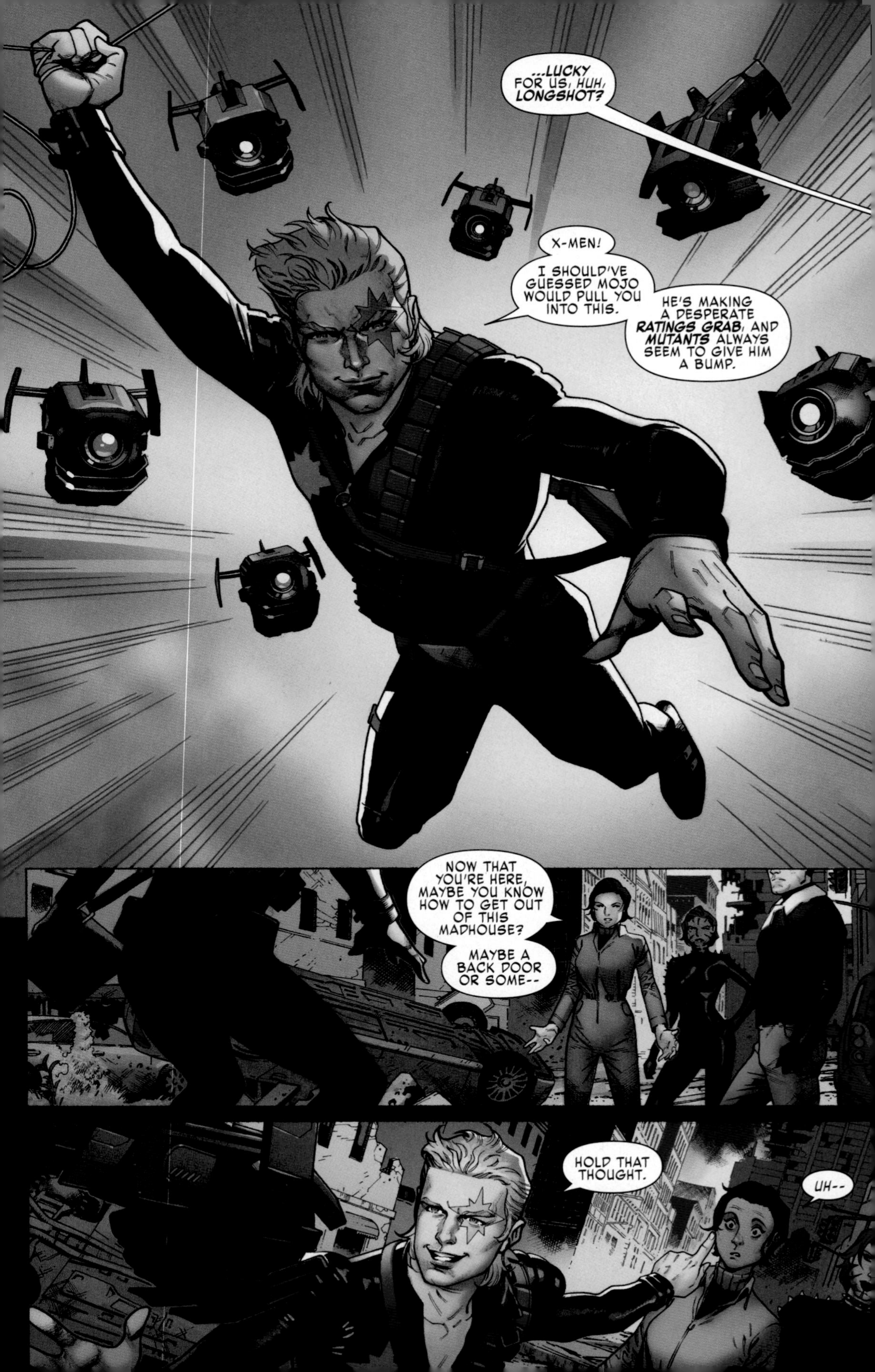

...LUCKY FOR US, HUH, LONGSHOT?
X-MEN!
I SHOULD'VE GUESSED MOJO WOULD PULL YOU INTO THIS.
HE'S MAKING A DESPERATE RATINGS GRAB, AND MUTANTS ALWAYS SEEM TO GIVE HIM A BUMP.
NOW THAT YOU'RE HERE, MAYBE YOU KNOW HOW TO GET OUT OF THIS MADHOUSE?
MAYBE A BACK DOOR OR SOME--
HOLD THAT THOUGHT.
UH--

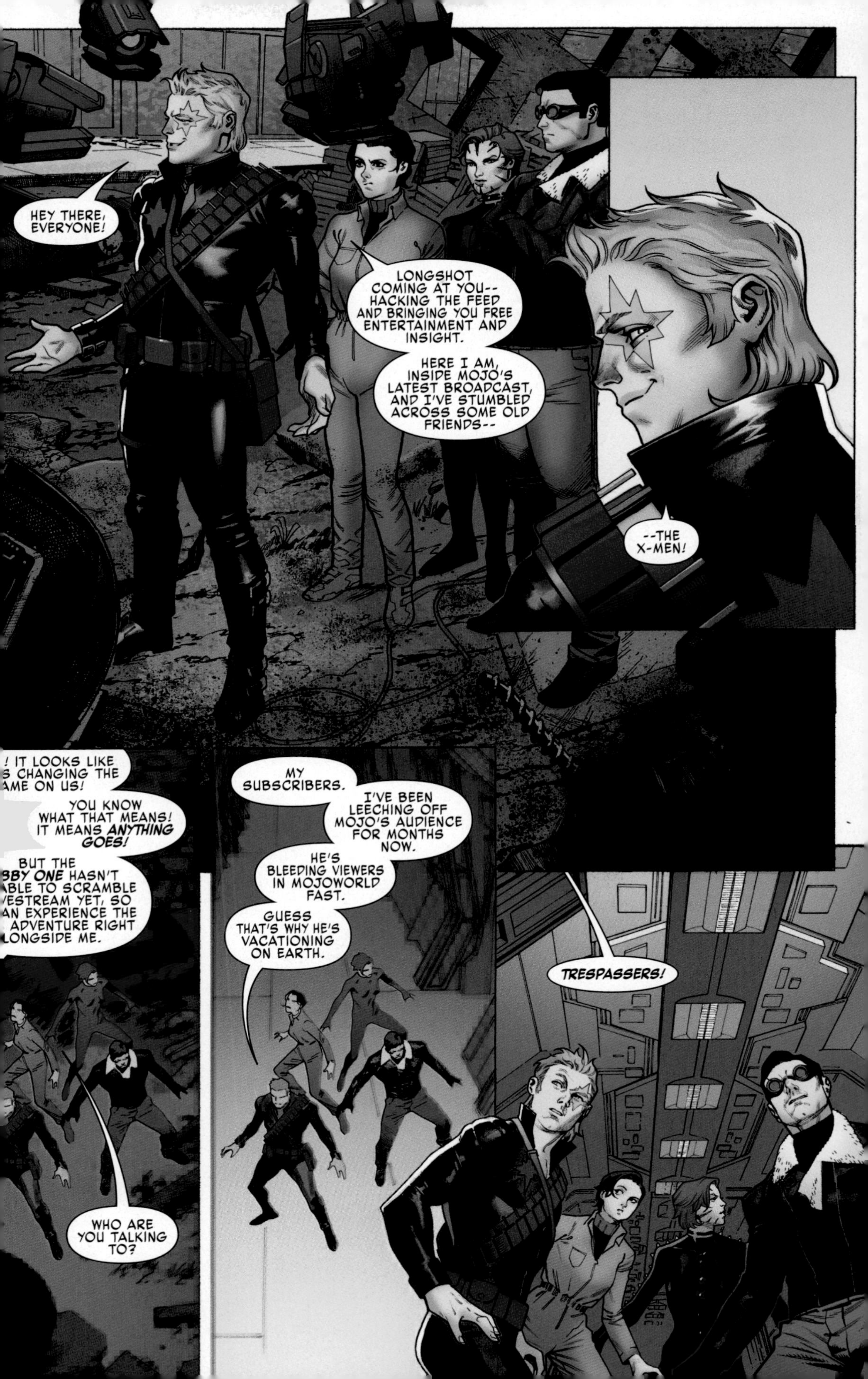
HEY THERE, EVERYONE!
LONGSHOT COMING AT YOU--HACKING THE FEED AND BRINGING YOU FREE ENTERTAINMENT AND INSIGHT.
HERE I AM, INSIDE MOJO'S LATEST BROADCAST, AND I'VE STUMBLED ACROSS SOME OLD FRIENDS--
--THE X-MEN!
! IT LOOKS LIKE S CHANGING THE AME ON US!
YOU KNOW WHAT THAT MEANS! IT MEANS ANYTHING GOES!
BUT THE BBY ONE HASN'T ABLE TO SCRAMBLE VESTREAM YET, SO AN EXPERIENCE THE ADVENTURE RIGHT LONGSIDE ME.
WHO ARE YOU TALKING TO?
MY SUBSCRIBERS.
I'VE BEEN LEECHING OFF MOJO'S AUDIENCE FOR MONTHS NOW.
HE'S BLEEDING VIEWERS IN MOJOWORLD FAST.
GUESS THAT'S WHY HE'S VACATIONING ON EARTH.
TRESPASSERS!

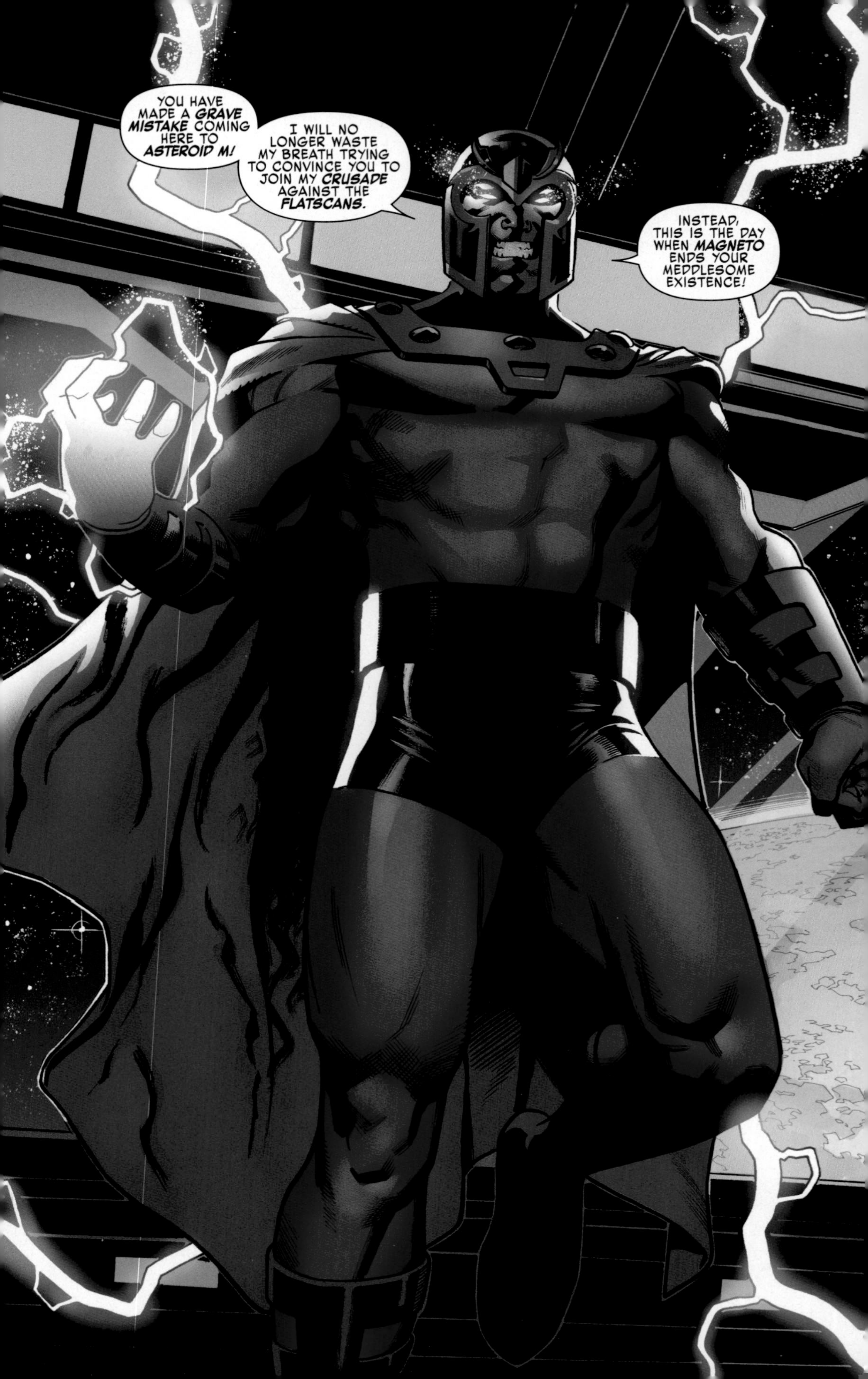
YOU HAVE MADE A GRAVE MISTAKE COMING HERE TO ASTEROID M!
I WILL NO LONGER WASTE MY BREATH TRYING TO CONVINCE YOU TO JOIN MY CRUSADE AGAINST THE FLATSCANS.
INSTEAD, THIS IS THE DAY WHEN MAGNETO ENDS YOUR MEDDLESOME EXISTENCE!

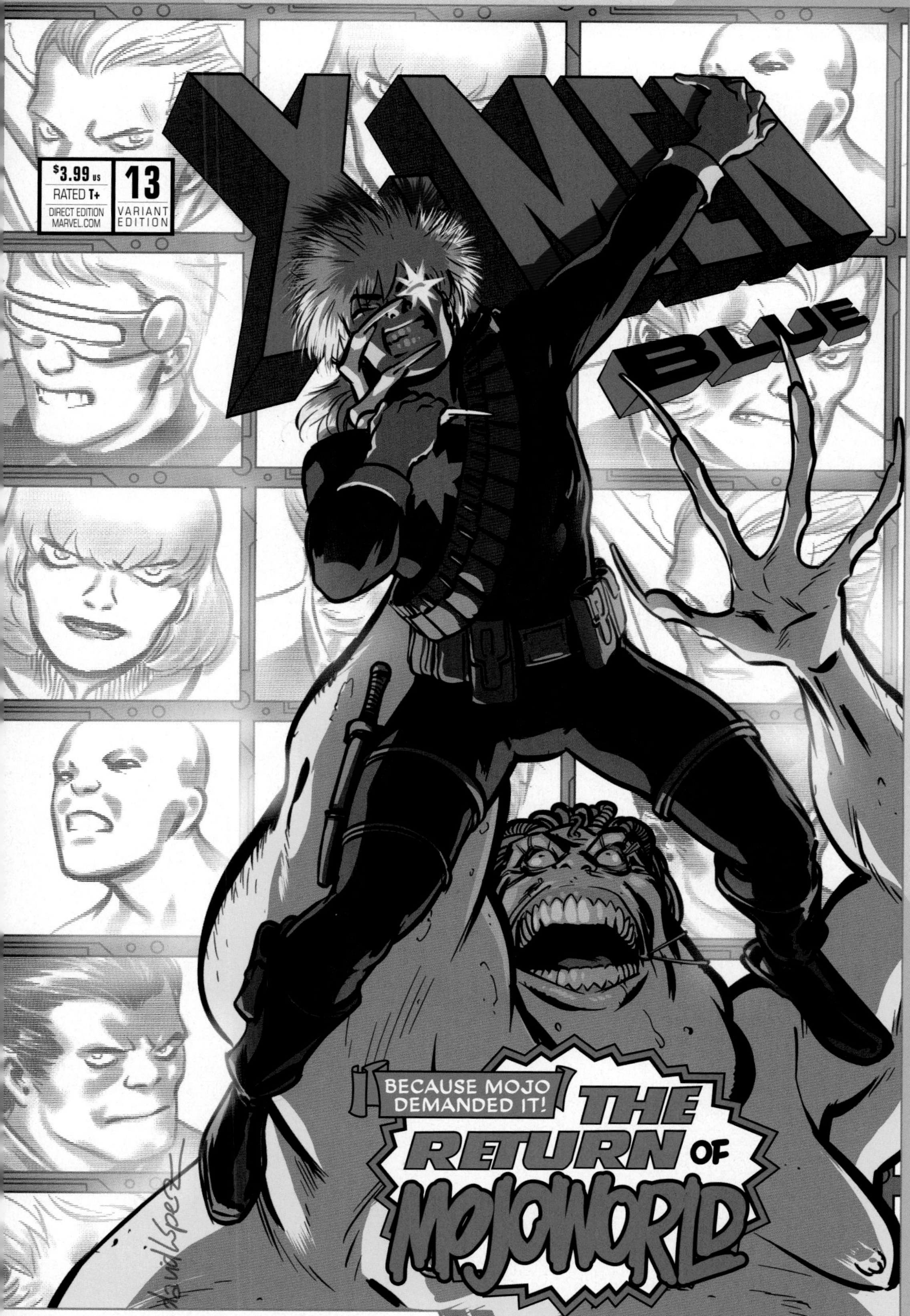
X-MEN
BLUE
$3.99 US
13
RATED T+
DIRECT EDITION
MARVEL.COM
VARIANT EDITION
BECAUSE MOJO DEMANDED IT!
THE RETURN OF MOJOWORLD

-MEN BLUE #13 *HOMAGE VARIANT*
BY ***DAVID LOPEZ***

X-MEN GOLD #14

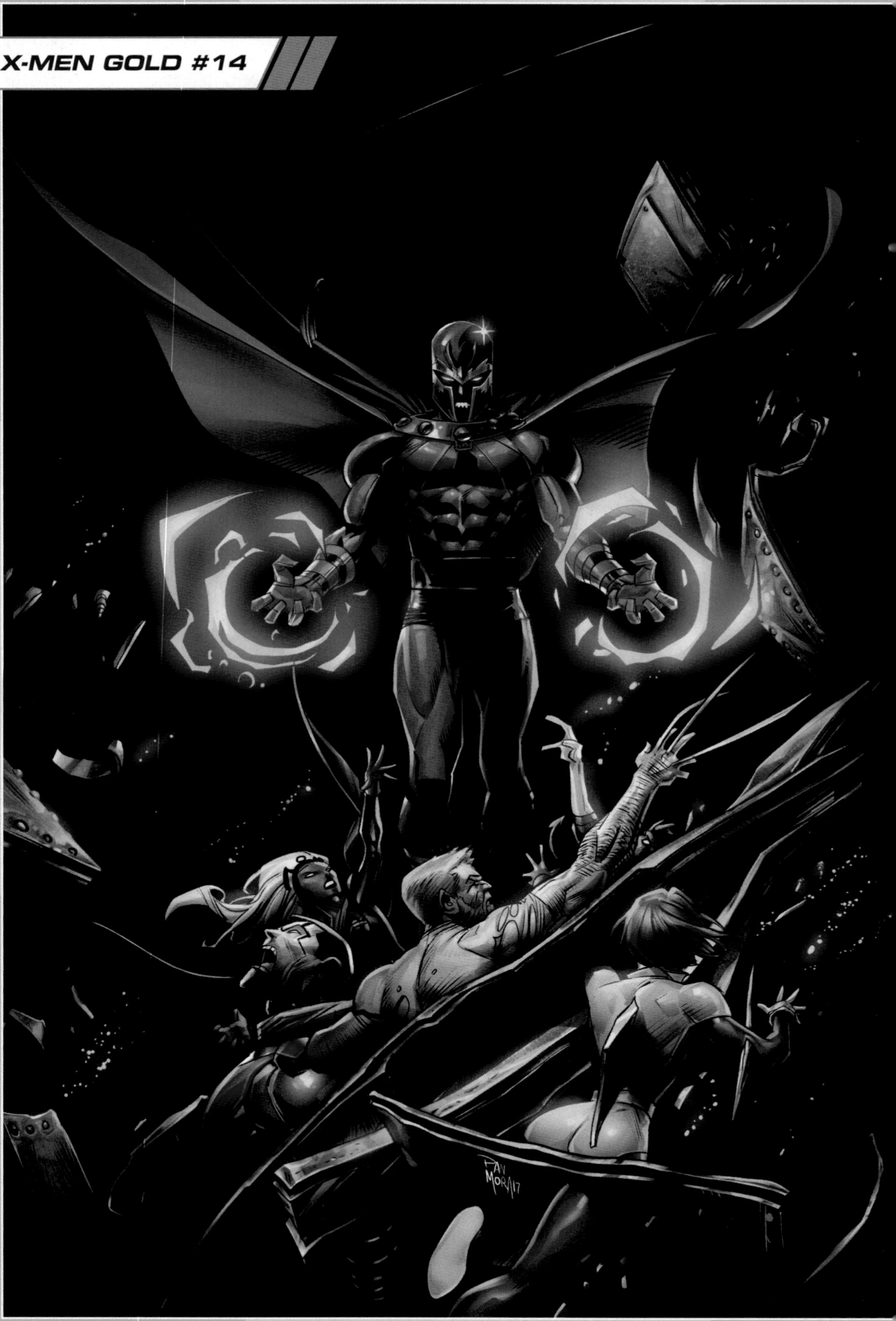
DAN MORA /17

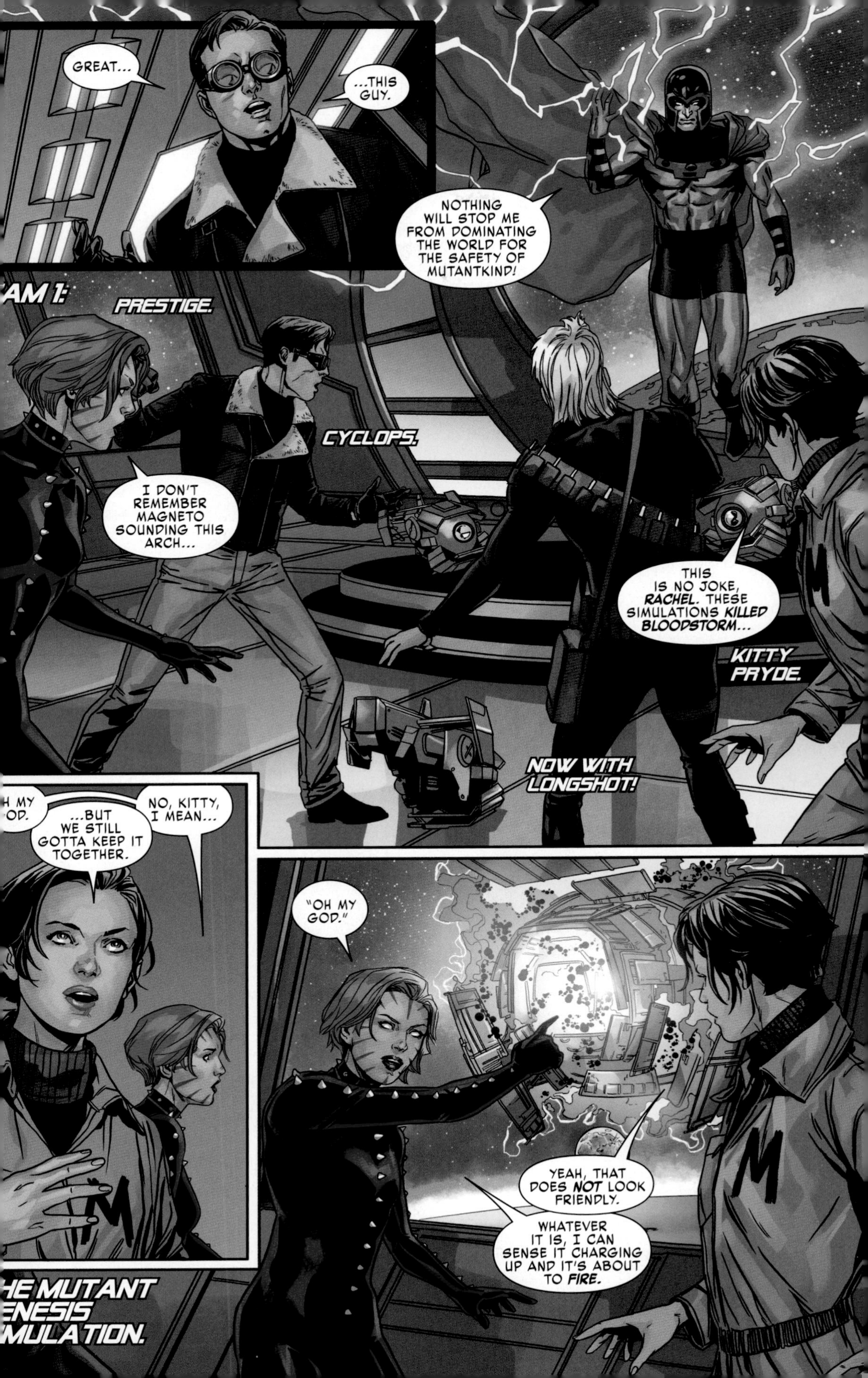

GREAT...
...THIS GUY.
NOTHING WILL STOP ME FROM DOMINATING THE WORLD FOR THE SAFETY OF MUTANTKIND!
AM 1:
PRESTIGE.
CYCLOPS.
I DON'T REMEMBER MAGNETO SOUNDING THIS ARCH...
THIS IS NO JOKE, RACHEL. THESE SIMULATIONS KILLED BLOODSTORM...
KITTY PRYDE.
NOW WITH LONGSHOT!
H MY OD.
...BUT WE STILL GOTTA KEEP IT TOGETHER.
NO, KITTY, I MEAN...
"OH MY GOD."
YEAH, THAT DOES NOT LOOK FRIENDLY.
WHATEVER IT IS, I CAN SENSE IT CHARGING UP AND IT'S ABOUT TO FIRE.
HE MUTANT ENESIS MULATION.

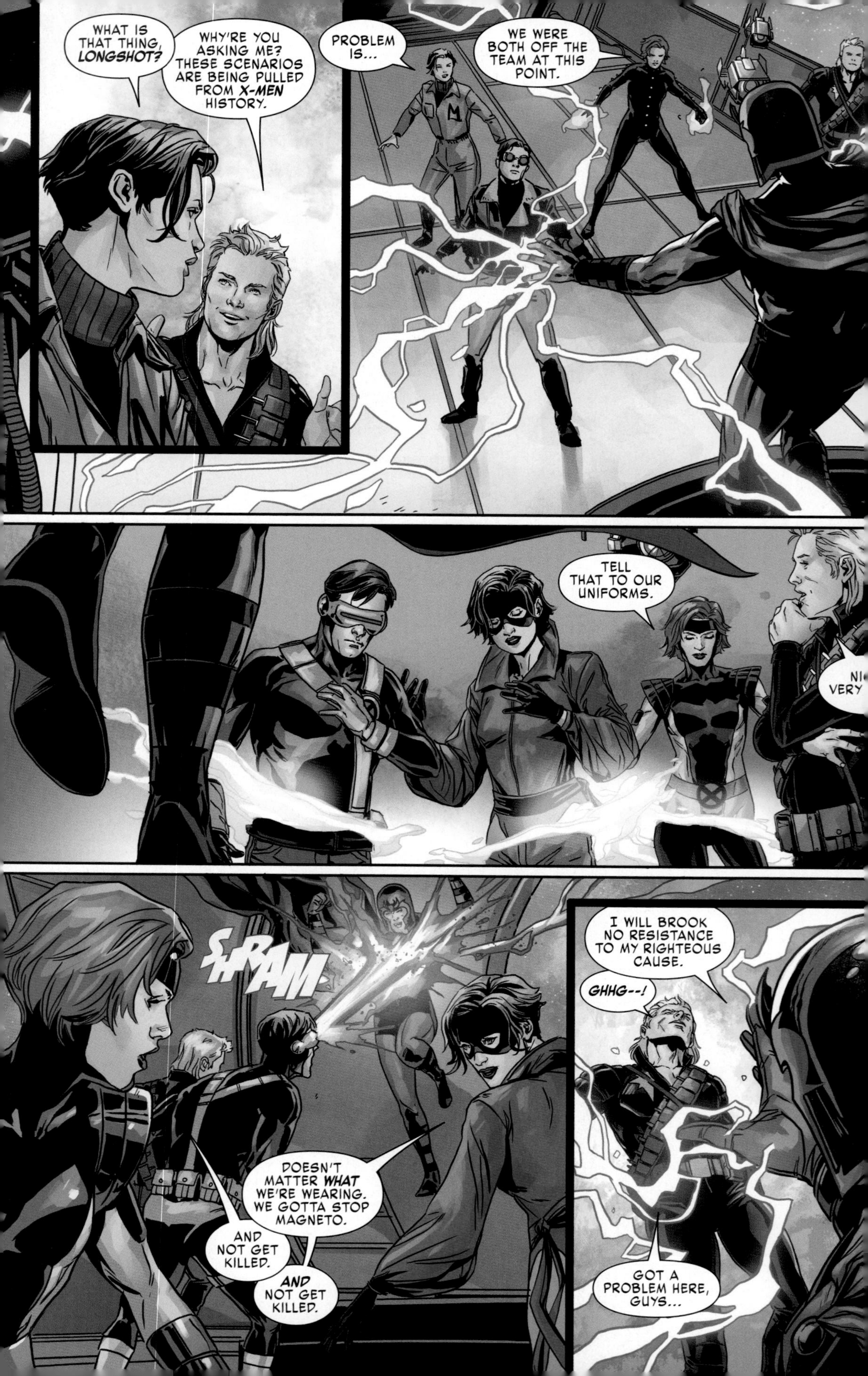
WHAT IS THAT THING, LONGSHOT?
WHY'RE YOU ASKING ME? THESE SCENARIOS ARE BEING PULLED FROM X-MEN HISTORY.
PROBLEM IS...
WE WERE BOTH OFF THE TEAM AT THIS POINT.
TELL THAT TO OUR UNIFORMS.
I WILL BROOK NO RESISTANCE TO MY RIGHTEOUS CAUSE.
GHHG--!
SHRAM
DOESN'T MATTER WHAT WE'RE WEARING. WE GOTTA STOP MAGNETO.
AND NOT GET KILLED.
AND NOT GET KILLED.
GOT A PROBLEM HERE, GUYS...

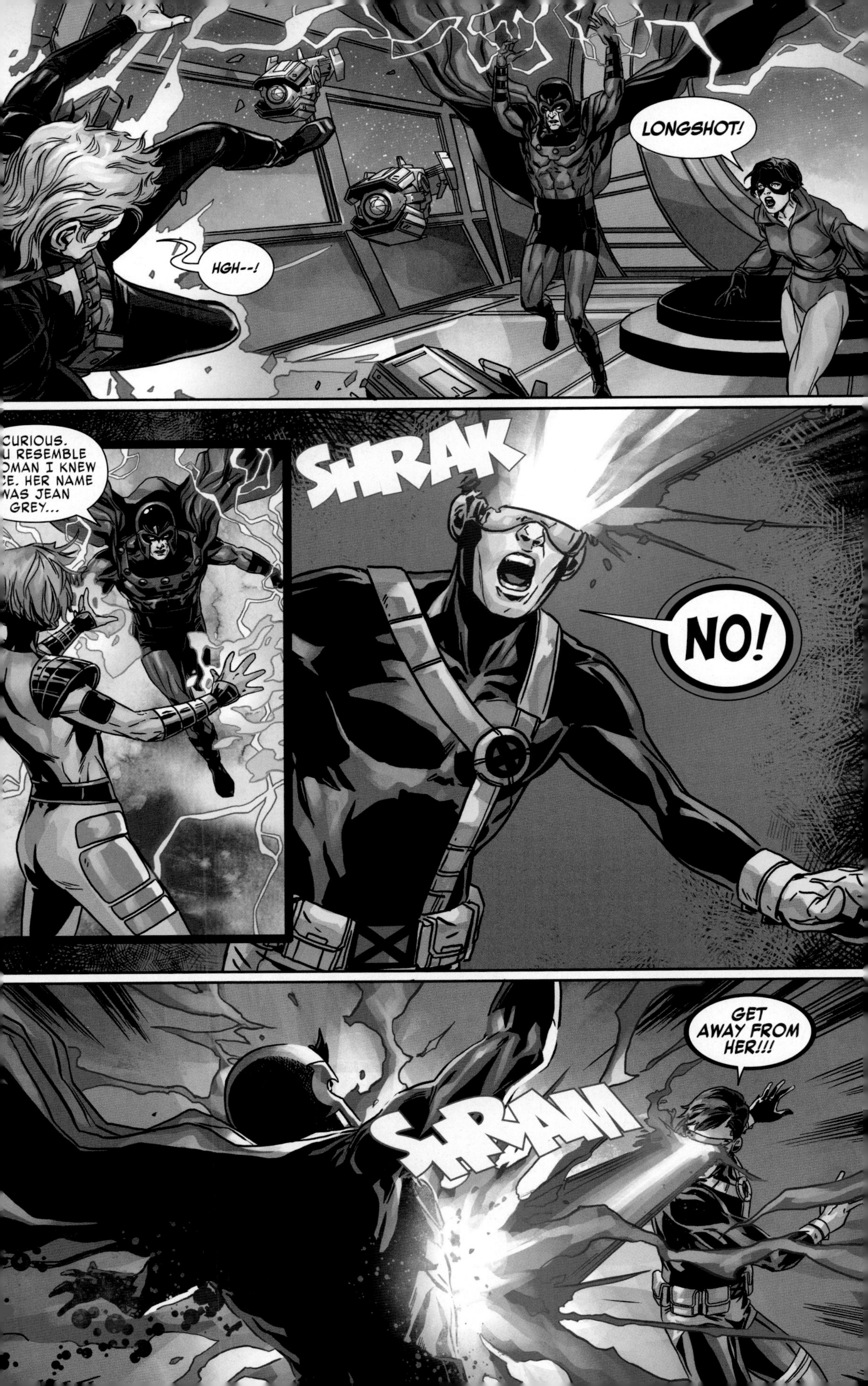
LONGSHOT!
HGH--!
CURIOUS.
U RESEMBLE
OMAN I KNEW
CE. HER NAME
WAS JEAN
GREY...
SHRAK
NO!
GET AWAY FROM HER!!!
SHRAM

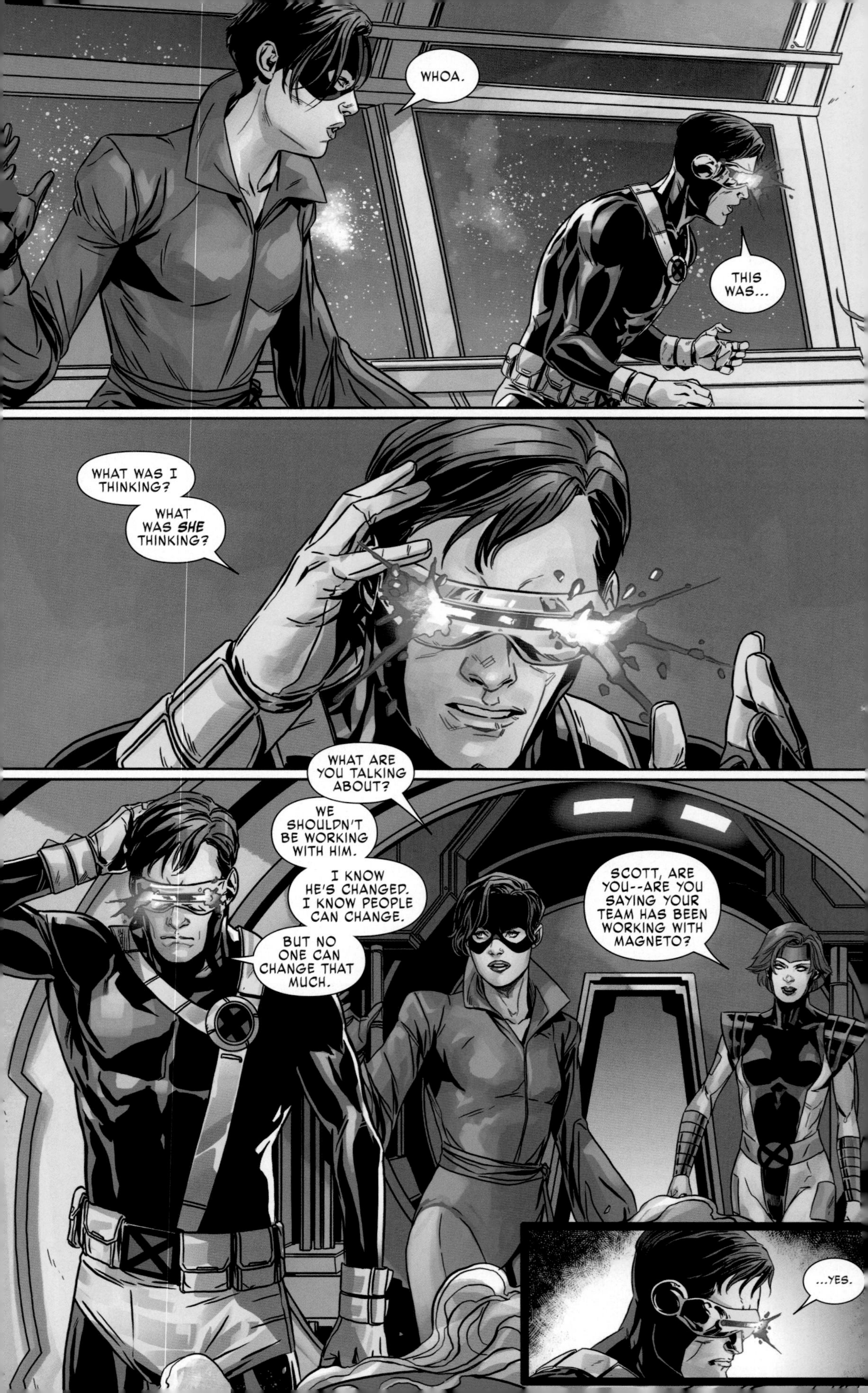
WHOA.
THIS WAS...
WHAT WAS I THINKING?
WHAT WAS *SHE* THINKING?
WHAT ARE YOU TALKING ABOUT?
WE SHOULDN'T BE WORKING WITH HIM.
I KNOW HE'S CHANGED. I KNOW PEOPLE CAN CHANGE.
BUT NO ONE CAN CHANGE THAT MUCH.
SCOTT, ARE YOU--ARE YOU SAYING YOUR TEAM HAS BEEN WORKING WITH MAGNETO?
...YES.

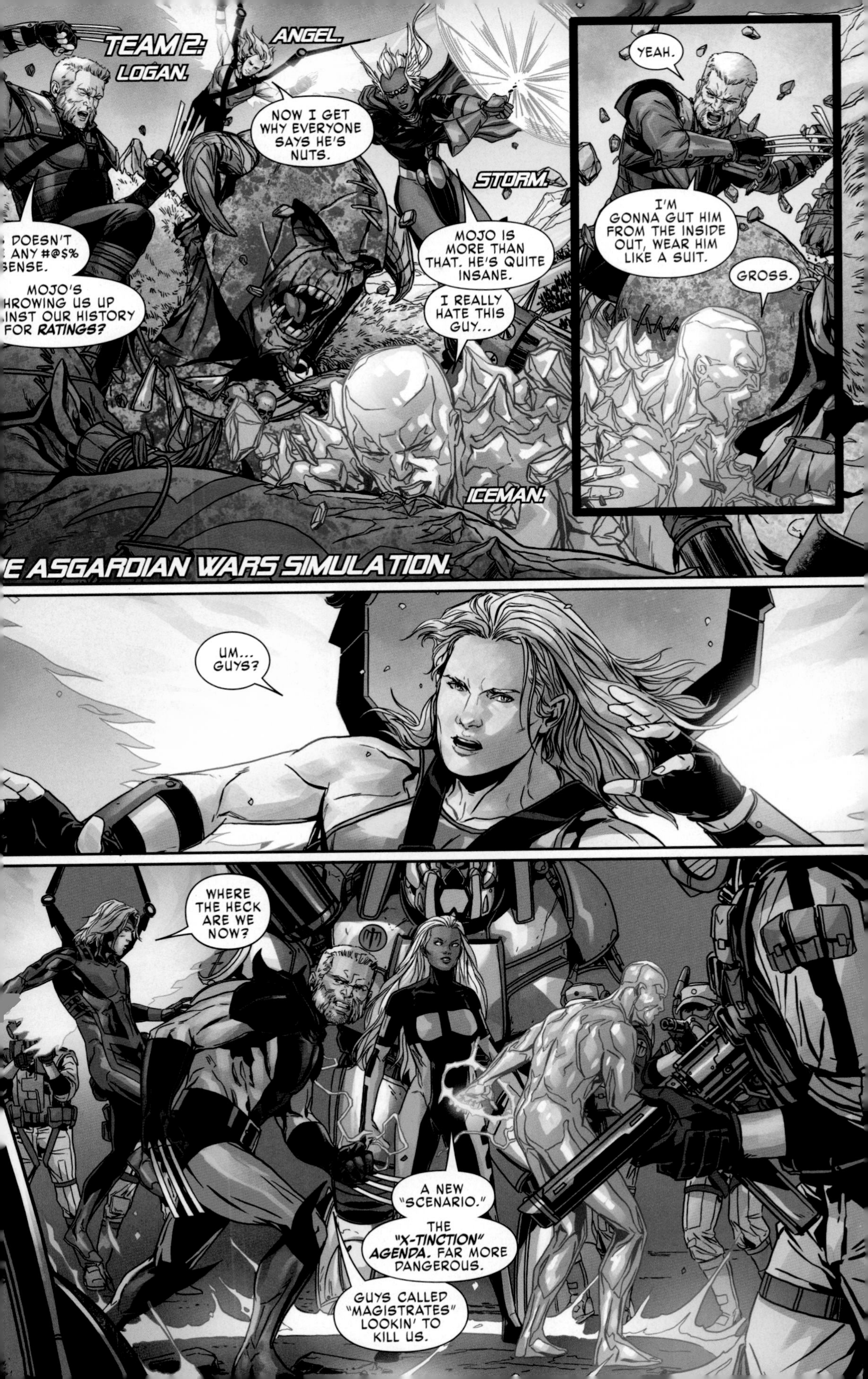

TEAM 2:
LOGAN.
ANGEL.
STORM.
ICEMAN.
E ASGARDIAN WARS SIMULATION.
DOESN'T ANY #@$% SENSE.
MOJO'S HROWING US UP INST OUR HISTORY FOR RATINGS?
NOW I GET WHY EVERYONE SAYS HE'S NUTS.
MOJO IS MORE THAN THAT. HE'S QUITE INSANE.
I REALLY HATE THIS GUY...
YEAH.
I'M GONNA GUT HIM FROM THE INSIDE OUT, WEAR HIM LIKE A SUIT.
GROSS.
UM... GUYS?
WHERE THE HECK ARE WE NOW?
A NEW "SCENARIO."
THE "X-TINCTION" AGENDA. FAR MORE DANGEROUS.
GUYS CALLED "MAGISTRATES" LOOKIN' TO KILL US.

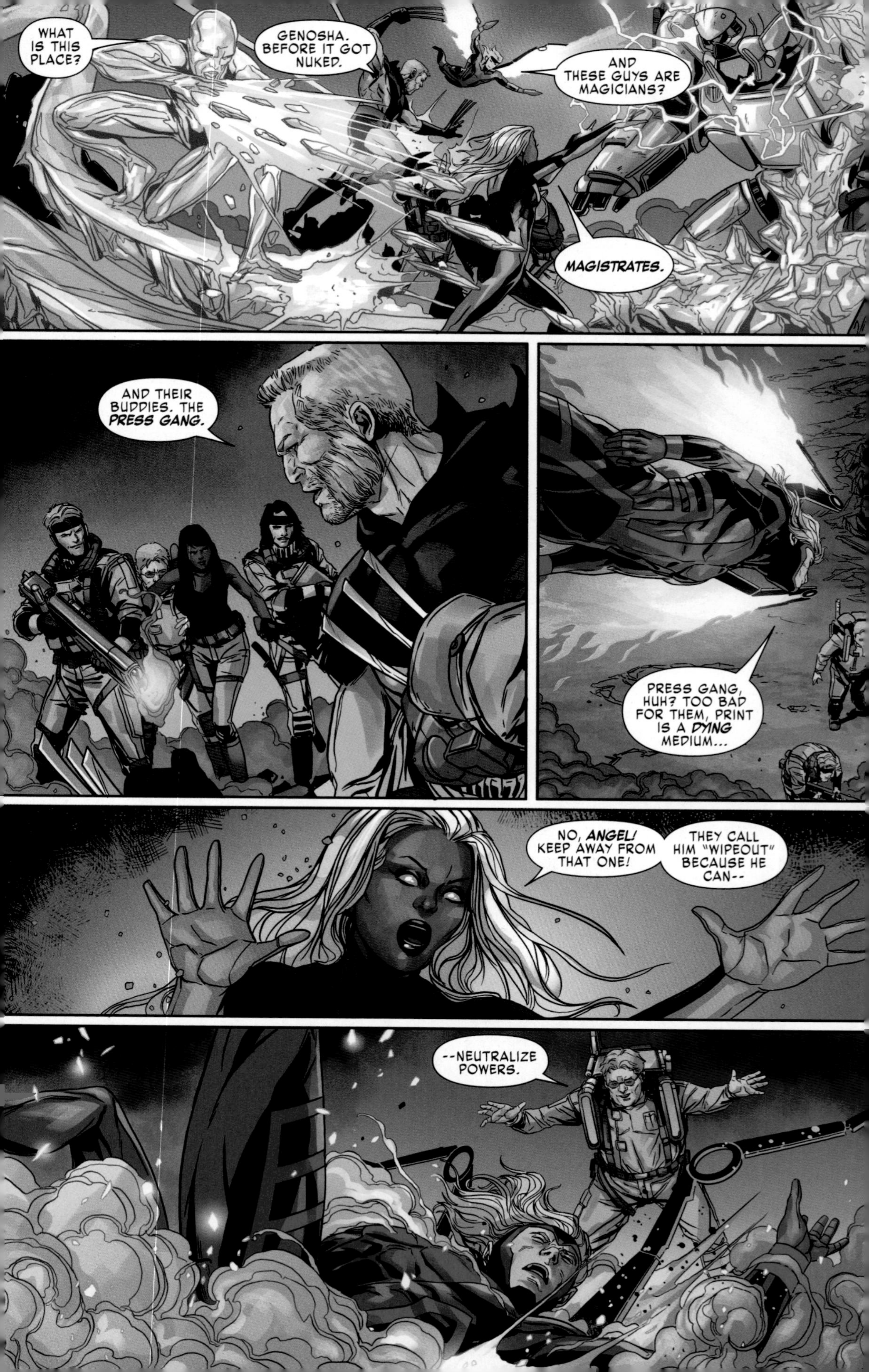
WHAT IS THIS PLACE?
GENOSHA. BEFORE IT GOT NUKED.
AND THESE GUYS ARE MAGICIANS?
MAGISTRATES.
AND THEIR BUDDIES. THE PRESS GANG.
PRESS GANG, HUH? TOO BAD FOR THEM, PRINT IS A DYING MEDIUM...
NO, ANGEL! KEEP AWAY FROM THAT ONE!
THEY CALL HIM "WIPEOUT" BECAUSE HE CAN--
--NEUTRALIZE POWERS.

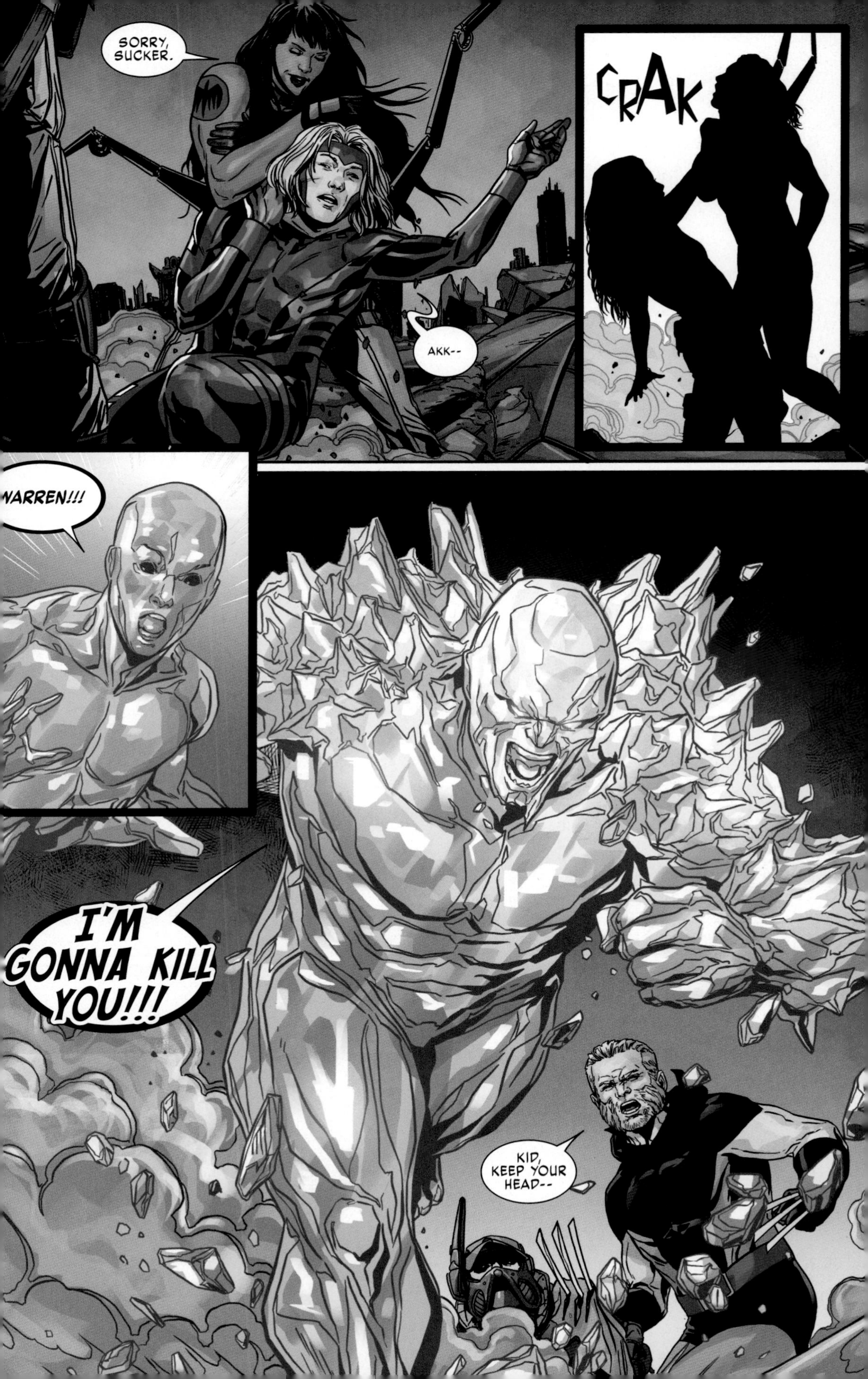
SORRY, SUCKER.
AKK--
CRAK
WARREN!!!
I'M GONNA KILL YOU!!!
KID, KEEP YOUR HEAD--

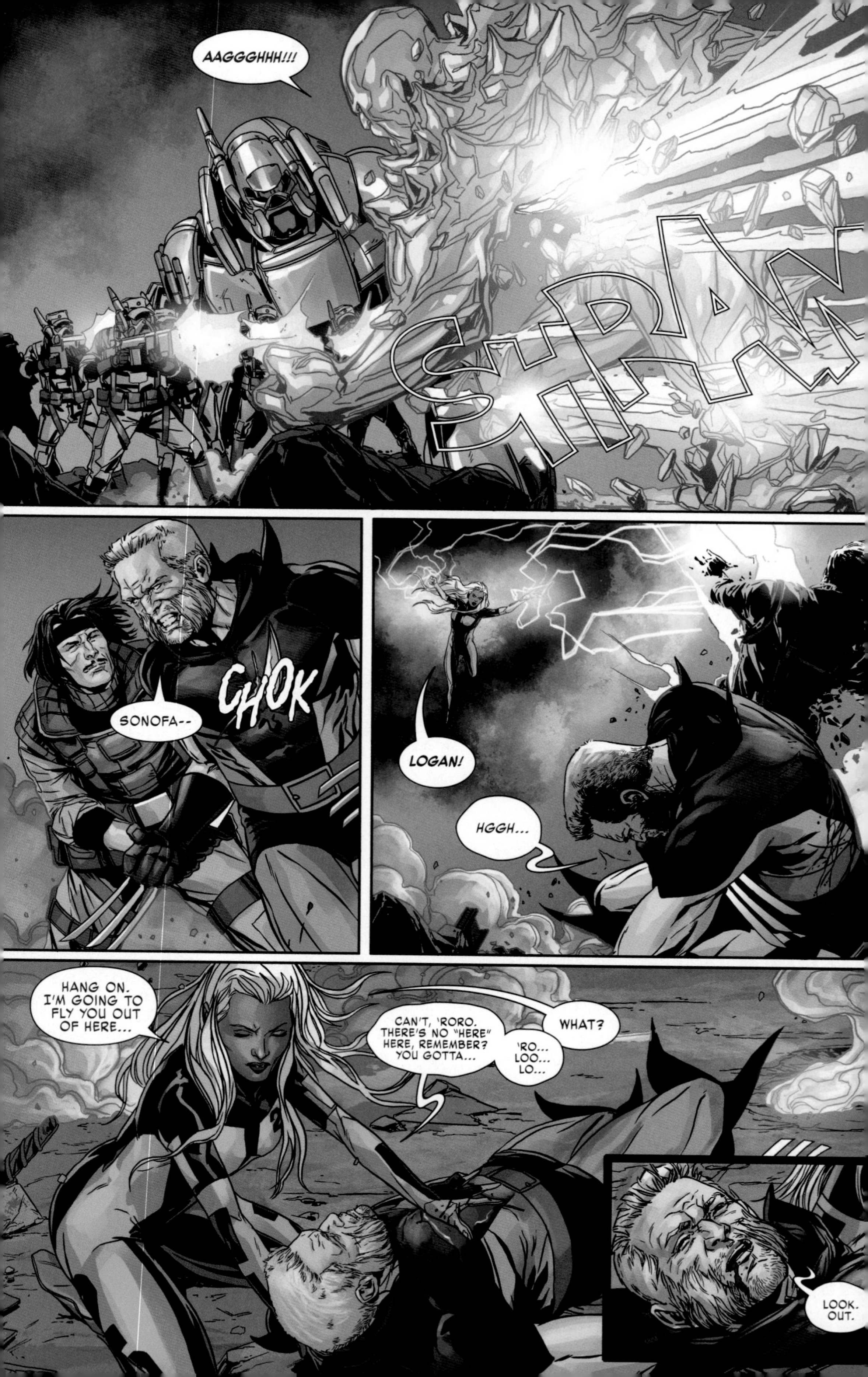
AAGGGHHH!!!
SHRAW
SONOFA--
CHOK
LOGAN!
HGGH...
HANG ON. I'M GOING TO FLY YOU OUT OF HERE...
CAN'T, 'RORO. THERE'S NO "HERE" HERE, REMEMBER? YOU GOTTA...
WHAT?
'RO... LOO... LO...
LOOK. OUT.

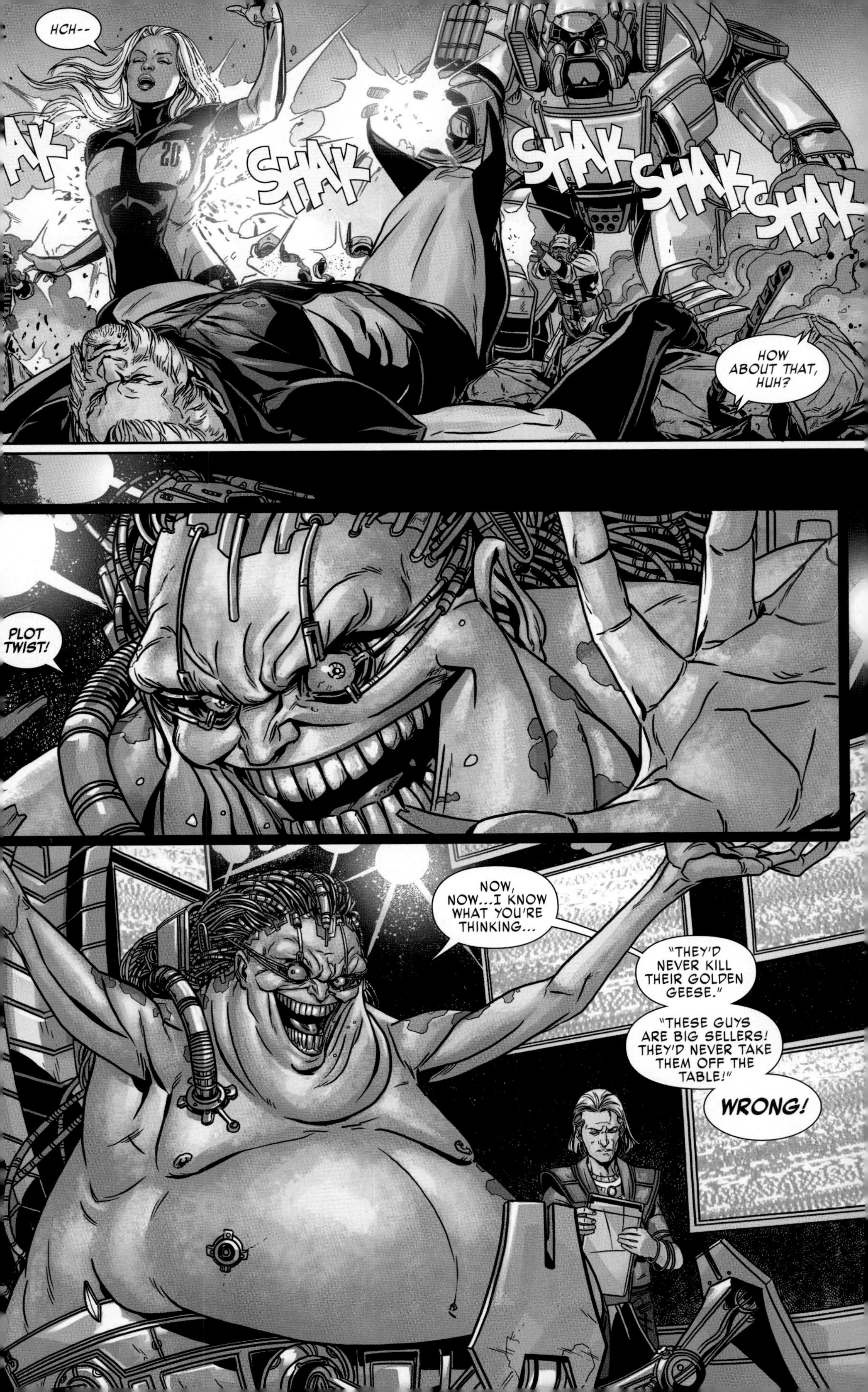
HCH--
AK
SHAK
SHAK
SHAK
SHAK
HOW ABOUT THAT, HUH?
PLOT TWIST!
NOW, NOW...I KNOW WHAT YOU'RE THINKING...
"THEY'D NEVER KILL THEIR GOLDEN GEESE."
"THESE GUYS ARE BIG SELLERS! THEY'D NEVER TAKE THEM OFF THE TABLE!"
WRONG!

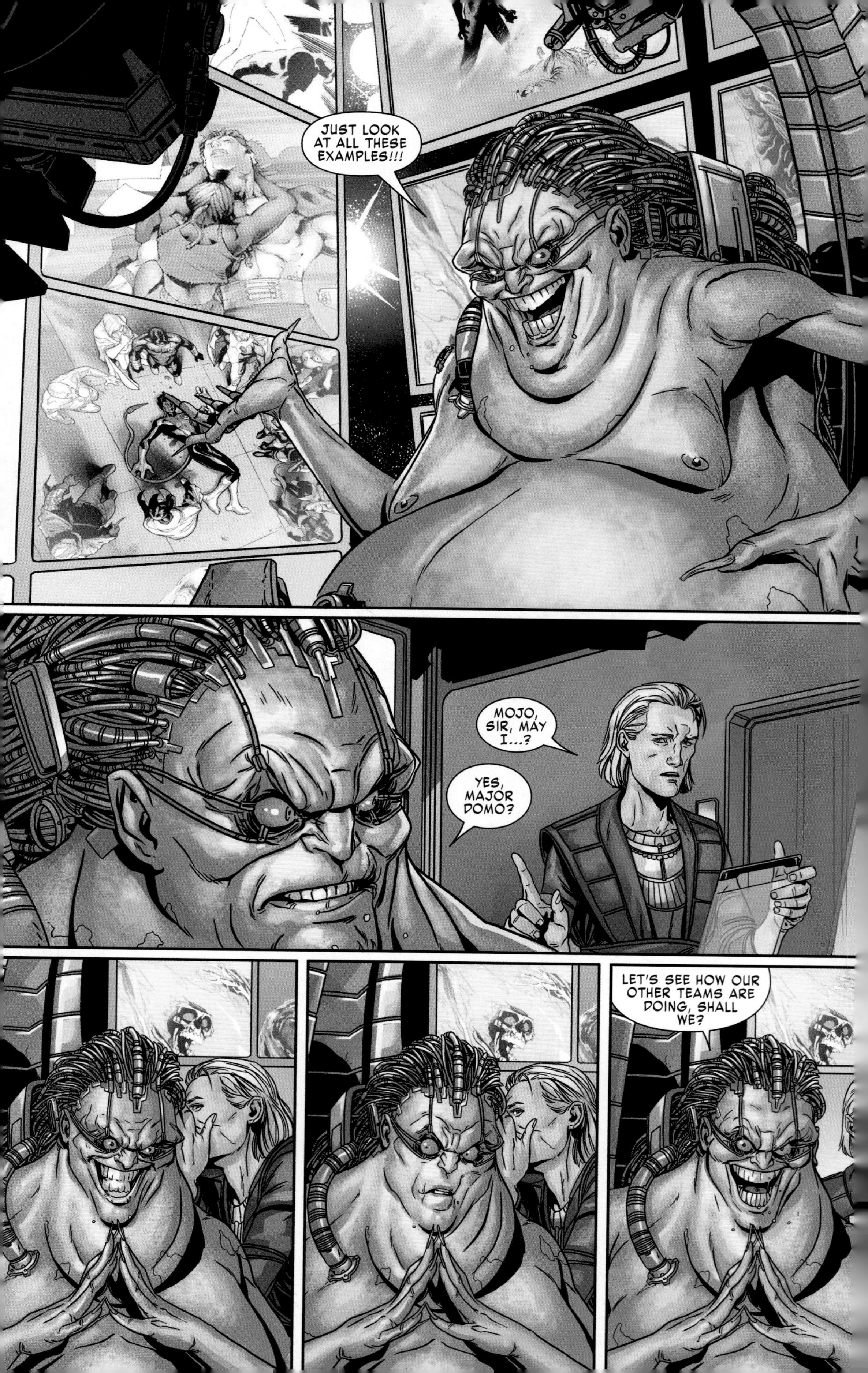
JUST LOOK AT ALL THESE EXAMPLES!!!
MOJO, SIR, MAY I...?
YES, MAJOR DOMO?
LET'S SEE HOW OUR OTHER TEAMS ARE DOING, SHALL WE?

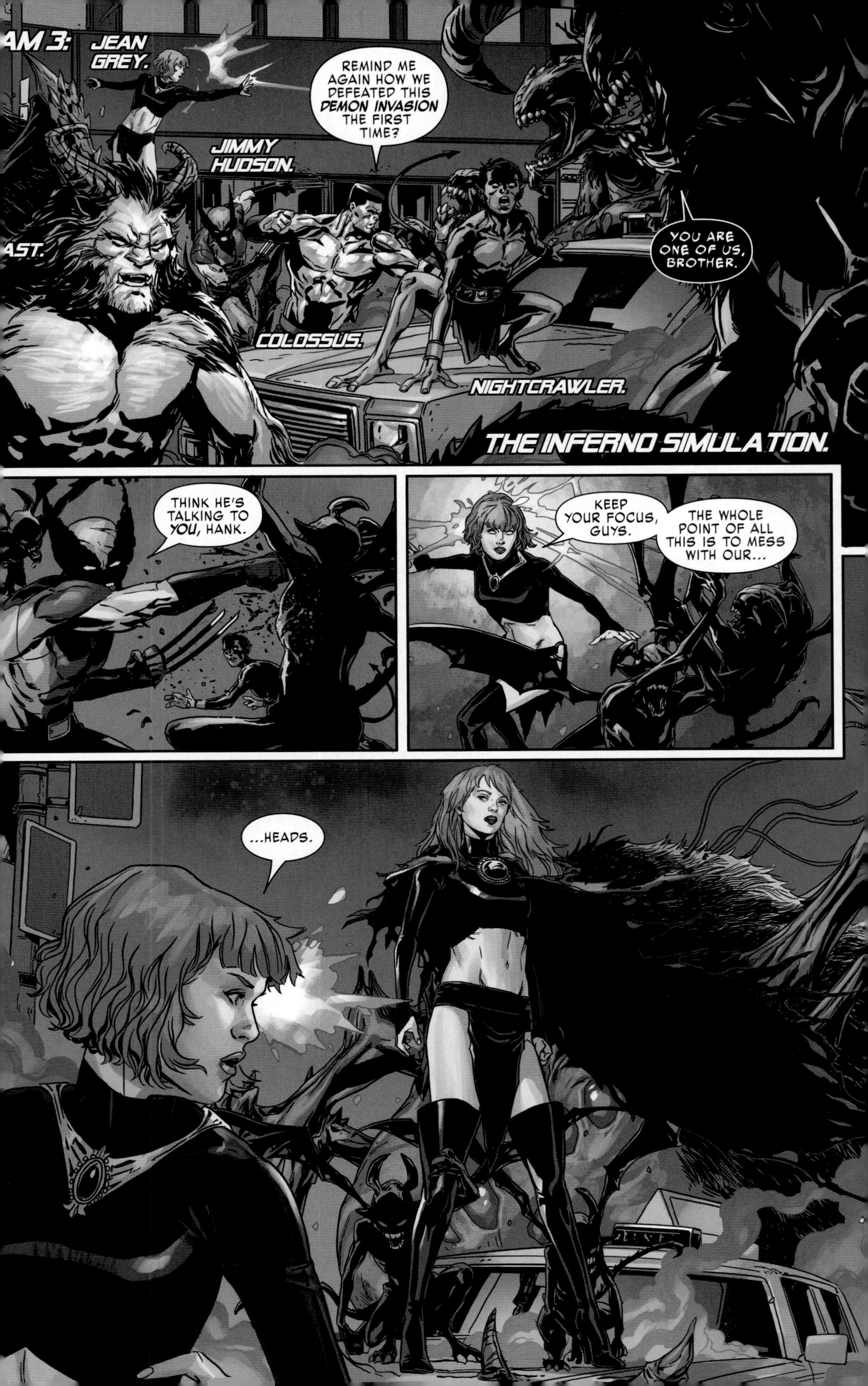
AM 3: JEAN GREY.
REMIND ME AGAIN HOW WE DEFEATED THIS DEMON INVASION THE FIRST TIME?
JIMMY HUDSON.
AST.
YOU ARE ONE OF US, BROTHER.
COLOSSUS.
NIGHTCRAWLER.
THE INFERNO SIMULATION.
THINK HE'S TALKING TO YOU, HANK.
KEEP YOUR FOCUS, GUYS.
THE WHOLE POINT OF ALL THIS IS TO MESS WITH OUR...
...HEADS.

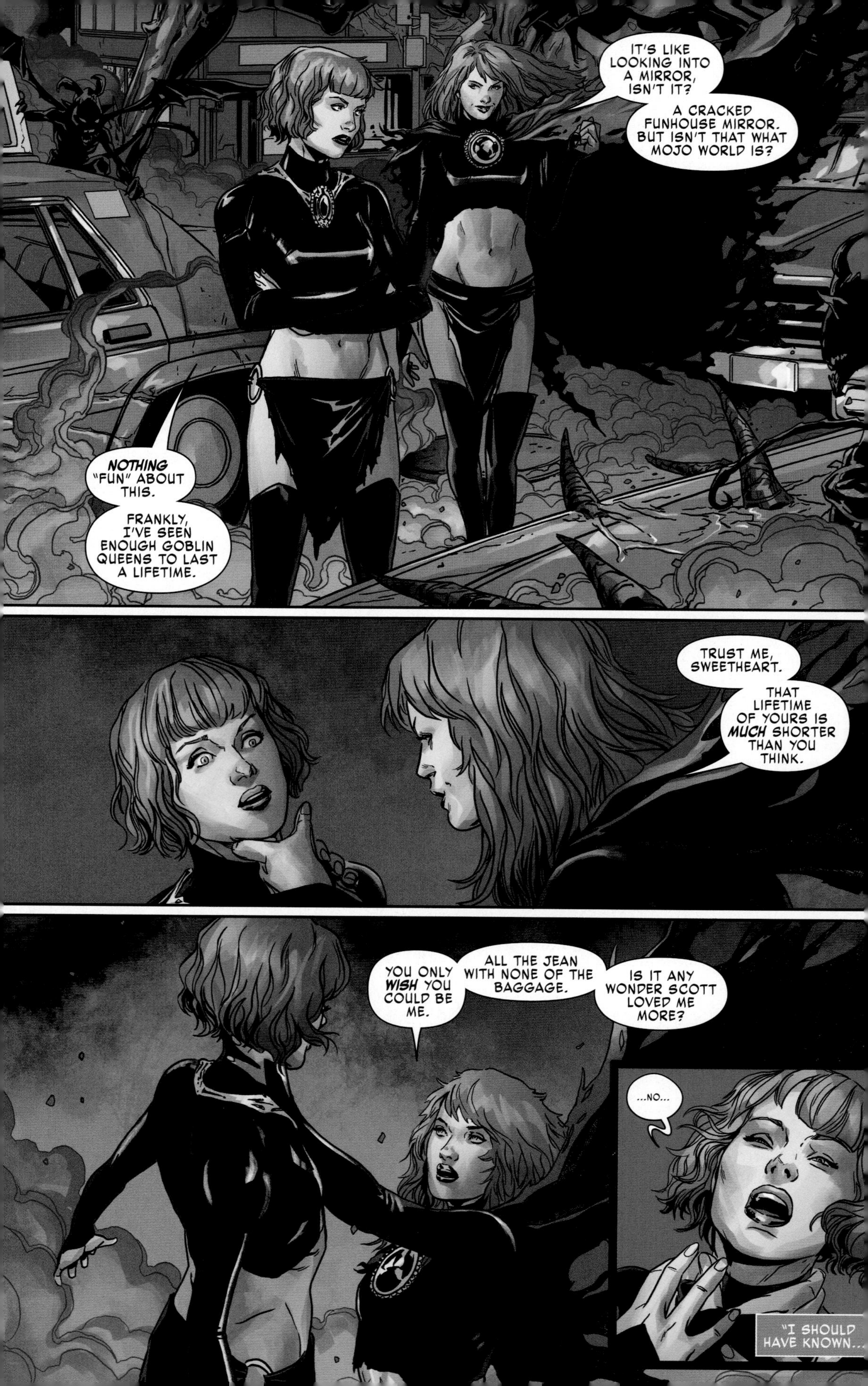
IT'S LIKE LOOKING INTO A MIRROR, ISN'T IT?
A CRACKED FUNHOUSE MIRROR. BUT ISN'T THAT WHAT MOJO WORLD IS?
NOTHING "FUN" ABOUT THIS.
FRANKLY, I'VE SEEN ENOUGH GOBLIN QUEENS TO LAST A LIFETIME.
TRUST ME, SWEETHEART.
THAT LIFETIME OF YOURS IS MUCH SHORTER THAN YOU THINK.
YOU ONLY WISH YOU COULD BE ME.
ALL THE JEAN WITH NONE OF THE BAGGAGE.
IS IT ANY WONDER SCOTT LOVED ME MORE?
...NO...
"I SHOULD HAVE KNOWN...

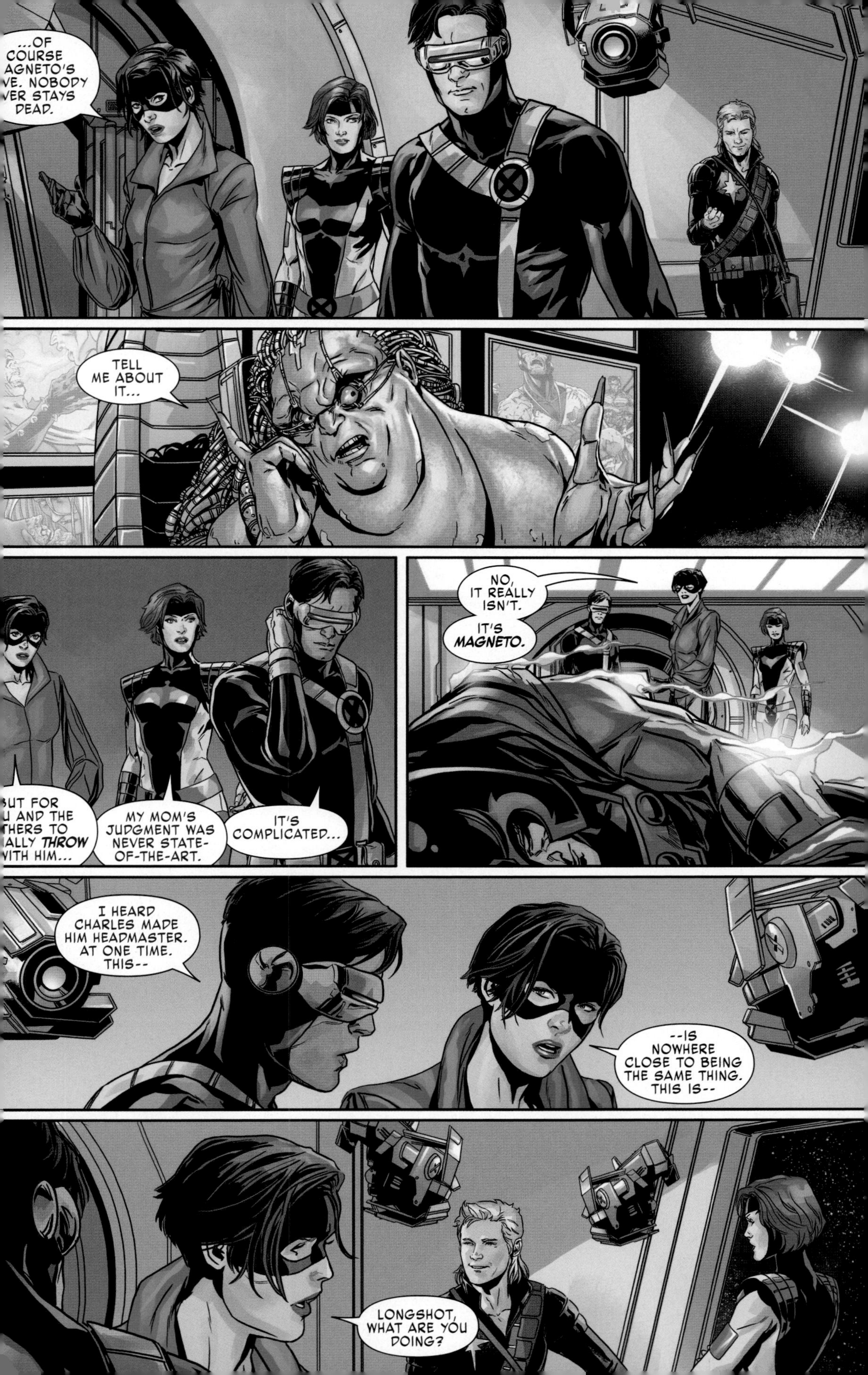
...OF COURSE AGNETO'S VE. NOBODY VER STAYS DEAD.
TELL ME ABOUT IT...
UT FOR U AND THE THERS TO ALLY THROW WITH HIM...
MY MOM'S JUDGMENT WAS NEVER STATE-OF-THE-ART.
IT'S COMPLICATED...
NO, IT REALLY ISN'T.
IT'S MAGNETO.
I HEARD CHARLES MADE HIM HEADMASTER. AT ONE TIME. THIS--
--IS NOWHERE CLOSE TO BEING THE SAME THING. THIS IS--
LONGSHOT, WHAT ARE YOU DOING?

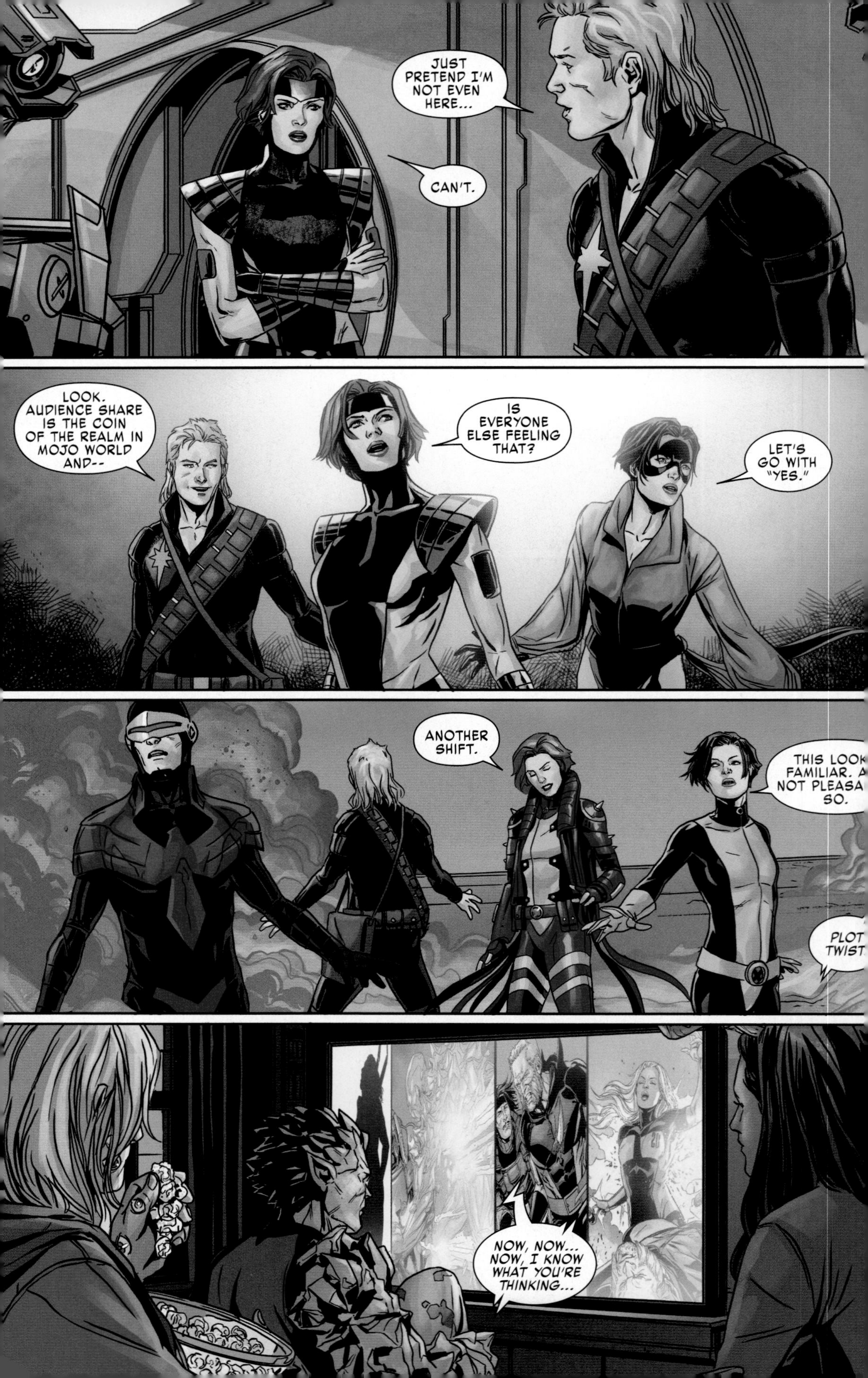
JUST PRETEND I'M NOT EVEN HERE...
CAN'T.
LOOK. AUDIENCE SHARE IS THE COIN OF THE REALM IN MOJO WORLD AND--
IS EVERYONE ELSE FEELING THAT?
LET'S GO WITH "YES."
ANOTHER SHIFT.
THIS LOOK FAMILIAR. A NOT PLEASA SO.
PLOT TWIST
NOW, NOW... NOW, I KNOW WHAT YOU'RE THINKING...

"THEY'D NEVER KILL THEIR GOLDEN GEESE."

"THESE GUYS ARE BIG SELLERS! THEY'D NEVER TAKE THEM OFF THE TABLE!"

AND *I* NEVER THOUGHT I'D HOPE MOJO WAS TELLING THE TRUTH.

E XAVIER INSTITUTE FOR
NTANT EDUCATION AND OUTREACH.

WE SHOULD BE OUT THERE.

DOING WHAT? THE OTHERS ARE HANDLING CROWD CONTROL.

AND WE'VE TRIED GETTING THROUGH THE FORCE SHIELDS SURROUNDING THOSE SPIRES.

EVERYBODY AS. WE'RE STUCK SITTING HERE WATCHING.

WE JUST GOTTA WAIT. AND HOPE.

NOT EASY WHEN YOUR FRIENDS ARE DYING ON TV, THOUGH.

NO, IT'S NOT.

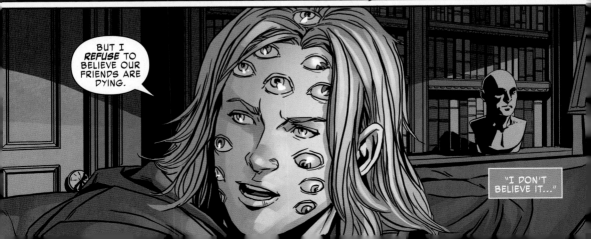

BUT I *REFUSE* TO BELIEVE OUR FRIENDS ARE DYING.

"I DON'T BELIEVE IT..."

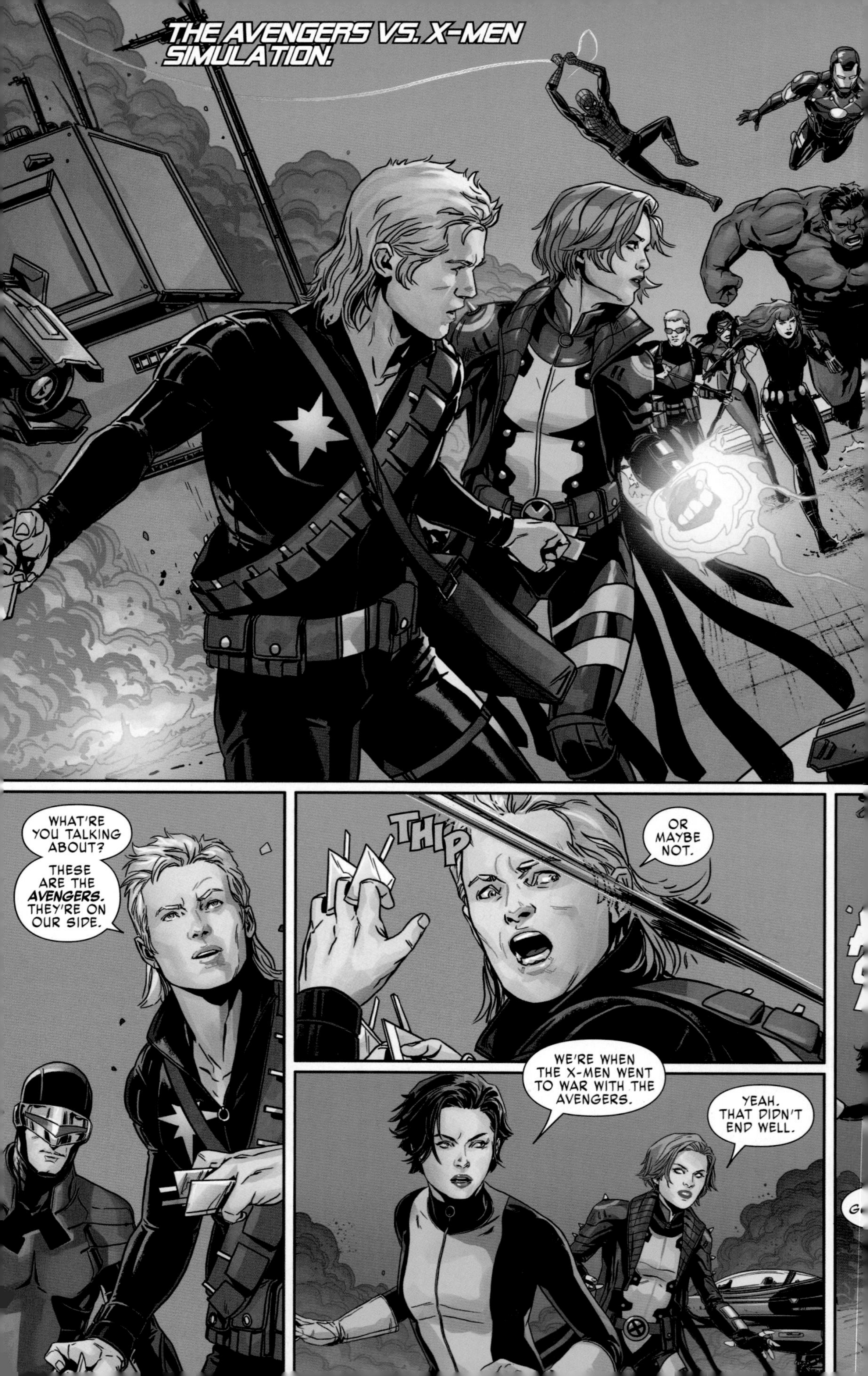
THE AVENGERS VS. X-MEN SIMULATION.
WHAT'RE YOU TALKING ABOUT?
THESE ARE THE AVENGERS. THEY'RE ON OUR SIDE.
THIP
OR MAYBE NOT.
WE'RE WHEN THE X-MEN WENT TO WAR WITH THE AVENGERS.
YEAH. THAT DIDN'T END WELL.

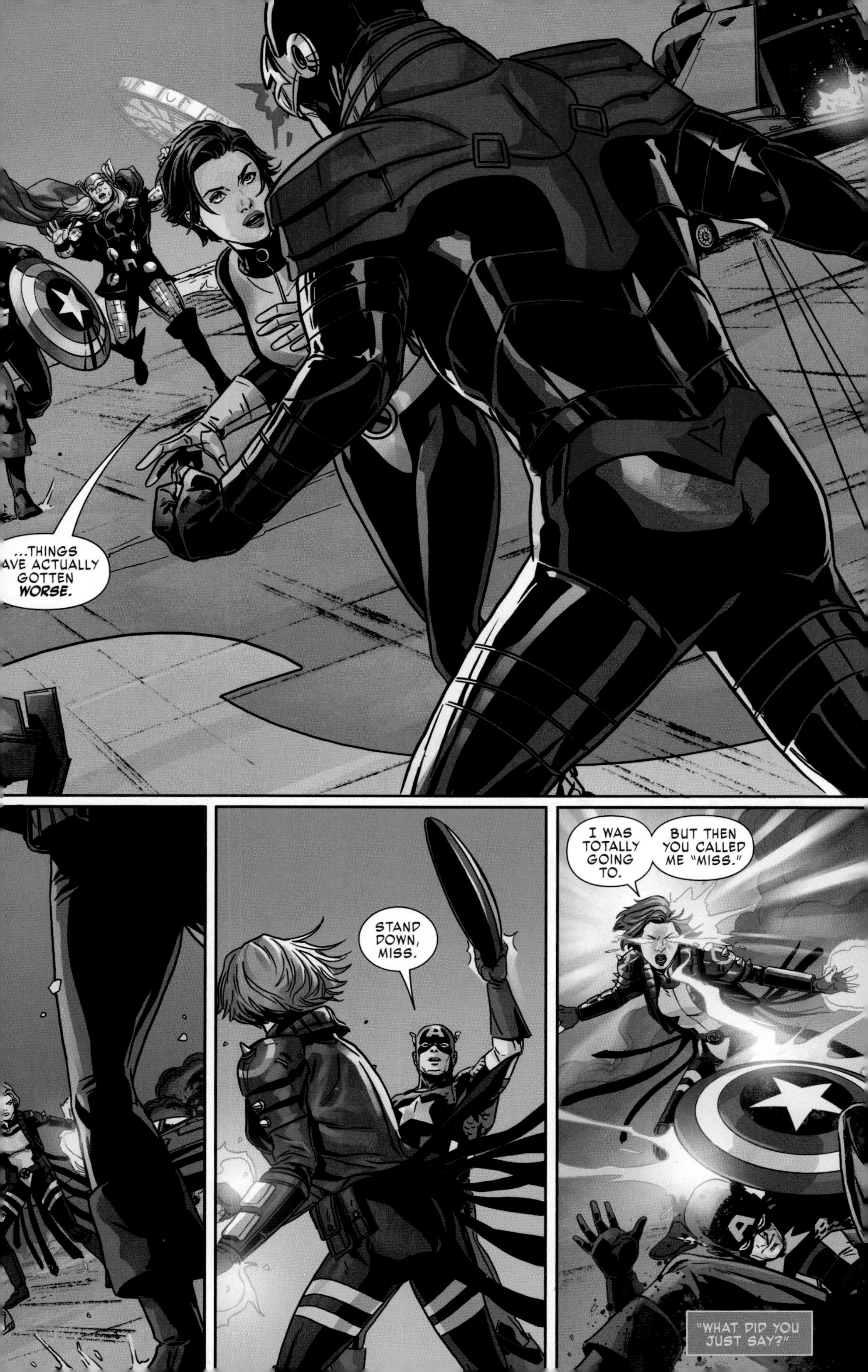
...THINGS AVE ACTUALLY GOTTEN *WORSE.*
STAND DOWN, MISS.
I WAS TOTALLY GOING TO.
BUT THEN YOU CALLED ME "MISS."
"WHAT DID YOU JUST SAY?"

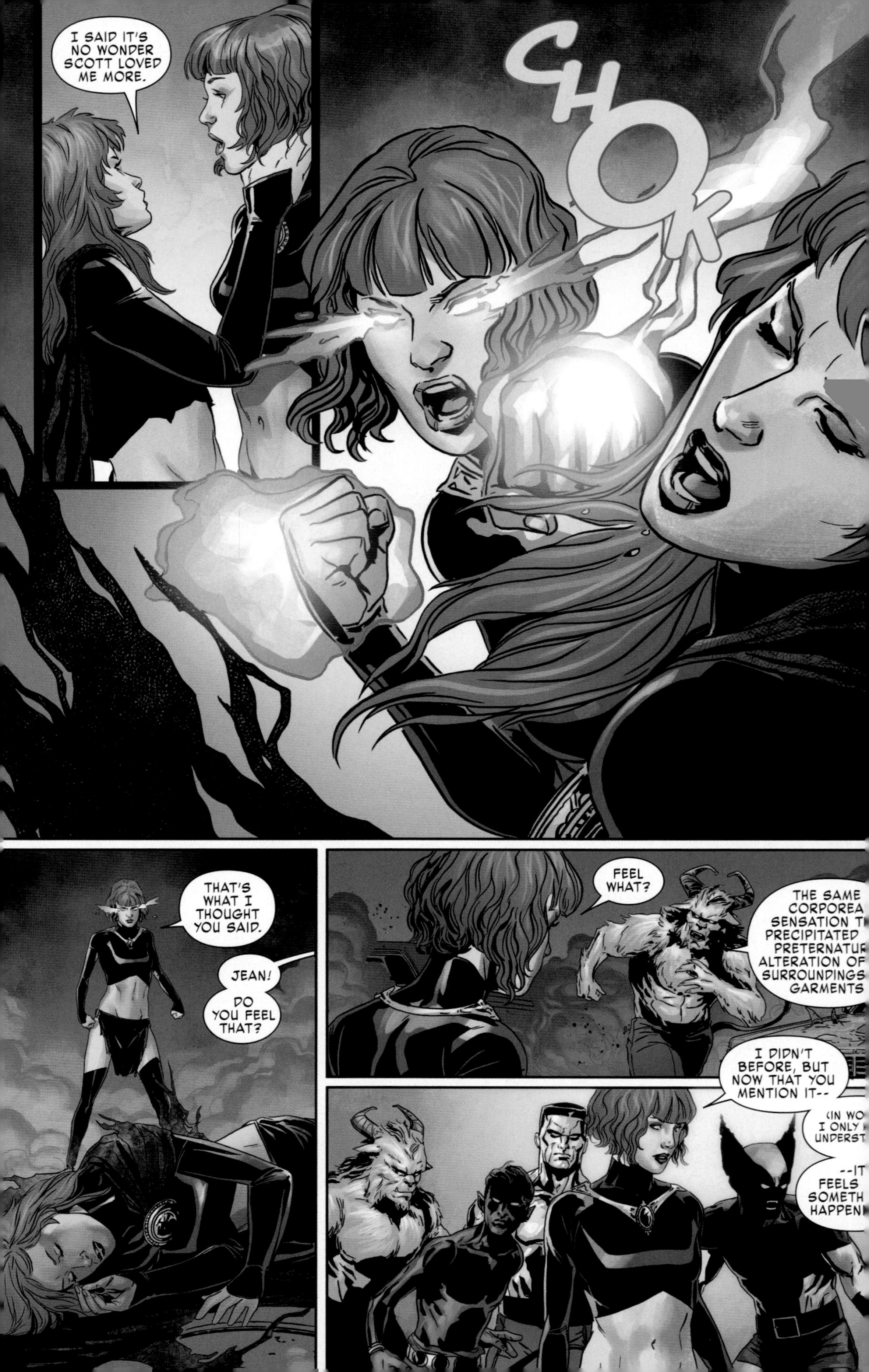
I SAID IT'S NO WONDER SCOTT LOVED ME MORE.
CHOK
THAT'S WHAT I THOUGHT YOU SAID.
JEAN!
DO YOU FEEL THAT?
FEEL WHAT?
THE SAME CORPOREA SENSATION T PRECIPITATED PRETERNATUR ALTERATION OF SURROUNDINGS GARMENTS
I DIDN'T BEFORE, BUT NOW THAT YOU MENTION IT--
(IN WO I ONLY UNDERST
--IT FEELS SOMETH HAPPEN

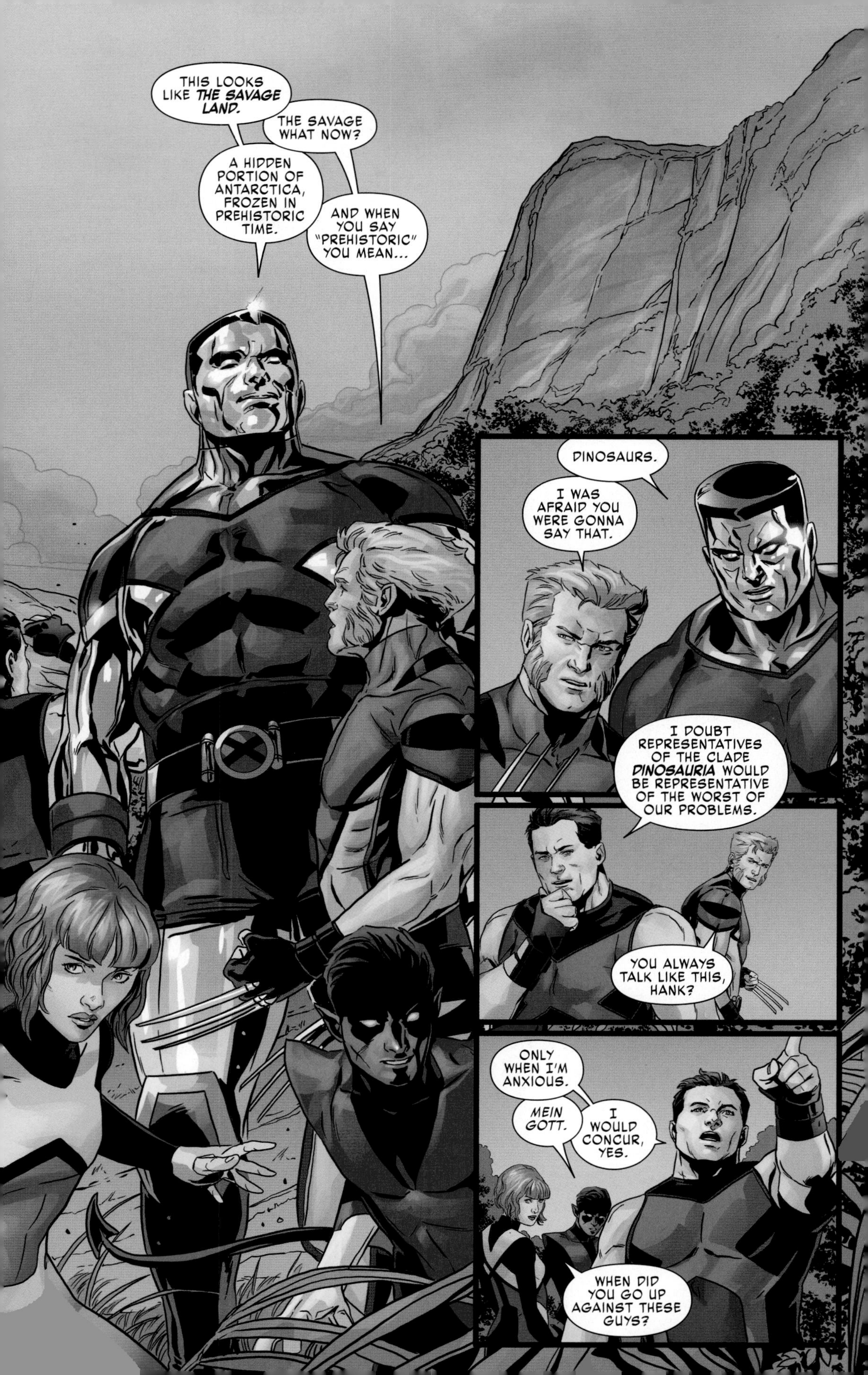
THIS LOOKS LIKE *THE SAVAGE LAND.*
THE SAVAGE WHAT NOW?
A HIDDEN PORTION OF ANTARCTICA, FROZEN IN PREHISTORIC TIME.
AND WHEN YOU SAY "PREHISTORIC" YOU MEAN...
DINOSAURS.
I WAS AFRAID YOU WERE GONNA SAY THAT.
I DOUBT REPRESENTATIVES OF THE CLADE *DINOSAURIA* WOULD BE REPRESENTATIVE OF THE WORST OF OUR PROBLEMS.
YOU ALWAYS TALK LIKE THIS, HANK?
ONLY WHEN I'M ANXIOUS.
MEIN GOTT.
I WOULD CONCUR, YES.
WHEN DID YOU GO UP AGAINST THESE GUYS?

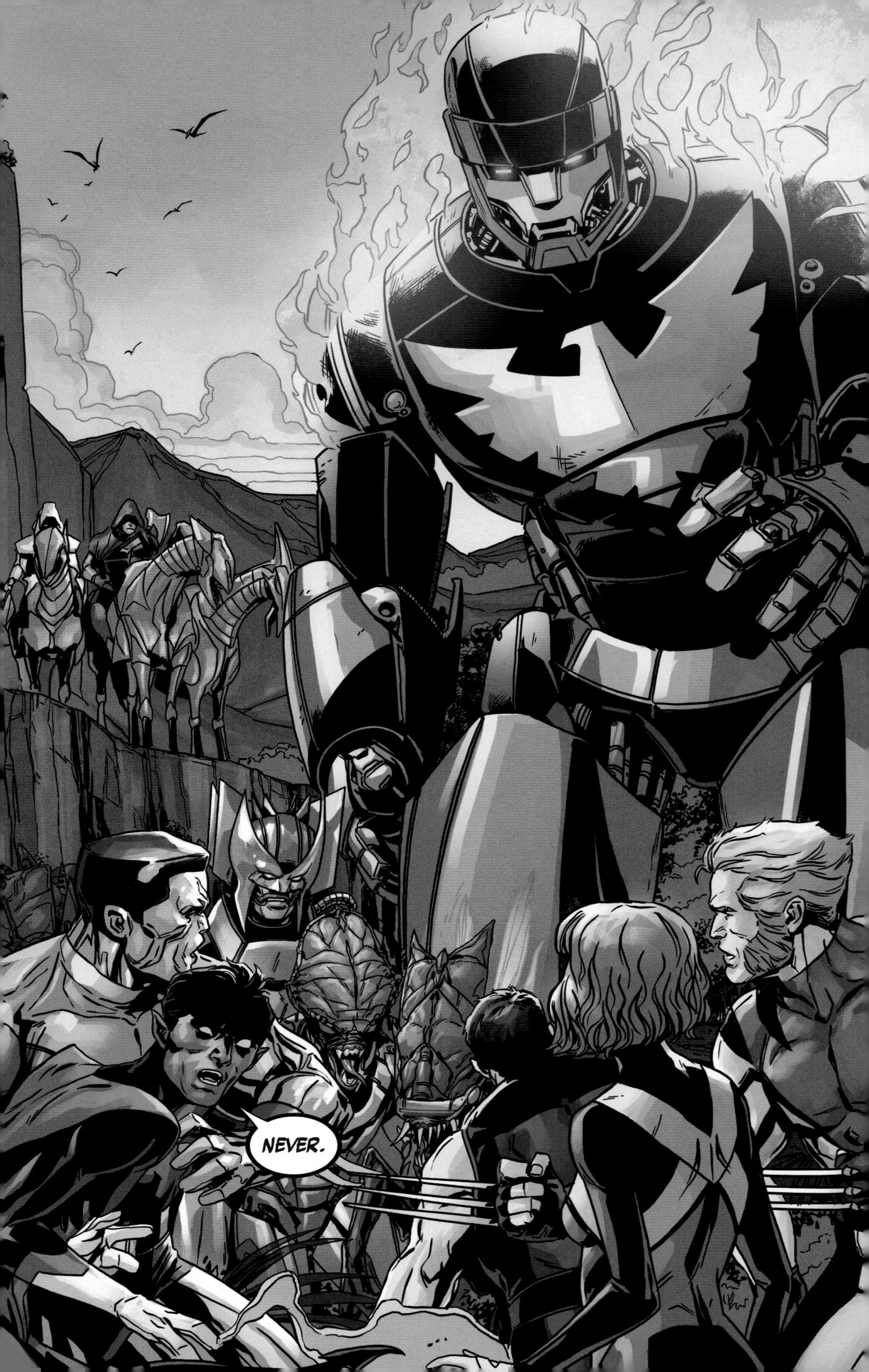
NEVER.

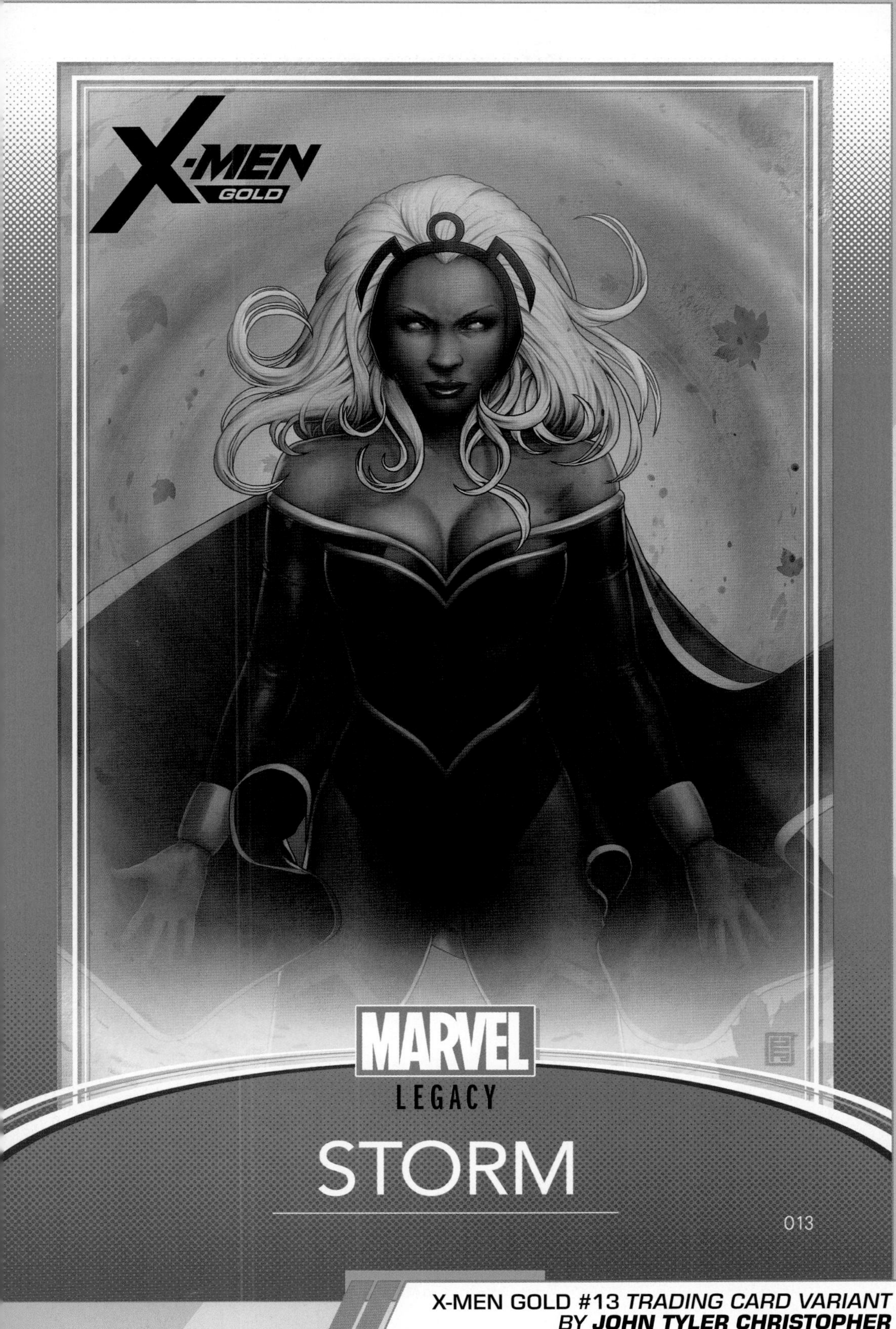
X-MEN GOLD
MARVEL
LEGACY
STORM
013

X-MEN GOLD #13 *TRADING CARD VARIANT*
BY **JOHN TYLER CHRISTOPHER**

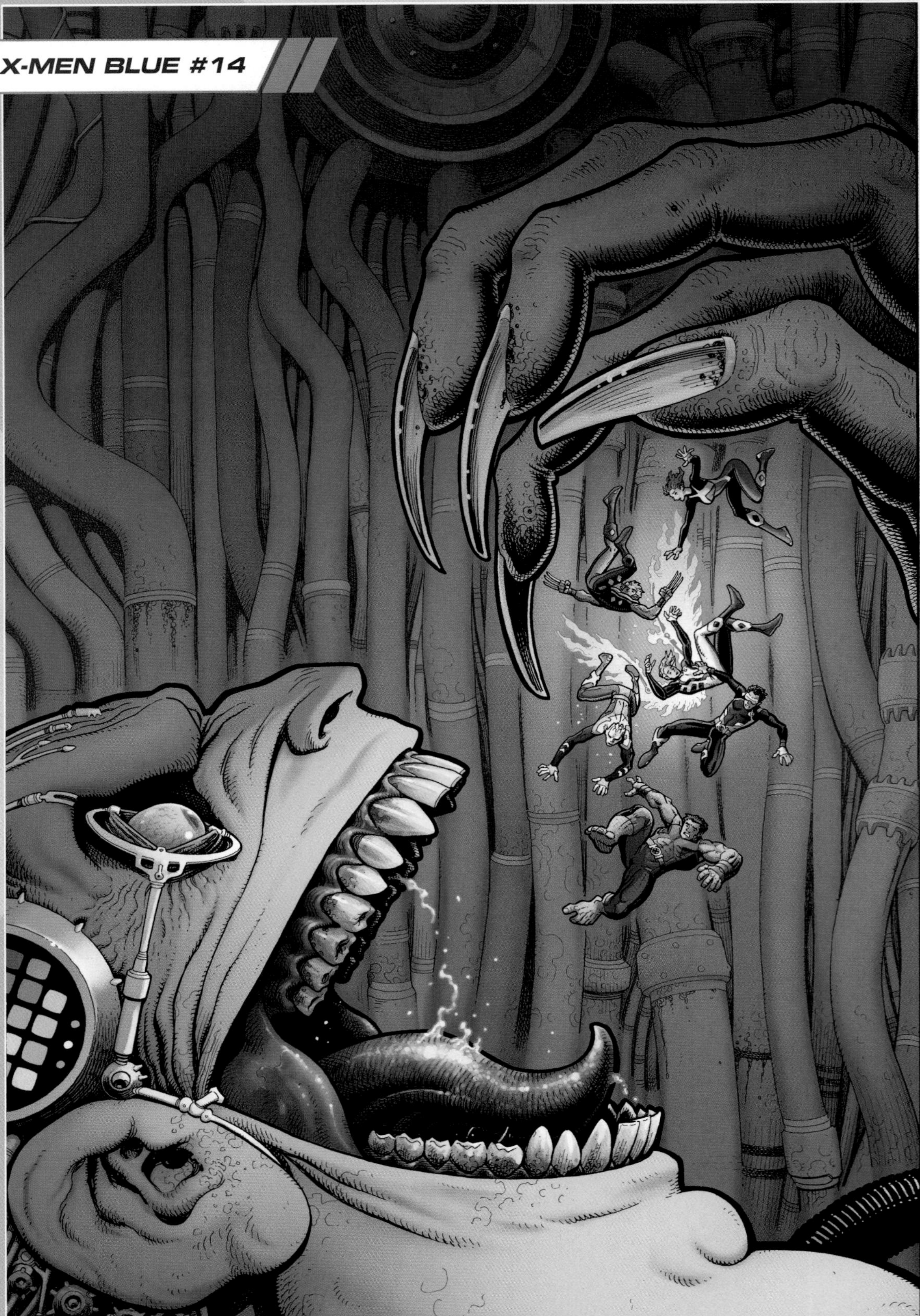

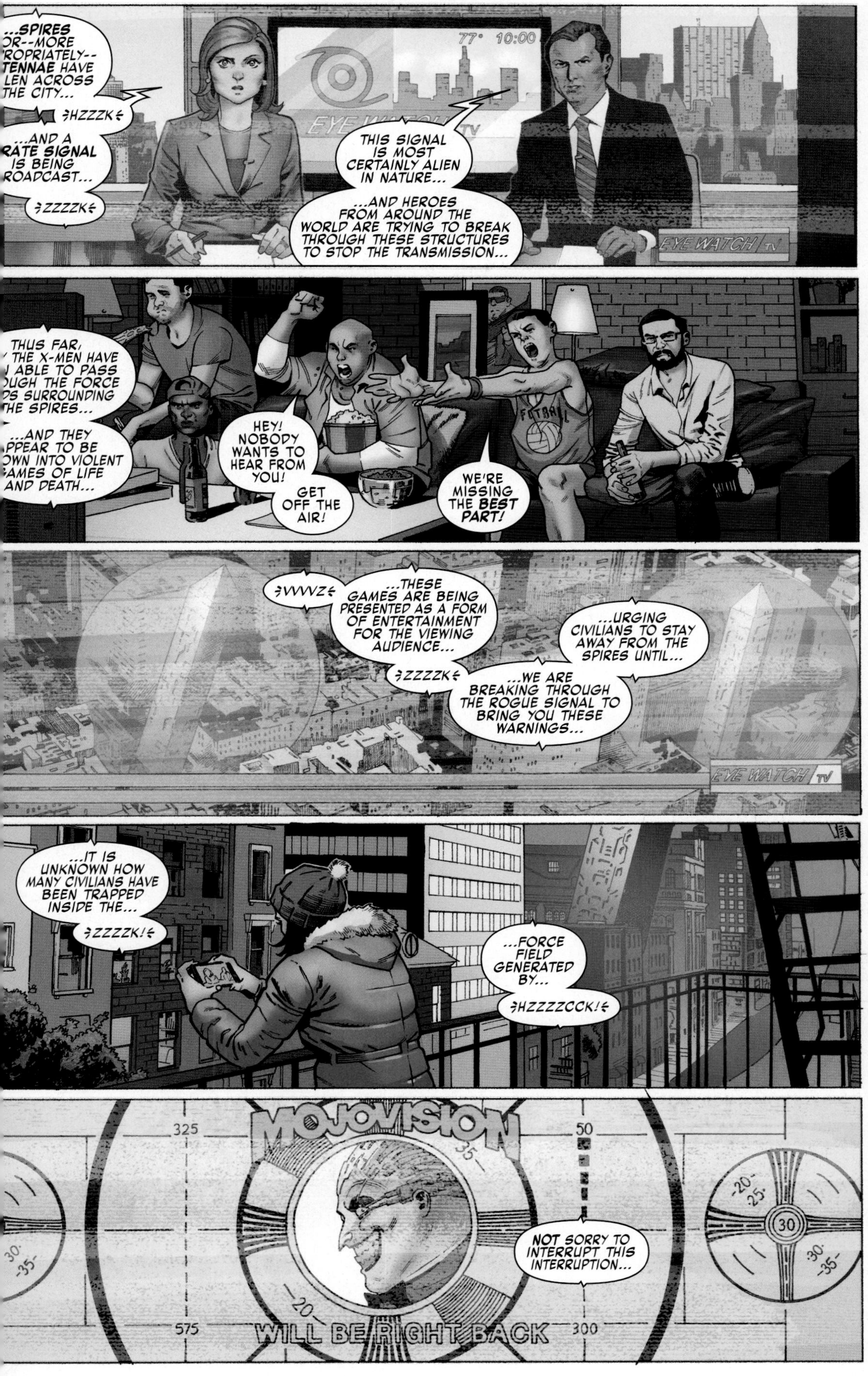
...SPIRES OR--MORE PROPRIATELY--TENNAE HAVE LEN ACROSS THE CITY...
77° 10:00
EYE WATCH TV
ƎHZZZKƐ
...AND A RATE SIGNAL IS BEING ROADCAST...
ƎZZZZKƐ
THIS SIGNAL IS MOST CERTAINLY ALIEN IN NATURE...
...AND HEROES FROM AROUND THE WORLD ARE TRYING TO BREAK THROUGH THESE STRUCTURES TO STOP THE TRANSMISSION...
EYE WATCH TV
THUS FAR, THE X-MEN HAVE N ABLE TO PASS OUGH THE FORCE DS SURROUNDING THE SPIRES...
...AND THEY PPEAR TO BE OWN INTO VIOLENT GAMES OF LIFE AND DEATH...
HEY! NOBODY WANTS TO HEAR FROM YOU!
GET OFF THE AIR!
WE'RE MISSING THE BEST PART!
ƎVVVVZƐ
...THESE GAMES ARE BEING PRESENTED AS A FORM OF ENTERTAINMENT FOR THE VIEWING AUDIENCE...
ƎZZZZKƐ
...URGING CIVILIANS TO STAY AWAY FROM THE SPIRES UNTIL...
...WE ARE BREAKING THROUGH THE ROGUE SIGNAL TO BRING YOU THESE WARNINGS...
EYE WATCH TV
...IT IS UNKNOWN HOW MANY CIVILIANS HAVE BEEN TRAPPED INSIDE THE...
ƎZZZZK!Ɛ
...FORCE FIELD GENERATED BY...
ƎHZZZZCCK!Ɛ
MOJOVISION
325
50
NOT SORRY TO INTERRUPT THIS INTERRUPTION...
575
300
WILL BE RIGHT BACK

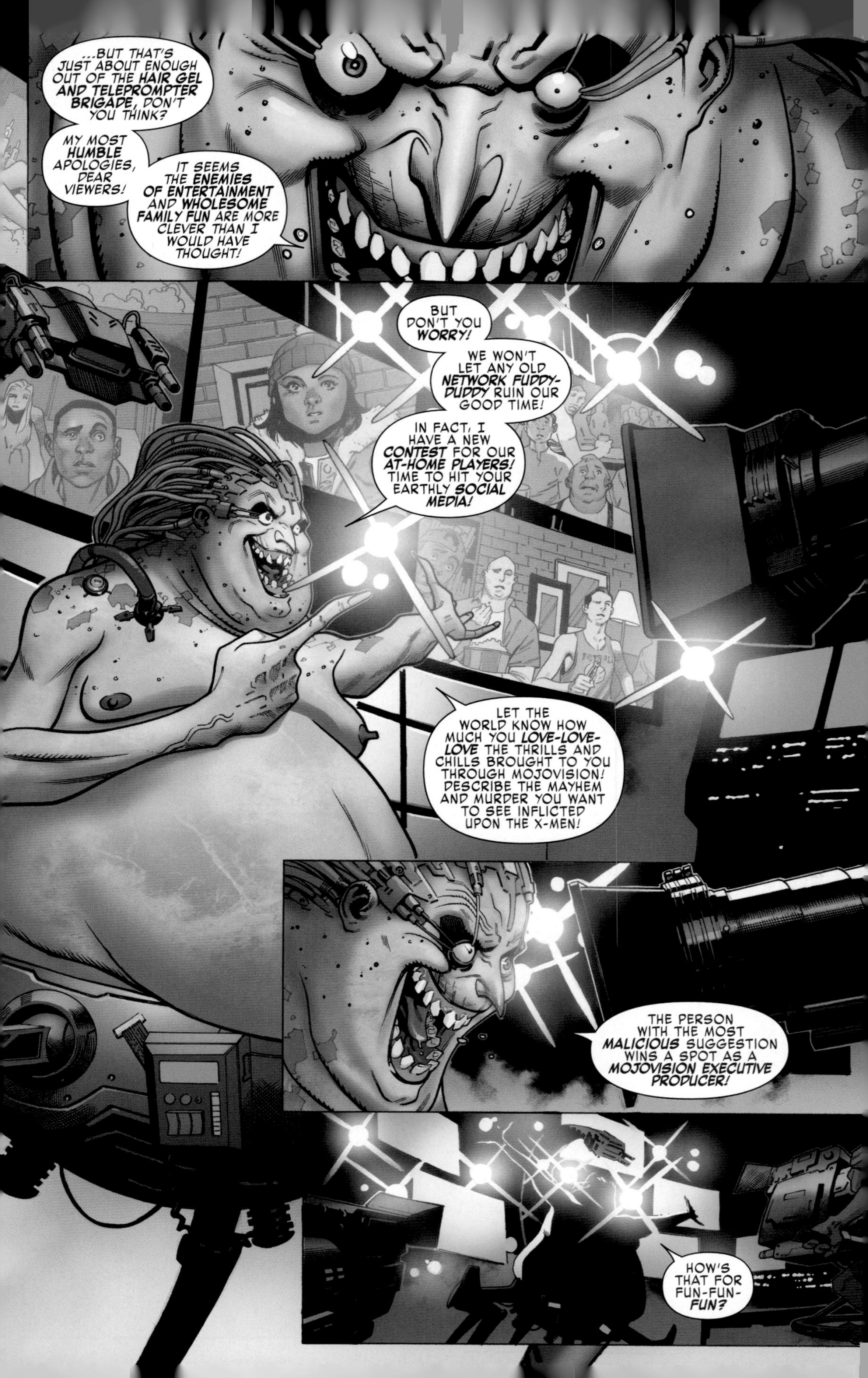
...BUT THAT'S JUST ABOUT ENOUGH OUT OF THE HAIR GEL AND TELEPROMPTER BRIGADE, DON'T YOU THINK?
MY MOST HUMBLE APOLOGIES, DEAR VIEWERS!
IT SEEMS THE ENEMIES OF ENTERTAINMENT AND WHOLESOME FAMILY FUN ARE MORE CLEVER THAN I WOULD HAVE THOUGHT!
BUT DON'T YOU WORRY!
WE WON'T LET ANY OLD NETWORK FUDDY-DUDDY RUIN OUR GOOD TIME!
IN FACT, I HAVE A NEW CONTEST FOR OUR AT-HOME PLAYERS! TIME TO HIT YOUR EARTHLY SOCIAL MEDIA!
LET THE WORLD KNOW HOW MUCH YOU LOVE-LOVE-LOVE THE THRILLS AND CHILLS BROUGHT TO YOU THROUGH MOJOVISION! DESCRIBE THE MAYHEM AND MURDER YOU WANT TO SEE INFLICTED UPON THE X-MEN!
THE PERSON WITH THE MOST MALICIOUS SUGGESTION WINS A SPOT AS A MOJOVISION EXECUTIVE PRODUCER!
HOW'S THAT FOR FUN-FUN-FUN?

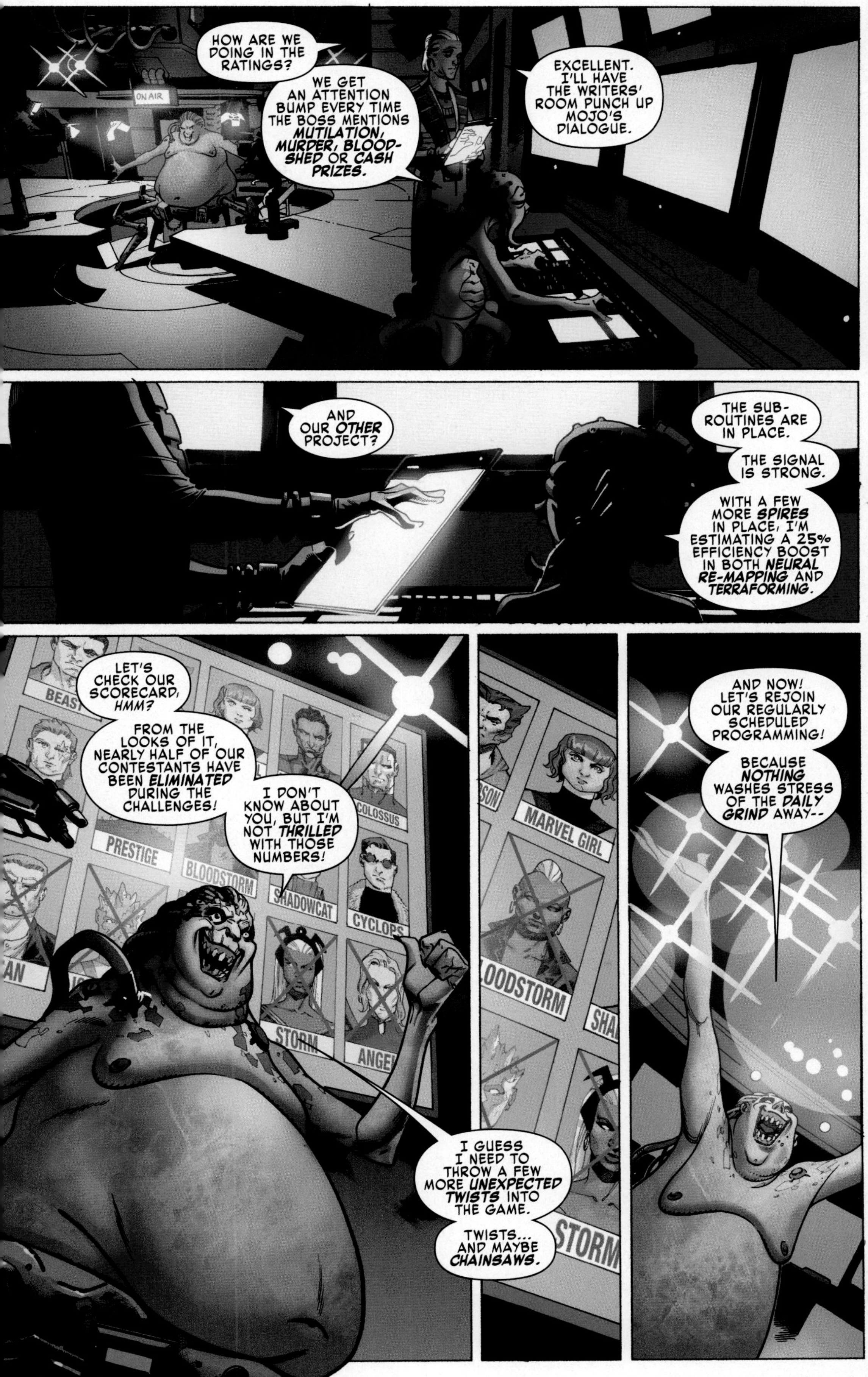
HOW ARE WE DOING IN THE RATINGS?
WE GET AN ATTENTION BUMP EVERY TIME THE BOSS MENTIONS MUTILATION, MURDER, BLOODSHED OR CASH PRIZES.
EXCELLENT. I'LL HAVE THE WRITERS' ROOM PUNCH UP MOJO'S DIALOGUE.
ON AIR
AND OUR OTHER PROJECT?
THE SUB-ROUTINES ARE IN PLACE.
THE SIGNAL IS STRONG.
WITH A FEW MORE SPIRES IN PLACE, I'M ESTIMATING A 25% EFFICIENCY BOOST IN BOTH NEURAL RE-MAPPING AND TERRAFORMING.
LET'S CHECK OUR SCORECARD, HMM?
FROM THE LOOKS OF IT, NEARLY HALF OF OUR CONTESTANTS HAVE BEEN ELIMINATED DURING THE CHALLENGES!
I DON'T KNOW ABOUT YOU, BUT I'M NOT THRILLED WITH THOSE NUMBERS!
BEAST
COLOSSUS
PRESTIGE
BLOODSTORM
SHADOWCAT
CYCLOPS
STORM
MARVEL GIRL
I GUESS I NEED TO THROW A FEW MORE UNEXPECTED TWISTS INTO THE GAME.
TWISTS... AND MAYBE CHAINSAWS.
AND NOW! LET'S REJOIN OUR REGULARLY SCHEDULED PROGRAMMING!
BECAUSE NOTHING WASHES STRESS OF THE DAILY GRIND AWAY--

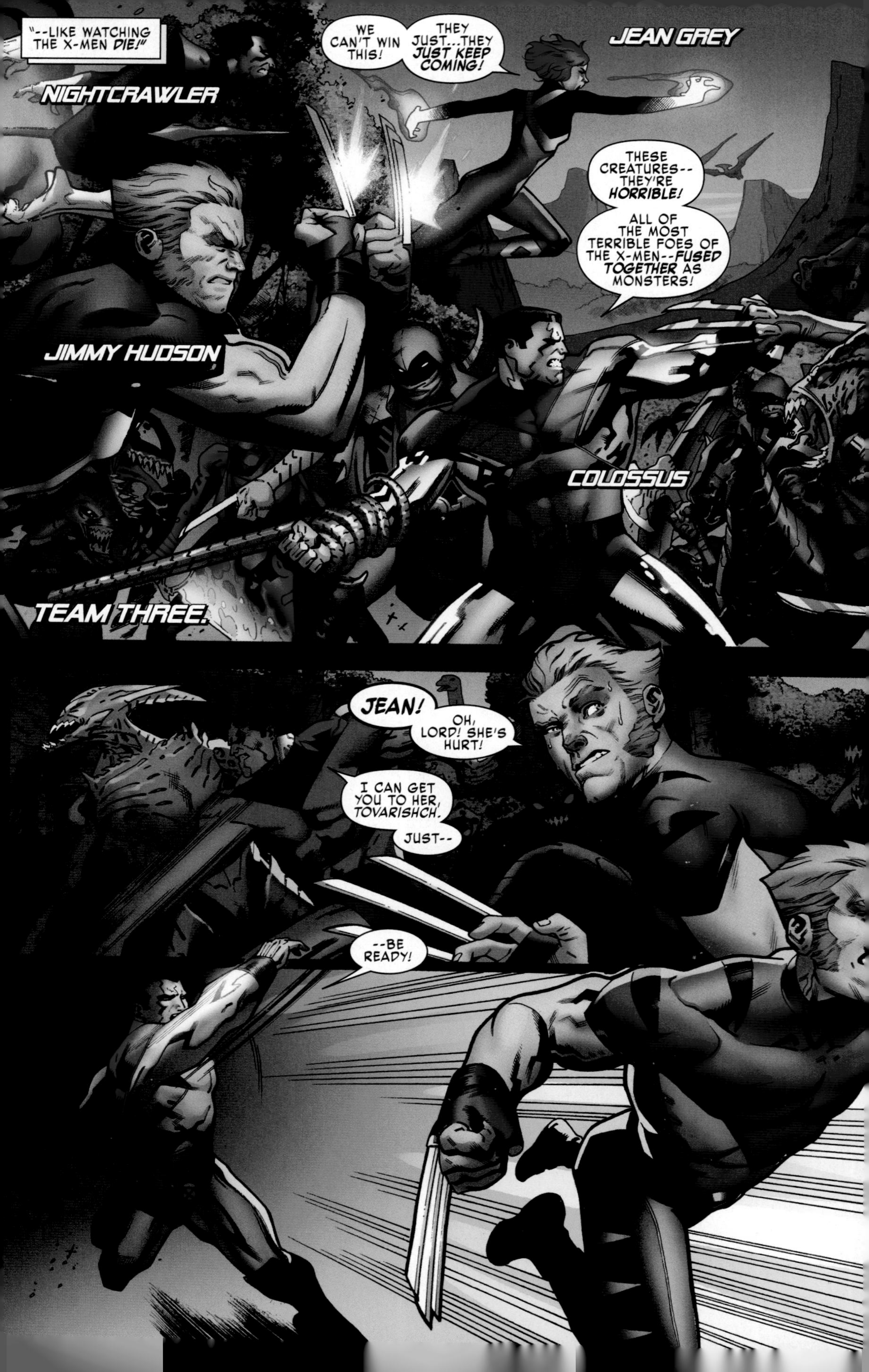
"--LIKE WATCHING THE X-MEN DIE!"
NIGHTCRAWLER
WE CAN'T WIN THIS!
THEY JUST...THEY JUST KEEP COMING!
JEAN GREY
THESE CREATURES-- THEY'RE HORRIBLE!
ALL OF THE MOST TERRIBLE FOES OF THE X-MEN--FUSED TOGETHER AS MONSTERS!
JIMMY HUDSON
COLOSSUS
TEAM THREE.
JEAN!
OH, LORD! SHE'S HURT!
I CAN GET YOU TO HER, TOVARISHCH.
JUST--
--BE READY!

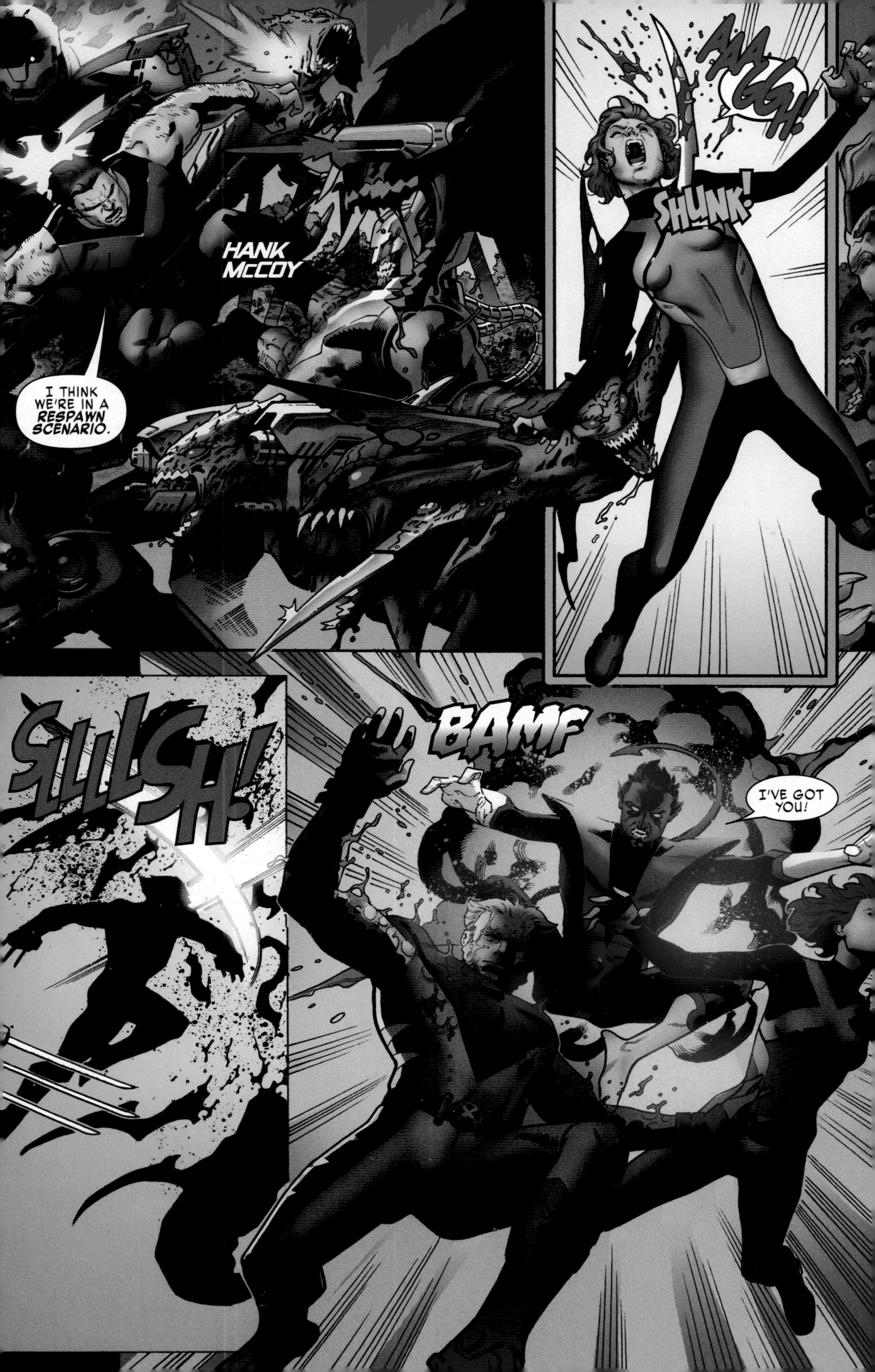

HANK McCOY
I THINK WE'RE IN A RESPAWN SCENARIO.
AAAGGH!
SHUNK!
SLLLSH!
BAMF
I'VE GOT YOU!

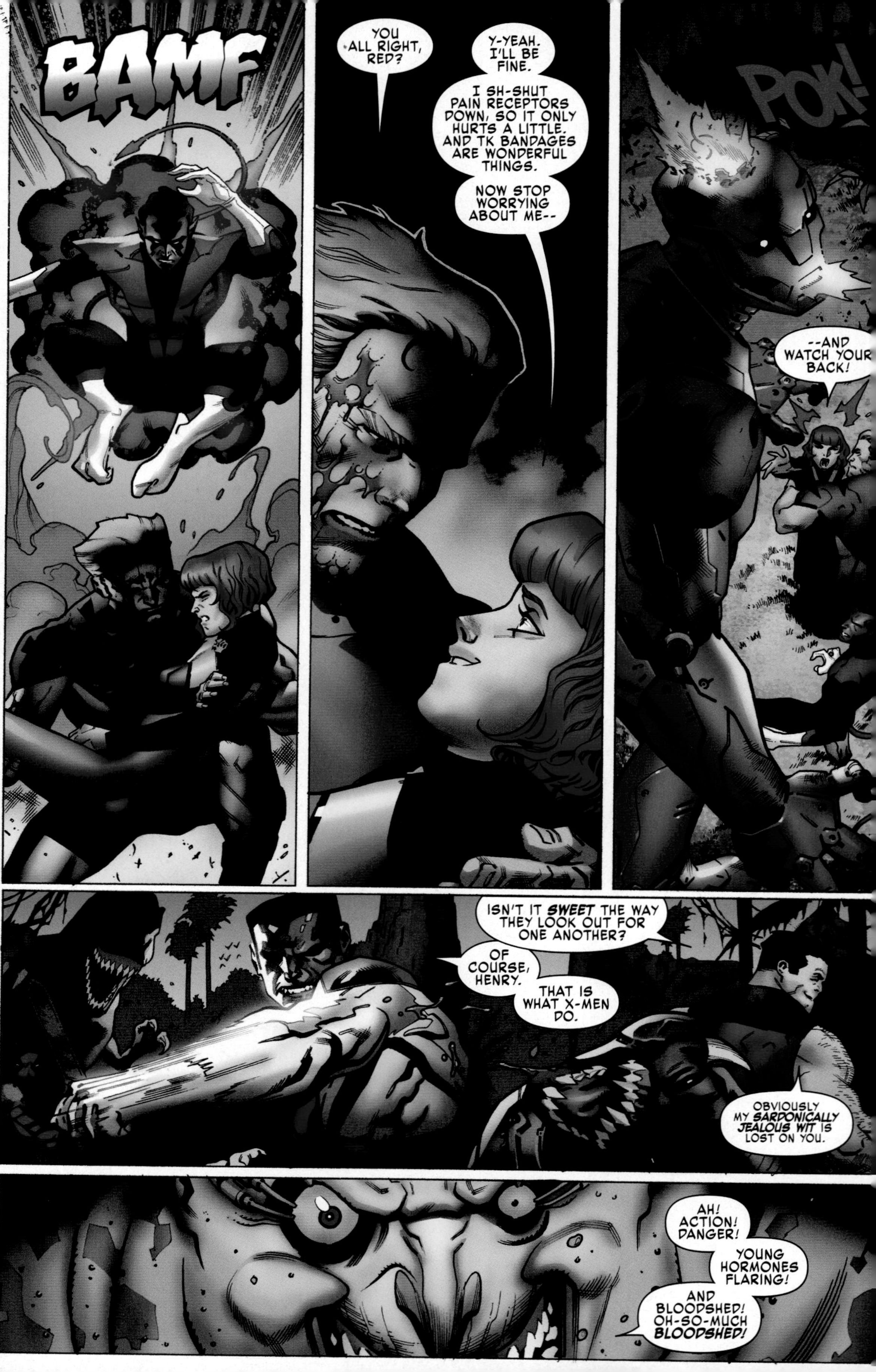
BAMF
YOU ALL RIGHT, RED?
Y-YEAH. I'LL BE FINE.
I SH-SHUT PAIN RECEPTORS DOWN, SO IT ONLY HURTS A LITTLE. AND TK BANDAGES ARE WONDERFUL THINGS.
NOW STOP WORRYING ABOUT ME--
POK!
--AND WATCH YOUR BACK!
ISN'T IT SWEET THE WAY THEY LOOK OUT FOR ONE ANOTHER?
OF COURSE, HENRY.
THAT IS WHAT X-MEN DO.
OBVIOUSLY MY SARDONICALLY JEALOUS WIT IS LOST ON YOU.
AH! ACTION! DANGER!
YOUNG HORMONES FLARING!
AND BLOODSHED! OH-SO-MUCH BLOODSHED!

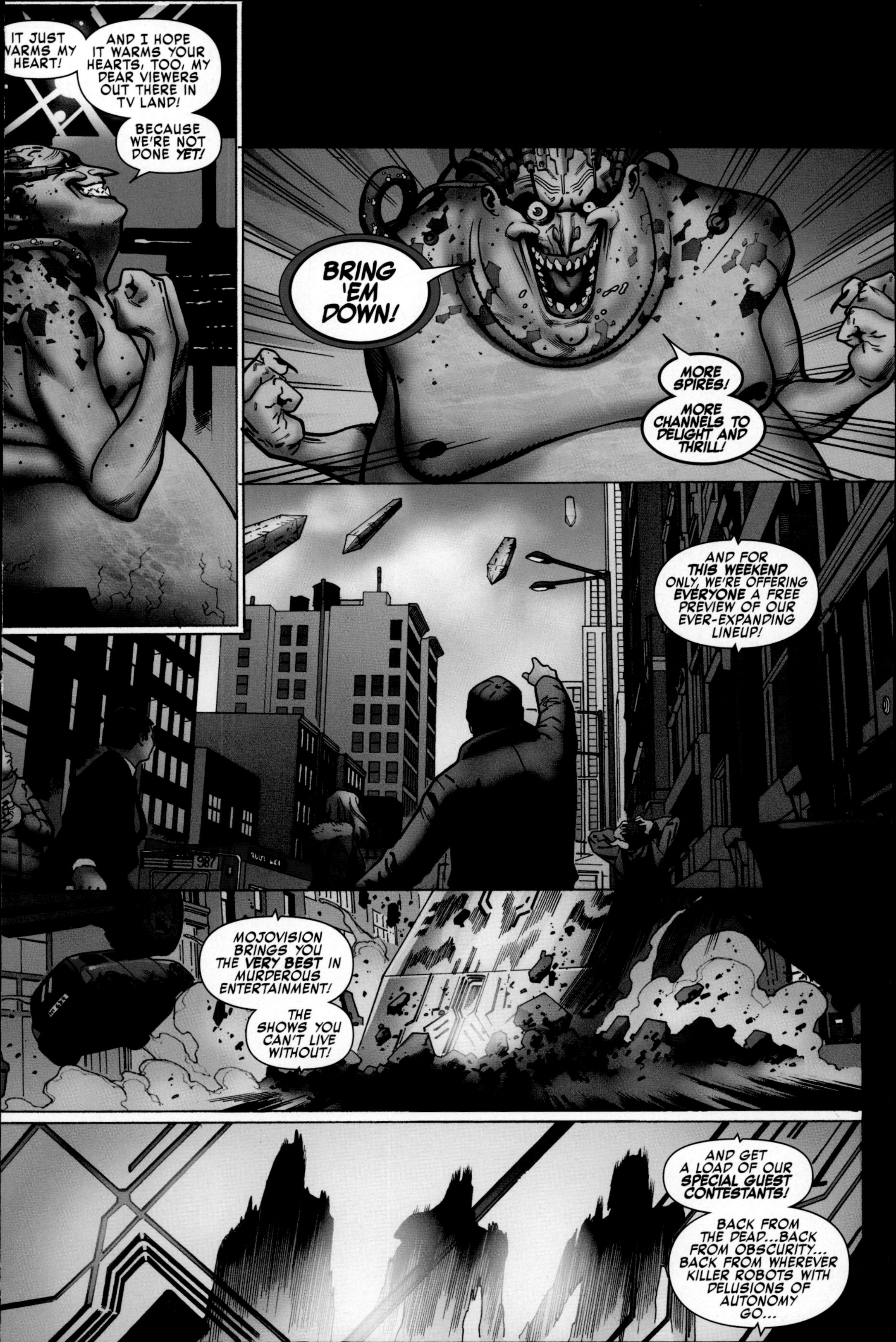

IT JUST WARMS MY HEART!
AND I HOPE IT WARMS YOUR HEARTS, TOO, MY DEAR VIEWERS OUT THERE IN TV LAND!
BECAUSE WE'RE NOT DONE YET!
BRING 'EM DOWN!
MORE SPIRES!
MORE CHANNELS TO DELIGHT AND THRILL!
AND FOR THIS WEEKEND ONLY, WE'RE OFFERING EVERYONE A FREE PREVIEW OF OUR EVER-EXPANDING LINEUP!
MOJOVISION BRINGS YOU THE VERY BEST IN MURDEROUS ENTERTAINMENT!
THE SHOWS YOU CAN'T LIVE WITHOUT!
AND GET A LOAD OF OUR SPECIAL GUEST CONTESTANTS!
BACK FROM THE DEAD...BACK FROM OBSCURITY... BACK FROM WHEREVER KILLER ROBOTS WITH DELUSIONS OF AUTONOMY GO...

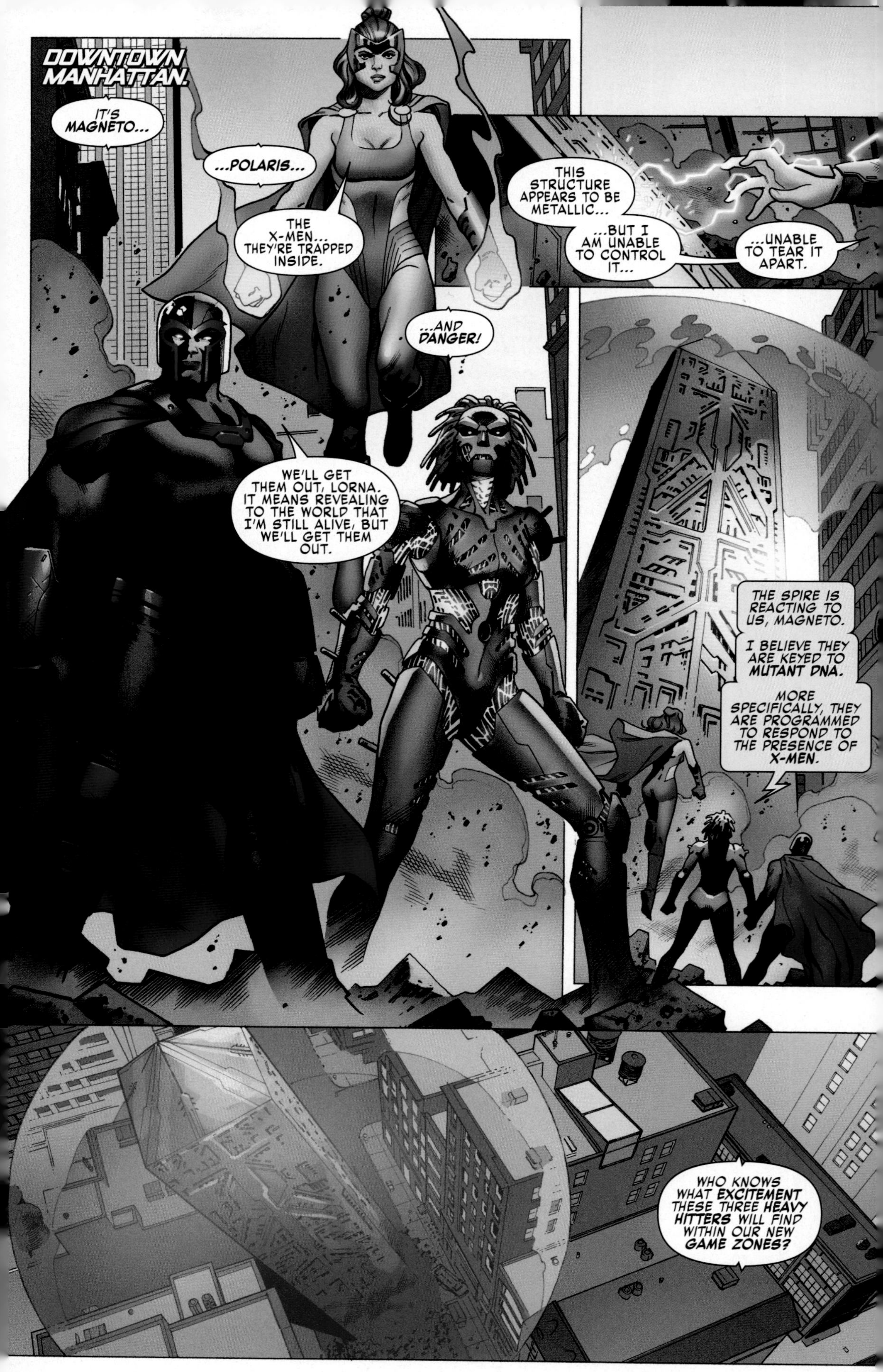
DOWNTOWN MANHATTAN.
IT'S MAGNETO...
...POLARIS...
THE X-MEN... THEY'RE TRAPPED INSIDE.
...AND DANGER!
THIS STRUCTURE APPEARS TO BE METALLIC...
...BUT I AM UNABLE TO CONTROL IT...
...UNABLE TO TEAR IT APART.
WE'LL GET THEM OUT, LORNA. IT MEANS REVEALING TO THE WORLD THAT I'M STILL ALIVE, BUT WE'LL GET THEM OUT.
THE SPIRE IS REACTING TO US, MAGNETO.
I BELIEVE THEY ARE KEYED TO MUTANT DNA.
MORE SPECIFICALLY, THEY ARE PROGRAMMED TO RESPOND TO THE PRESENCE OF X-MEN.
WHO KNOWS WHAT EXCITEMENT THESE THREE HEAVY HITTERS WILL FIND WITHIN OUR NEW GAME ZONES?

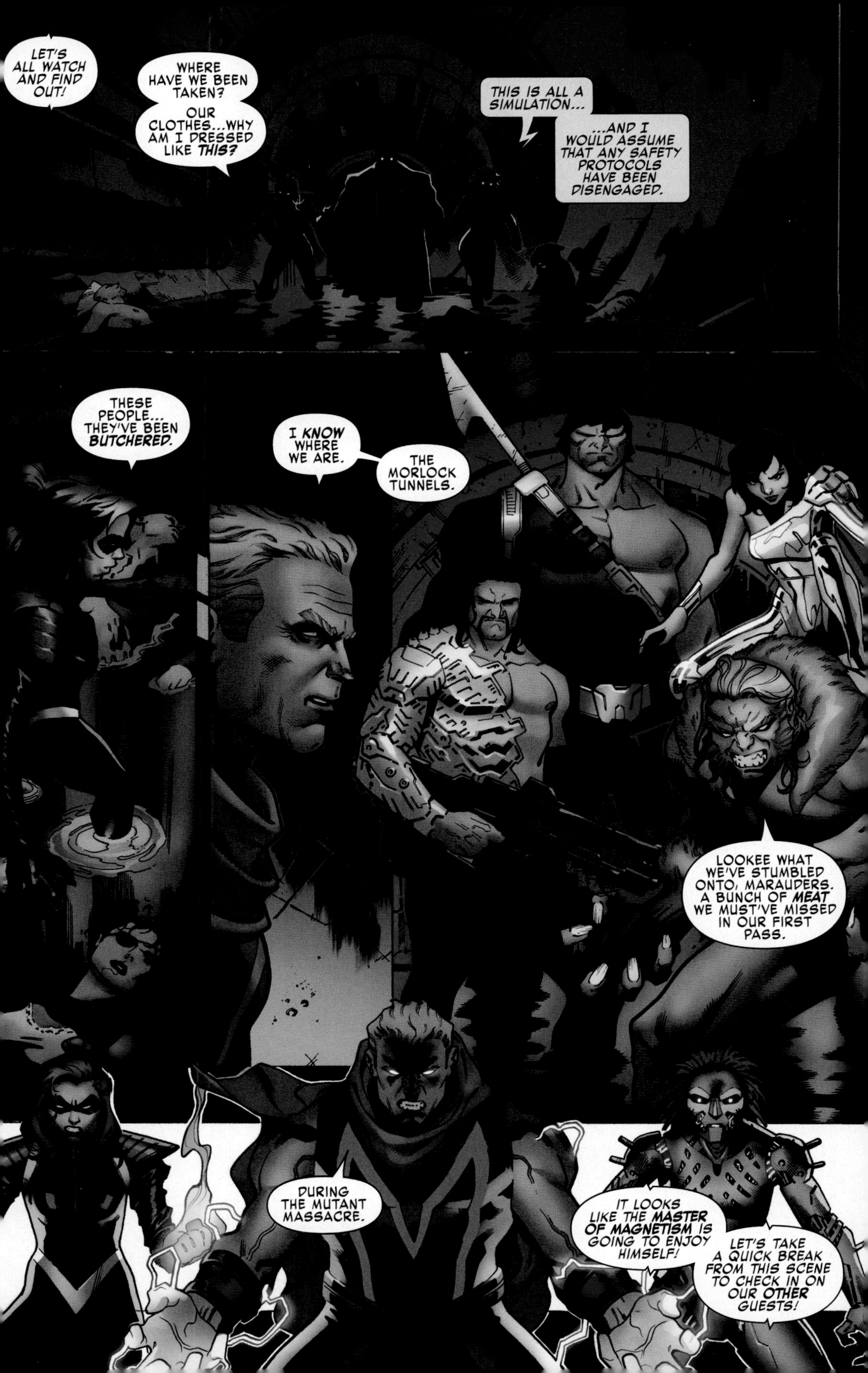
LET'S ALL WATCH AND FIND OUT!
WHERE HAVE WE BEEN TAKEN?
OUR CLOTHES...WHY AM I DRESSED LIKE *THIS?*
THIS IS ALL A SIMULATION...
...AND I WOULD ASSUME THAT ANY SAFETY PROTOCOLS HAVE BEEN DISENGAGED.
THESE PEOPLE... THEY'VE BEEN *BUTCHERED*.
I *KNOW* WHERE WE ARE.
THE MORLOCK TUNNELS.
LOOKEE WHAT WE'VE STUMBLED ONTO, MARAUDERS. A BUNCH OF *MEAT* WE MUST'VE MISSED IN OUR FIRST PASS.
DURING THE MUTANT MASSACRE.
IT LOOKS LIKE THE *MASTER OF MAGNETISM* IS GOING TO ENJOY HIMSELF!
LET'S TAKE A QUICK BREAK FROM THIS SCENE TO CHECK IN ON OUR *OTHER* GUESTS!

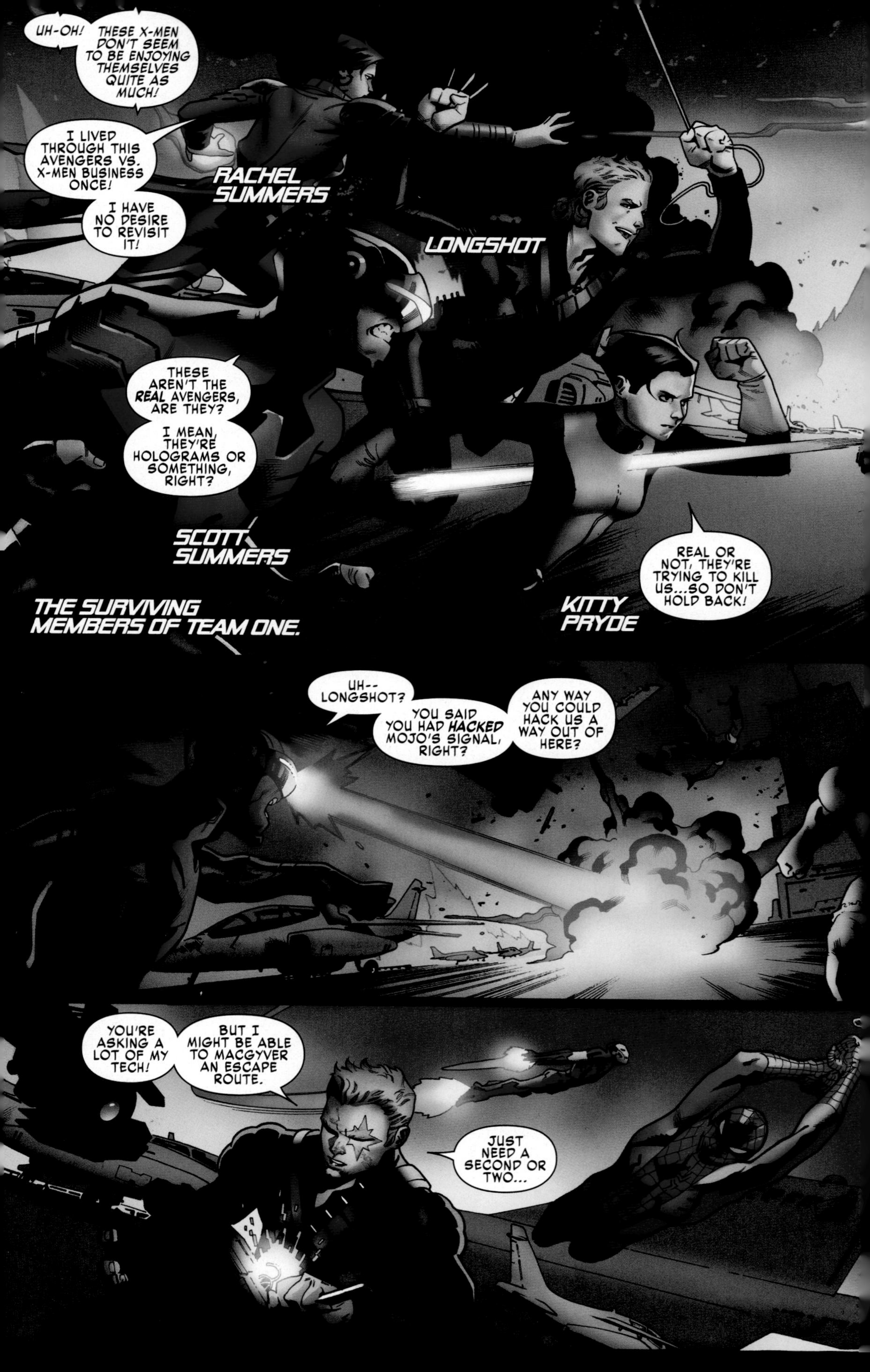
UH-OH!
THESE X-MEN DON'T SEEM TO BE ENJOYING THEMSELVES QUITE AS MUCH!
I LIVED THROUGH THIS AVENGERS VS. X-MEN BUSINESS ONCE!
I HAVE NO DESIRE TO REVISIT IT!
RACHEL SUMMERS
LONGSHOT
THESE AREN'T THE REAL AVENGERS, ARE THEY?
I MEAN, THEY'RE HOLOGRAMS OR SOMETHING, RIGHT?
SCOTT SUMMERS
THE SURVIVING MEMBERS OF TEAM ONE.
KITTY PRYDE
REAL OR NOT, THEY'RE TRYING TO KILL US...SO DON'T HOLD BACK!
UH-- LONGSHOT?
YOU SAID YOU HAD HACKED MOJO'S SIGNAL, RIGHT?
ANY WAY YOU COULD HACK US A WAY OUT OF HERE?
YOU'RE ASKING A LOT OF MY TECH!
BUT I MIGHT BE ABLE TO MACGYVER AN ESCAPE ROUTE.
JUST NEED A SECOND OR TWO...

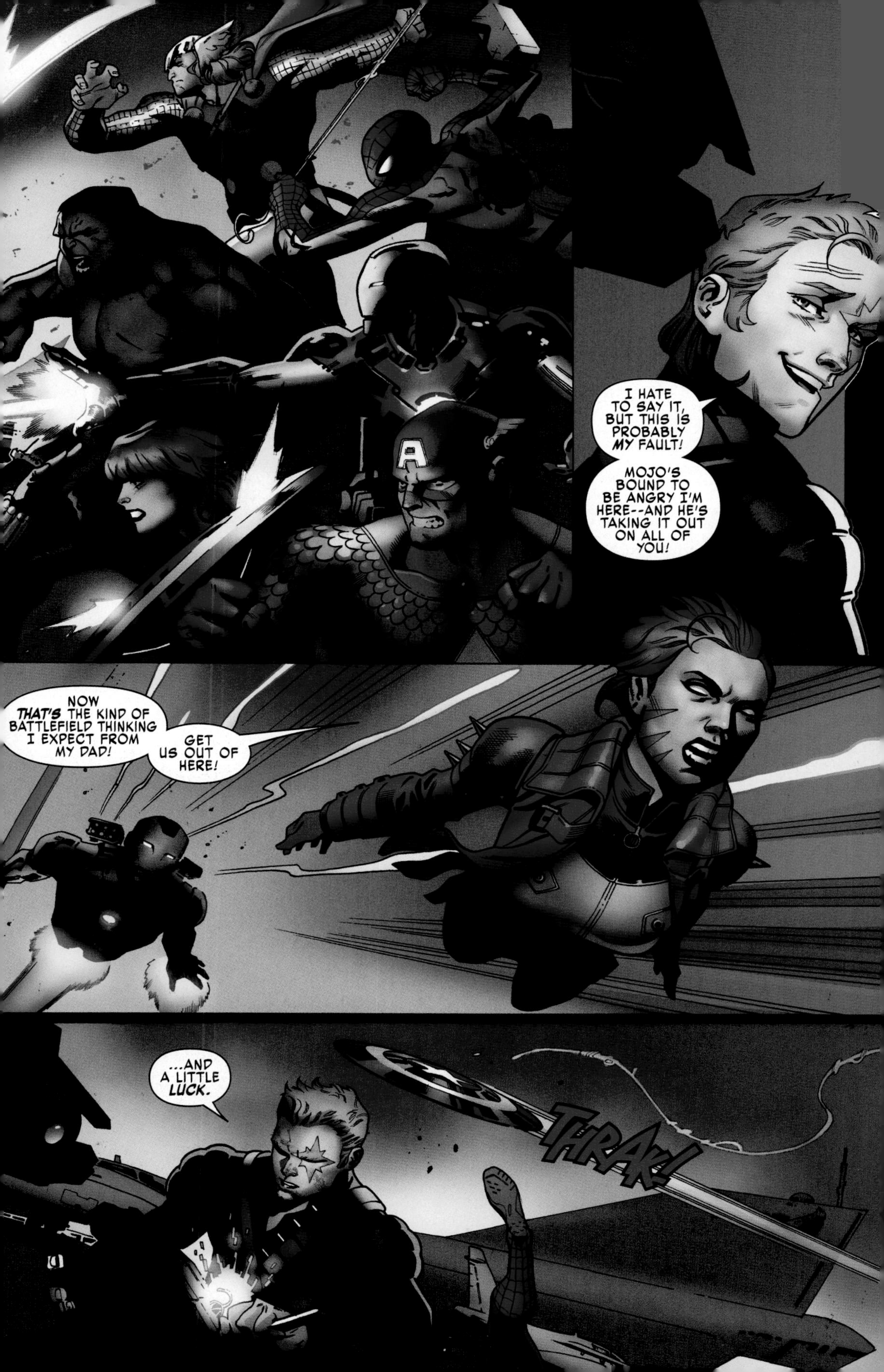

I HATE TO SAY IT, BUT THIS IS PROBABLY MY FAULT!
MOJO'S BOUND TO BE ANGRY I'M HERE--AND HE'S TAKING IT OUT ON ALL OF YOU!
NOW THAT'S THE KIND OF BATTLEFIELD THINKING I EXPECT FROM MY DAD!
GET US OUT OF HERE!
...AND A LITTLE LUCK.
THRAK!

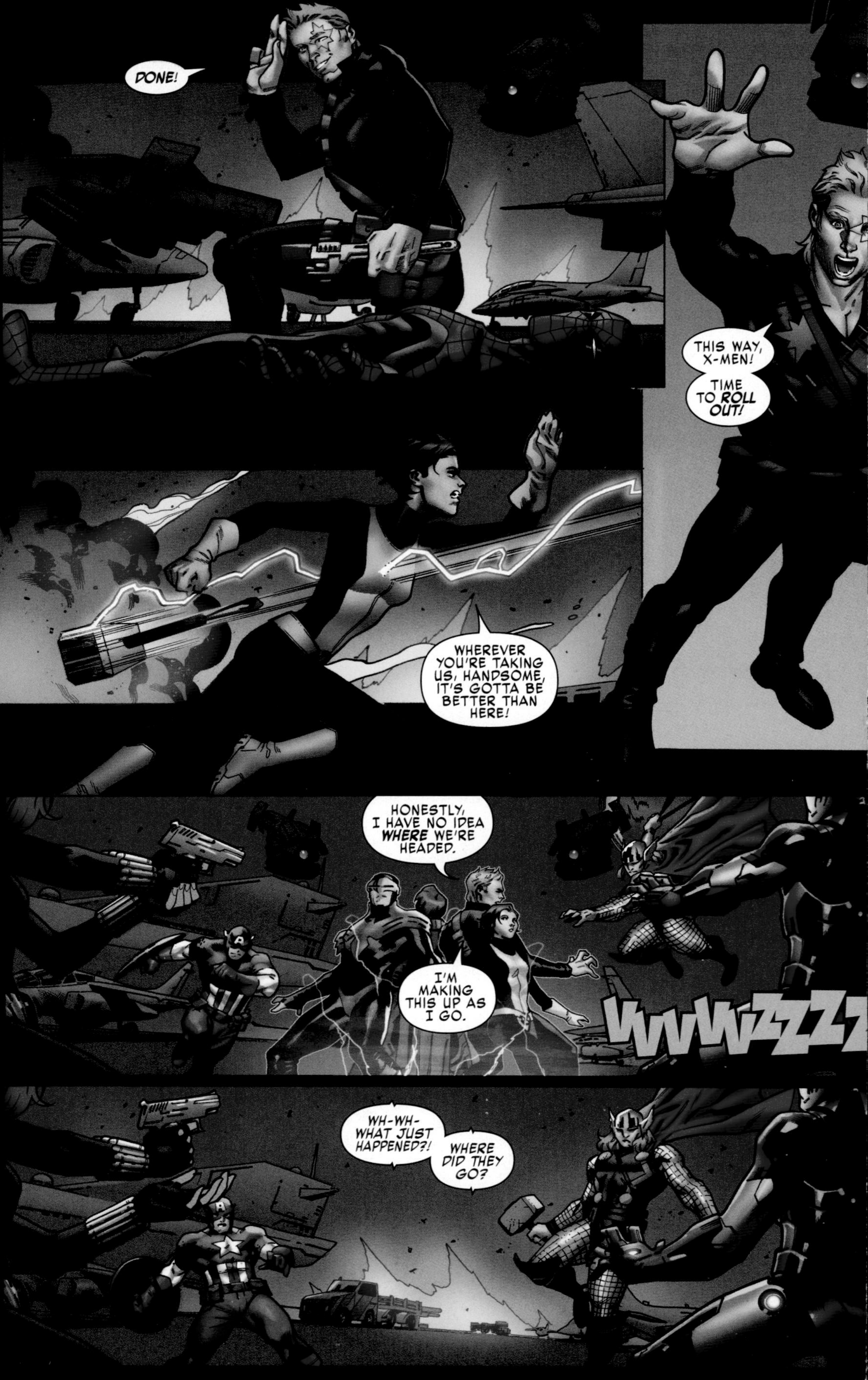
DONE!
THIS WAY, X-MEN!
TIME TO ROLL OUT!
WHEREVER YOU'RE TAKING US, HANDSOME, IT'S GOTTA BE BETTER THAN HERE!
HONESTLY, I HAVE NO IDEA WHERE WE'RE HEADED.
I'M MAKING THIS UP AS I GO.
WWWWZZZ
WH-WH-WHAT JUST HAPPENED?!
WHERE DID THEY GO?

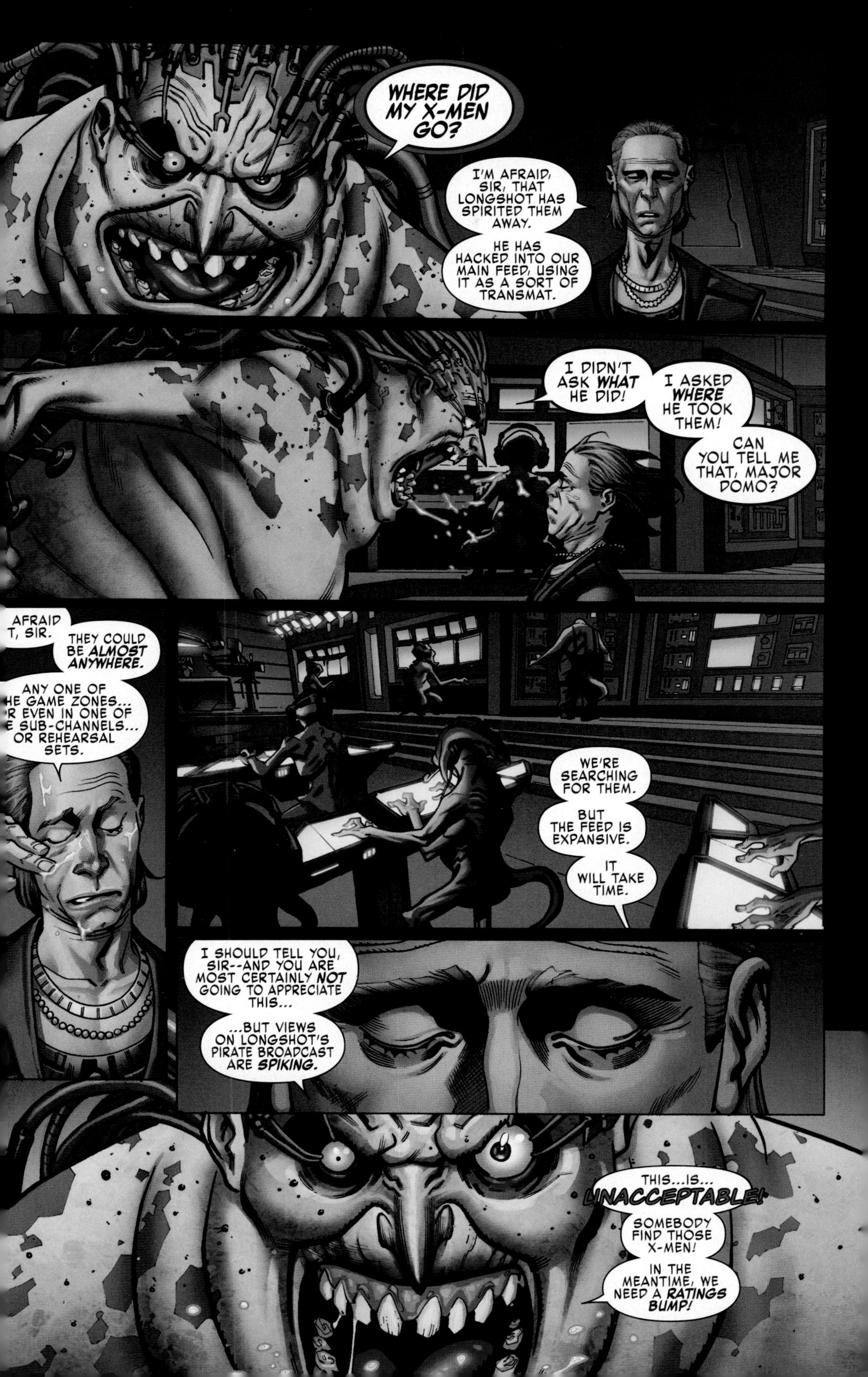

WHERE DID MY X-MEN GO?
I'M AFRAID, SIR, THAT LONGSHOT HAS SPIRITED THEM AWAY.
HE HAS HACKED INTO OUR MAIN FEED, USING IT AS A SORT OF TRANSMAT.
I DIDN'T ASK WHAT HE DID!
I ASKED WHERE HE TOOK THEM!
CAN YOU TELL ME THAT, MAJOR DOMO?
AFRAID T, SIR.
THEY COULD BE ALMOST ANYWHERE.
ANY ONE OF HE GAME ZONES... R EVEN IN ONE OF E SUB-CHANNELS... OR REHEARSAL SETS.
WE'RE SEARCHING FOR THEM.
BUT THE FEED IS EXPANSIVE.
IT WILL TAKE TIME.
I SHOULD TELL YOU, SIR--AND YOU ARE MOST CERTAINLY NOT GOING TO APPRECIATE THIS...
...BUT VIEWS ON LONGSHOT'S PIRATE BROADCAST ARE SPIKING.
THIS...IS... UNACCEPTABLE!
SOMEBODY FIND THOSE X-MEN!
IN THE MEANTIME, WE NEED A RATINGS BUMP!

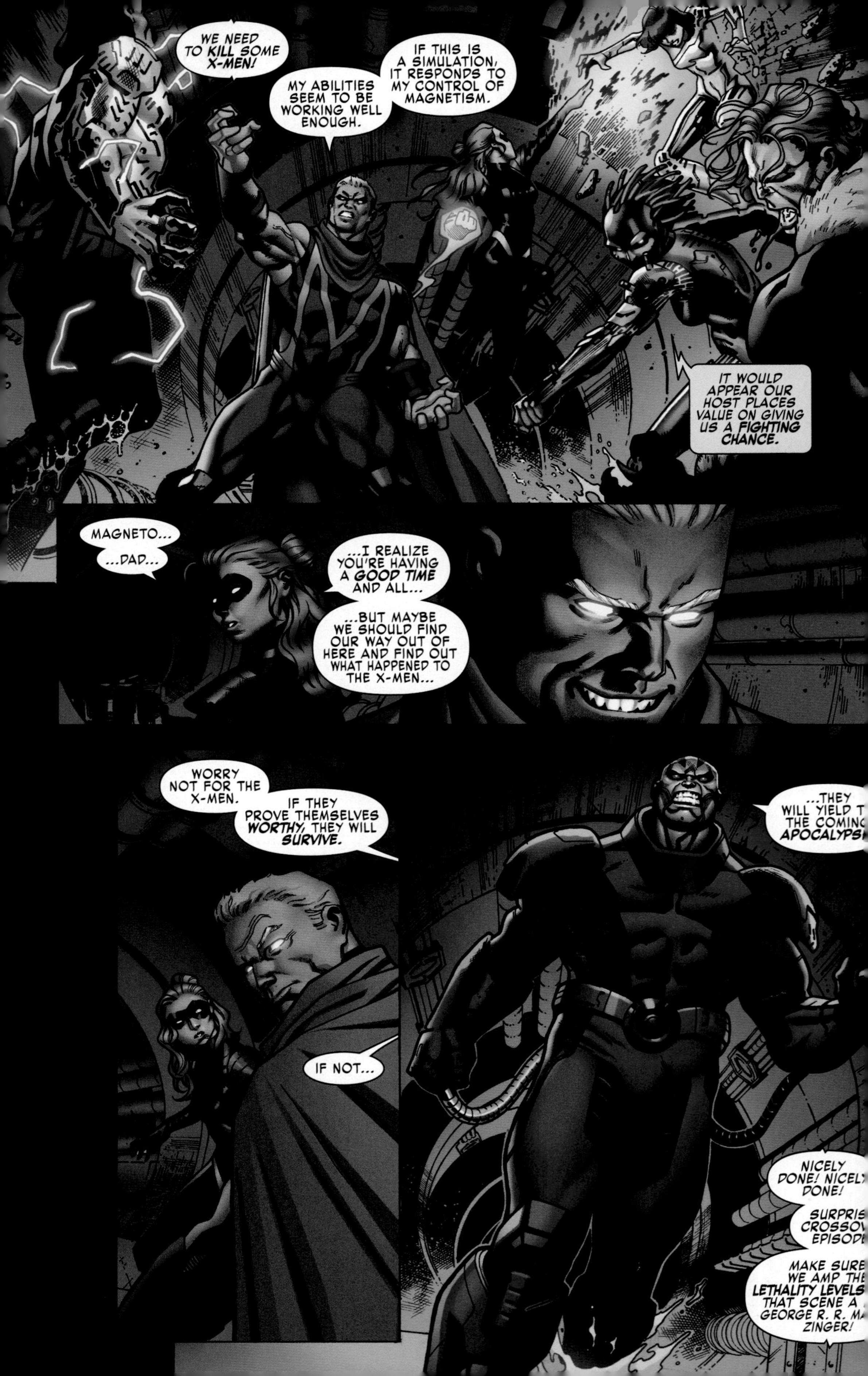
WE NEED TO KILL SOME X-MEN!
MY ABILITIES SEEM TO BE WORKING WELL ENOUGH.
IF THIS IS A SIMULATION, IT RESPONDS TO MY CONTROL OF MAGNETISM.
IT WOULD APPEAR OUR HOST PLACES VALUE ON GIVING US A FIGHTING CHANCE.
MAGNETO...
...DAD...
...I REALIZE YOU'RE HAVING A GOOD TIME AND ALL...
...BUT MAYBE WE SHOULD FIND OUR WAY OUT OF HERE AND FIND OUT WHAT HAPPENED TO THE X-MEN...
WORRY NOT FOR THE X-MEN.
IF THEY PROVE THEMSELVES WORTHY, THEY WILL SURVIVE.
IF NOT...
...THEY WILL YIELD T THE COMIN APOCALYPS
NICELY DONE! NICELY DONE!
SURPRIS CROSSOV EPISODE
MAKE SURE WE AMP THE LETHALITY LEVELS THAT SCENE A GEORGE R. R. MA ZINGER!

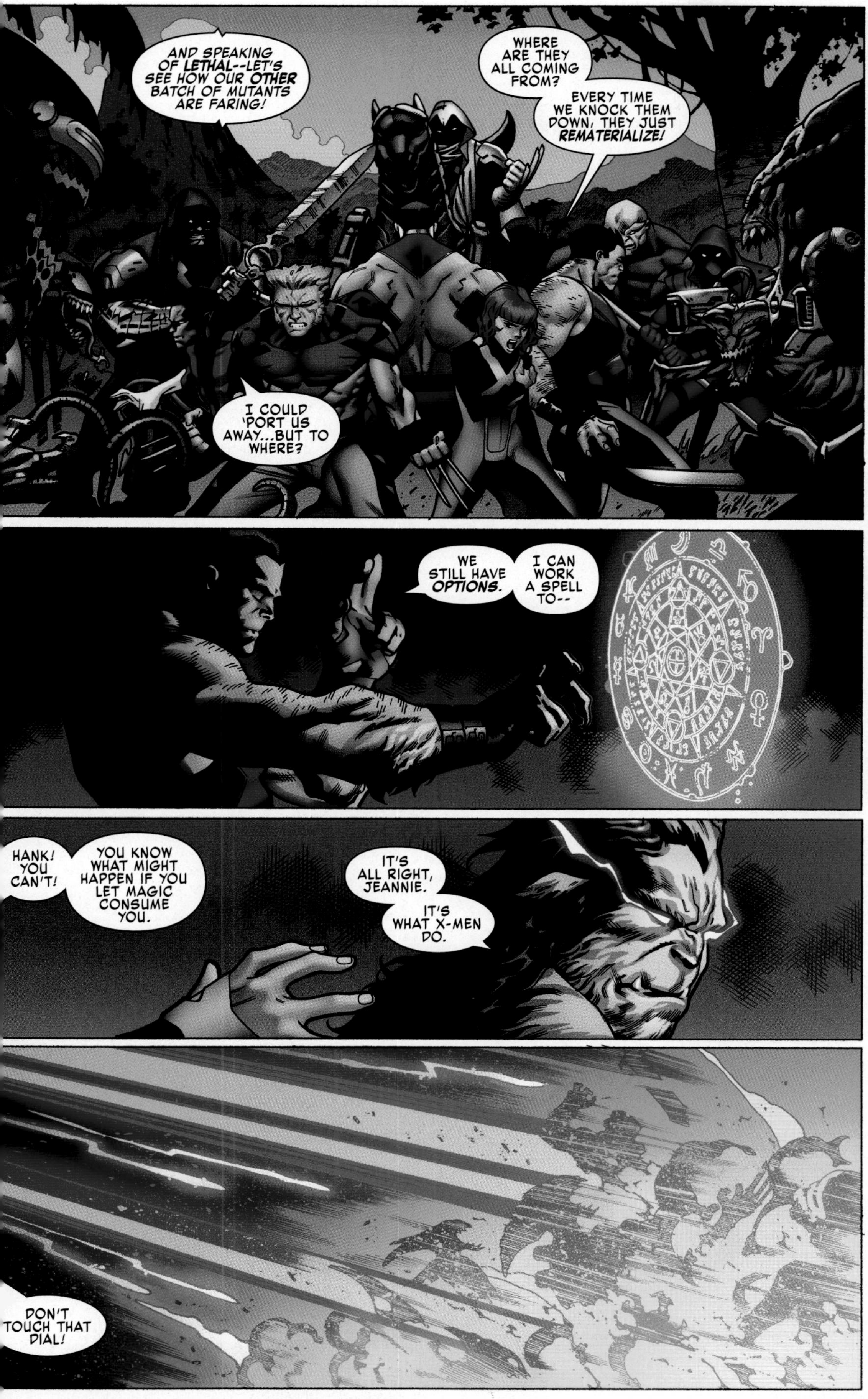
AND SPEAKING OF LETHAL--LET'S SEE HOW OUR OTHER BATCH OF MUTANTS ARE FARING!
WHERE ARE THEY ALL COMING FROM?
EVERY TIME WE KNOCK THEM DOWN, THEY JUST REMATERIALIZE!
I COULD 'PORT US AWAY...BUT TO WHERE?
WE STILL HAVE OPTIONS.
I CAN WORK A SPELL TO--
HANK! YOU CAN'T!
YOU KNOW WHAT MIGHT HAPPEN IF YOU LET MAGIC CONSUME YOU.
IT'S ALL RIGHT, JEANNIE.
IT'S WHAT X-MEN DO.
DON'T TOUCH THAT DIAL!

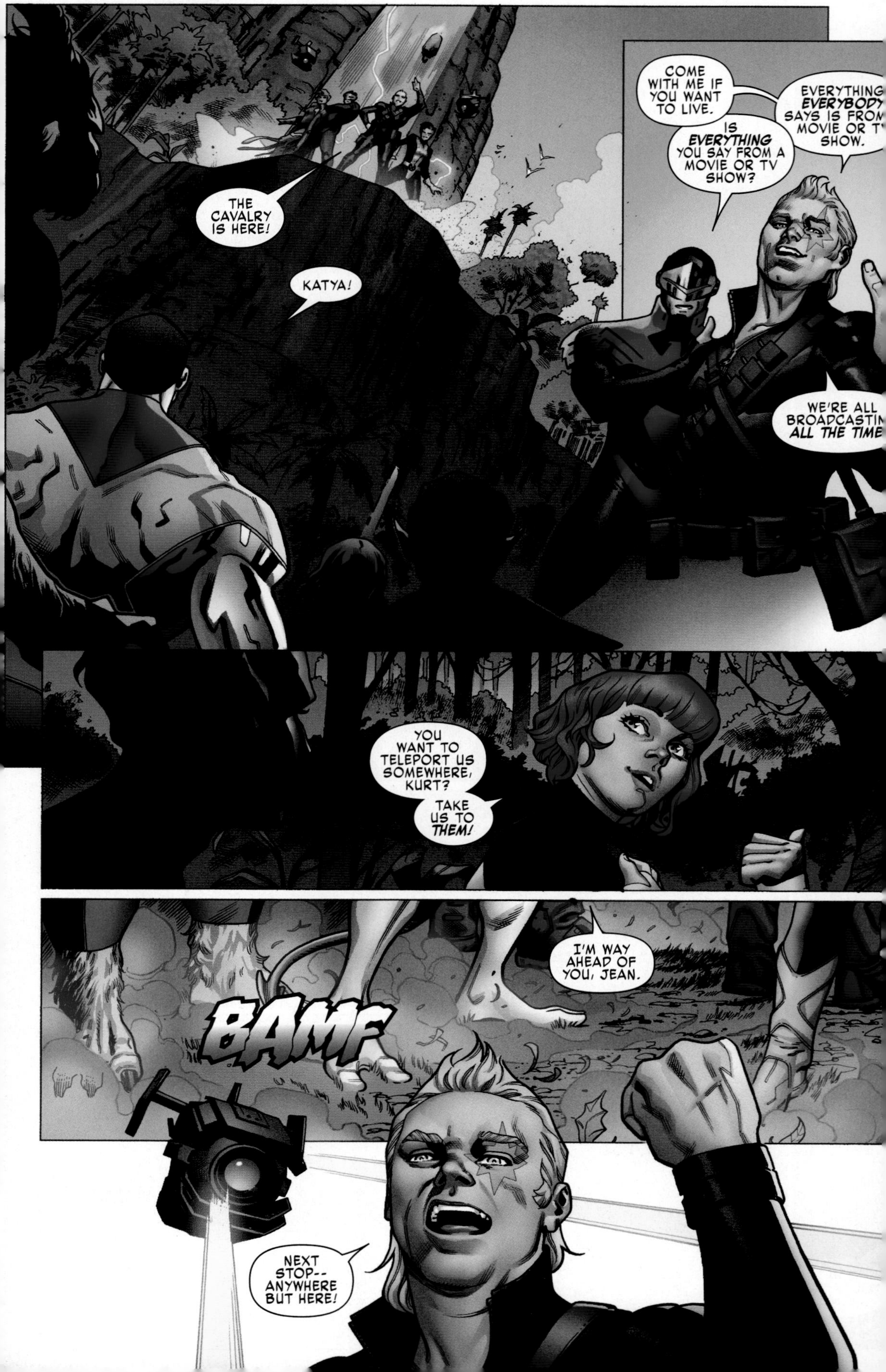
THE CAVALRY IS HERE!
KATYA!
COME WITH ME IF YOU WANT TO LIVE.
IS EVERYTHING YOU SAY FROM A MOVIE OR TV SHOW?
EVERYTHING EVERYBODY SAYS IS FROM MOVIE OR T SHOW.
WE'RE ALL BROADCASTIN ALL THE TIME
YOU WANT TO TELEPORT US SOMEWHERE, KURT?
TAKE US TO THEM!
I'M WAY AHEAD OF YOU, JEAN.
BAMF
NEXT STOP-- ANYWHERE BUT HERE!

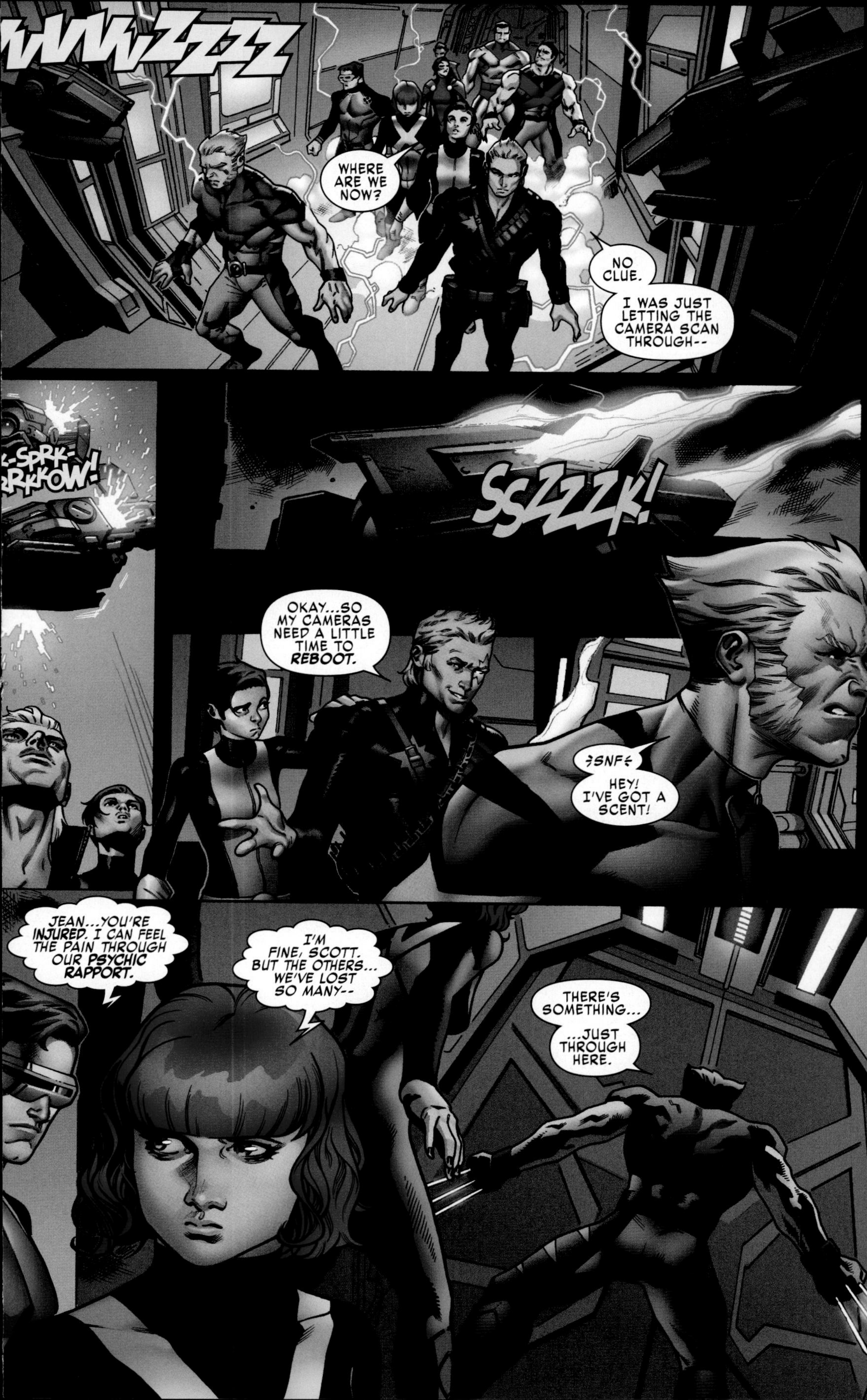
WWWZZZZ
WHERE ARE WE NOW?
NO CLUE.
I WAS JUST LETTING THE CAMERA SCAN THROUGH--
-SPRK-RKKOW!
SSZZZK!
OKAY...SO MY CAMERAS NEED A LITTLE TIME TO REBOOT.
SNF
HEY! I'VE GOT A SCENT!
JEAN...YOU'RE INJURED. I CAN FEEL THE PAIN THROUGH OUR PSYCHIC RAPPORT.
I'M FINE, SCOTT. BUT THE OTHERS... WE'VE LOST SO MANY--
THERE'S SOMETHING...
...JUST THROUGH HERE.

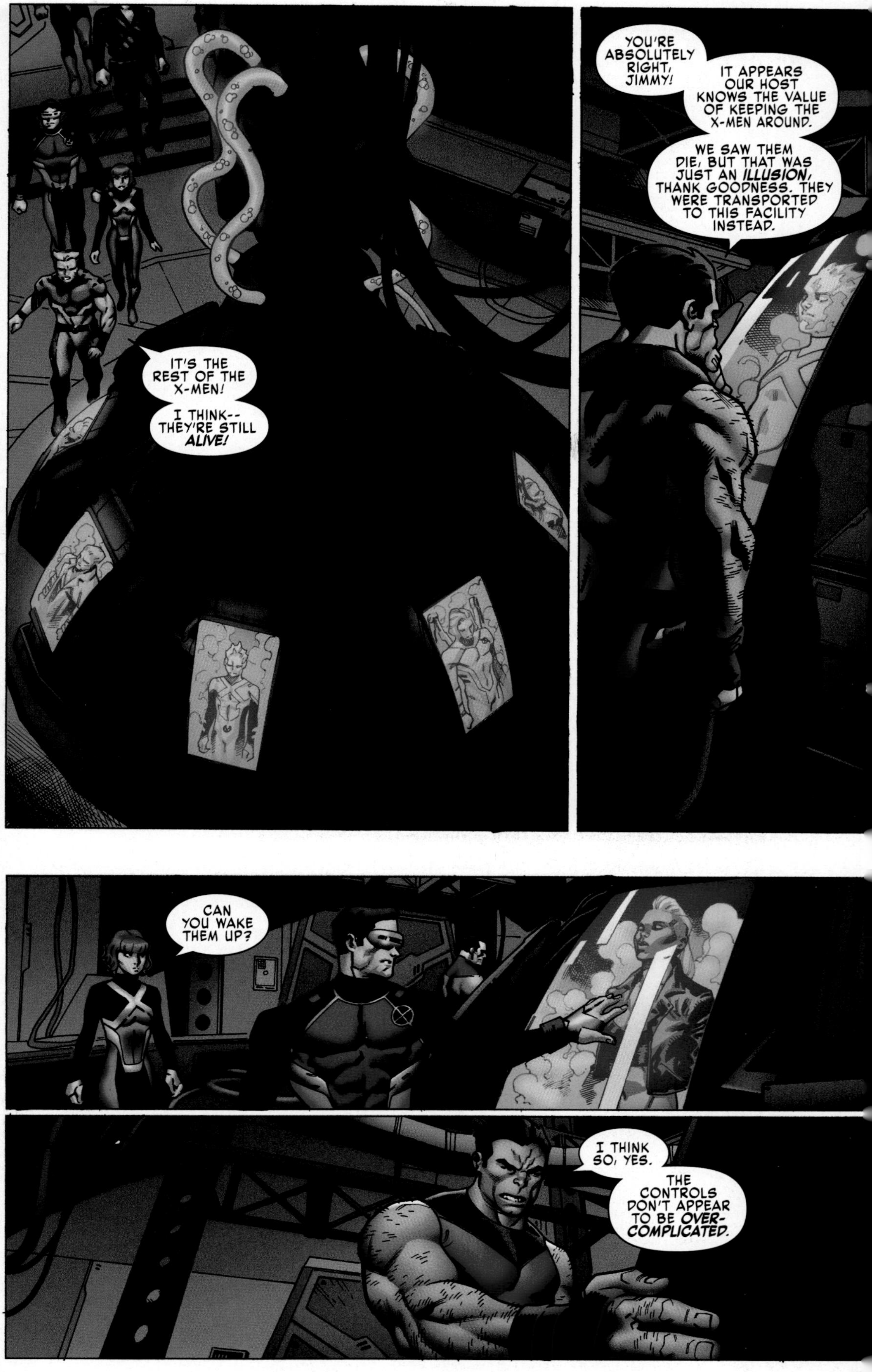
IT'S THE REST OF THE X-MEN!
I THINK-- THEY'RE STILL ALIVE!
YOU'RE ABSOLUTELY RIGHT, JIMMY!
IT APPEARS OUR HOST KNOWS THE VALUE OF KEEPING THE X-MEN AROUND.
WE SAW THEM DIE, BUT THAT WAS JUST AN ILLUSION, THANK GOODNESS. THEY WERE TRANSPORTED TO THIS FACILITY INSTEAD.
CAN YOU WAKE THEM UP?
I THINK SO, YES.
THE CONTROLS DON'T APPEAR TO BE OVER-COMPLICATED.

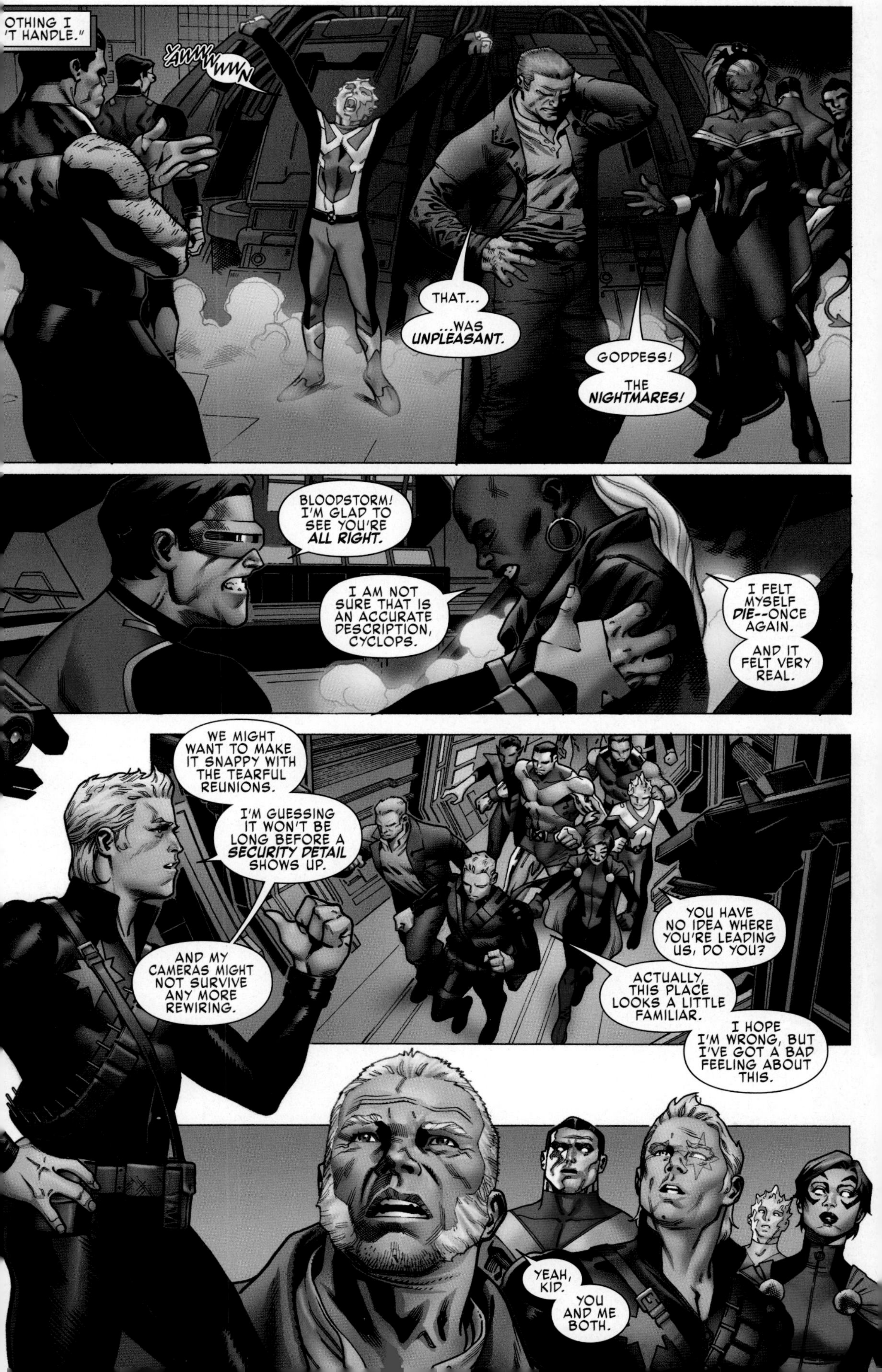

OTHING I
'T HANDLE."
YAWWWWWN
THAT...
...WAS UNPLEASANT.
GODDESS!
THE NIGHTMARES!
BLOODSTORM! I'M GLAD TO SEE YOU'RE ALL RIGHT.
I AM NOT SURE THAT IS AN ACCURATE DESCRIPTION, CYCLOPS.
I FELT MYSELF DIE--ONCE AGAIN.
AND IT FELT VERY REAL.
WE MIGHT WANT TO MAKE IT SNAPPY WITH THE TEARFUL REUNIONS.
I'M GUESSING IT WON'T BE LONG BEFORE A SECURITY DETAIL SHOWS UP.
AND MY CAMERAS MIGHT NOT SURVIVE ANY MORE REWIRING.
YOU HAVE NO IDEA WHERE YOU'RE LEADING US, DO YOU?
ACTUALLY, THIS PLACE LOOKS A LITTLE FAMILIAR.
I HOPE I'M WRONG, BUT I'VE GOT A BAD FEELING ABOUT THIS.
YEAH, KID.
YOU AND ME BOTH.

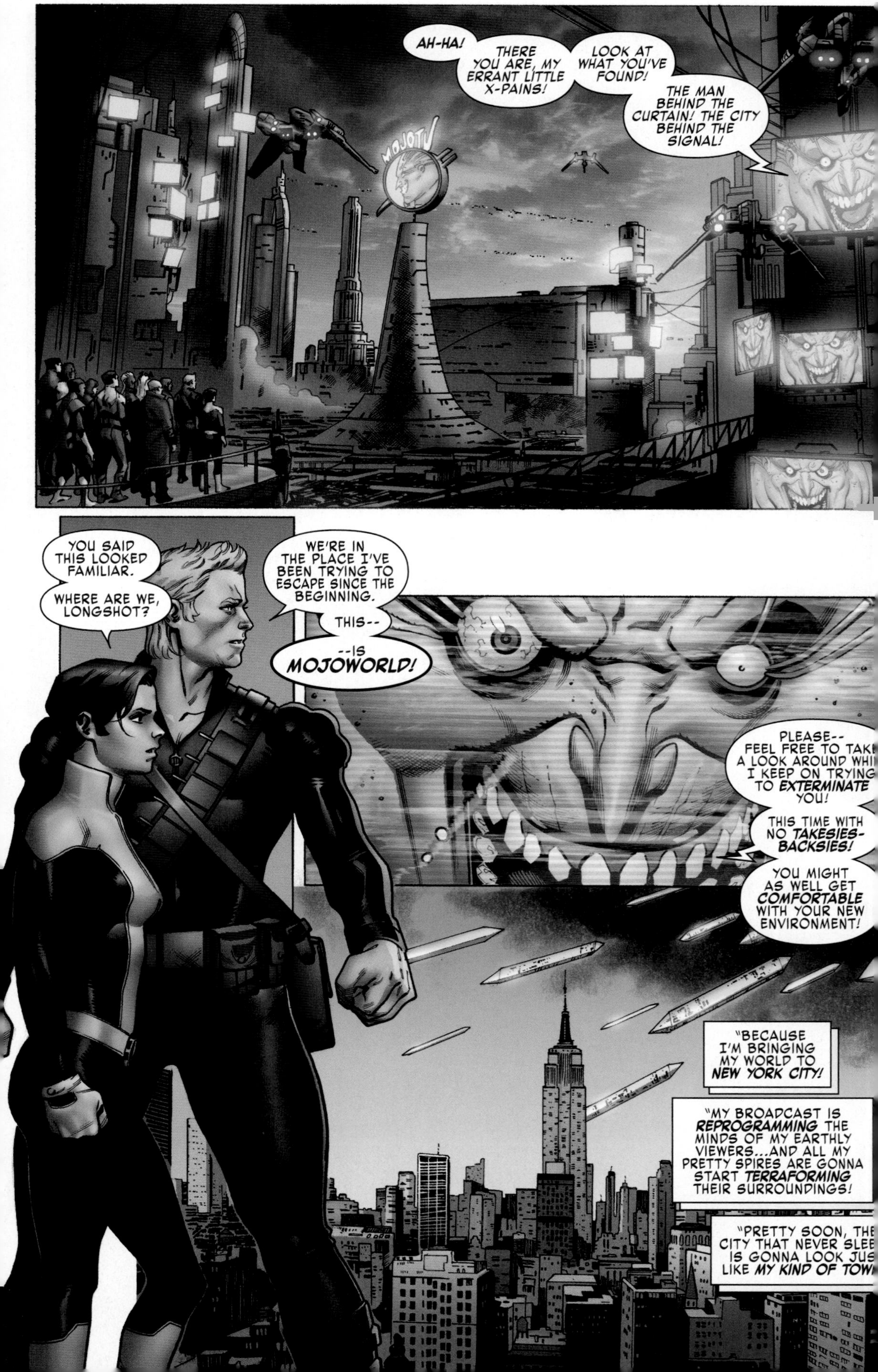
AH-HA!
THERE YOU ARE, MY ERRANT LITTLE X-PAINS!
LOOK AT WHAT YOU'VE FOUND!
THE MAN BEHIND THE CURTAIN! THE CITY BEHIND THE SIGNAL!
MOJOTV
YOU SAID THIS LOOKED FAMILIAR.
WHERE ARE WE, LONGSHOT?
WE'RE IN THE PLACE I'VE BEEN TRYING TO ESCAPE SINCE THE BEGINNING.
THIS--
--IS MOJOWORLD!
PLEASE-- FEEL FREE TO TAK A LOOK AROUND WHI I KEEP ON TRYING TO EXTERMINATE YOU!
THIS TIME WITH NO TAKESIES-BACKSIES!
YOU MIGHT AS WELL GET COMFORTABLE WITH YOUR NEW ENVIRONMENT!
"BECAUSE I'M BRINGING MY WORLD TO NEW YORK CITY!
"MY BROADCAST IS REPROGRAMMING THE MINDS OF MY EARTHLY VIEWERS...AND ALL MY PRETTY SPIRES ARE GONNA START TERRAFORMING THEIR SURROUNDINGS!
"PRETTY SOON, THE CITY THAT NEVER SLEE IS GONNA LOOK JUS LIKE MY KIND OF TOW

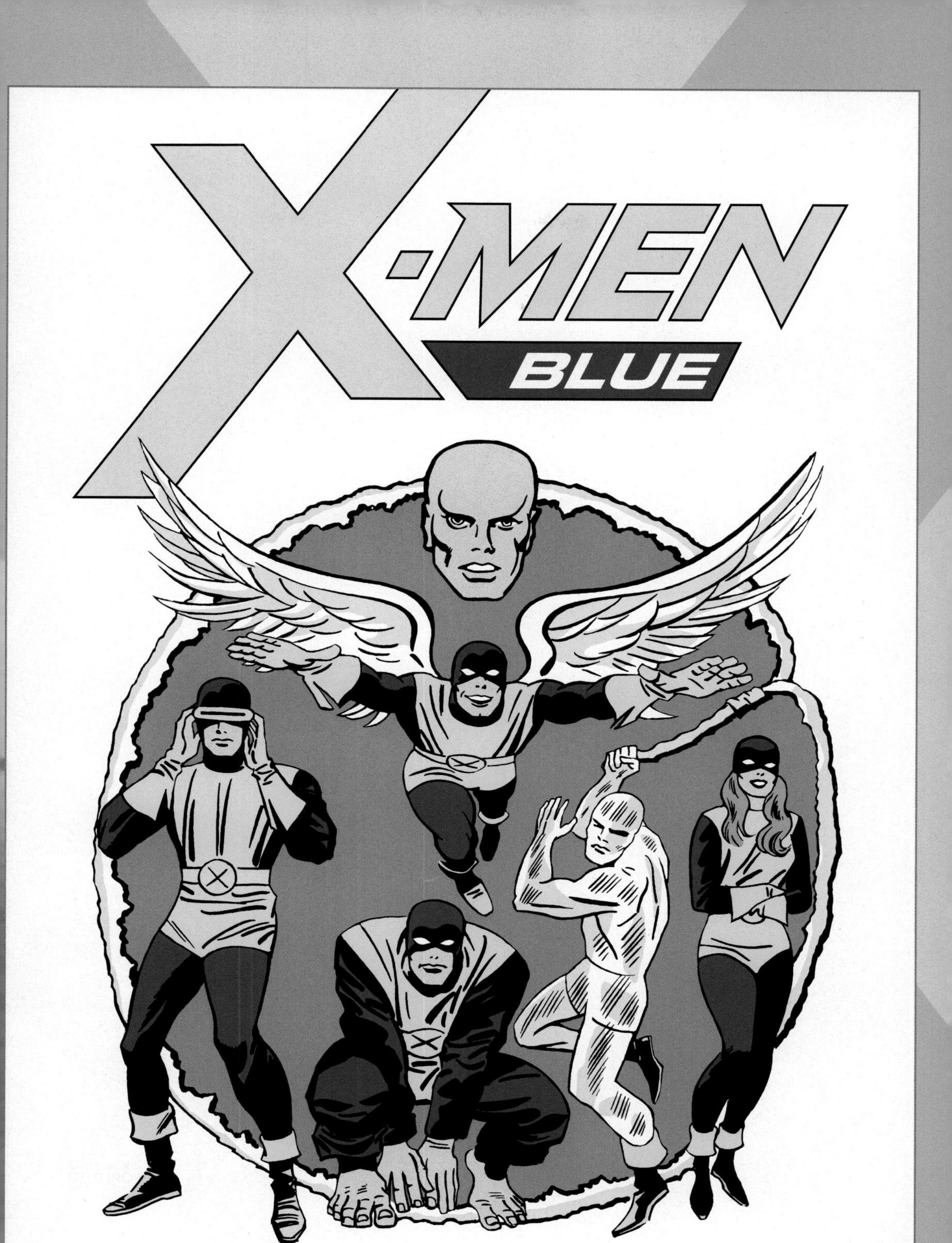
X-MEN
BLUE

X-MEN BLUE #13 *T-SHIRT VARIANT*
BY **JACK KIRBY**

X-MEN GOLD #15

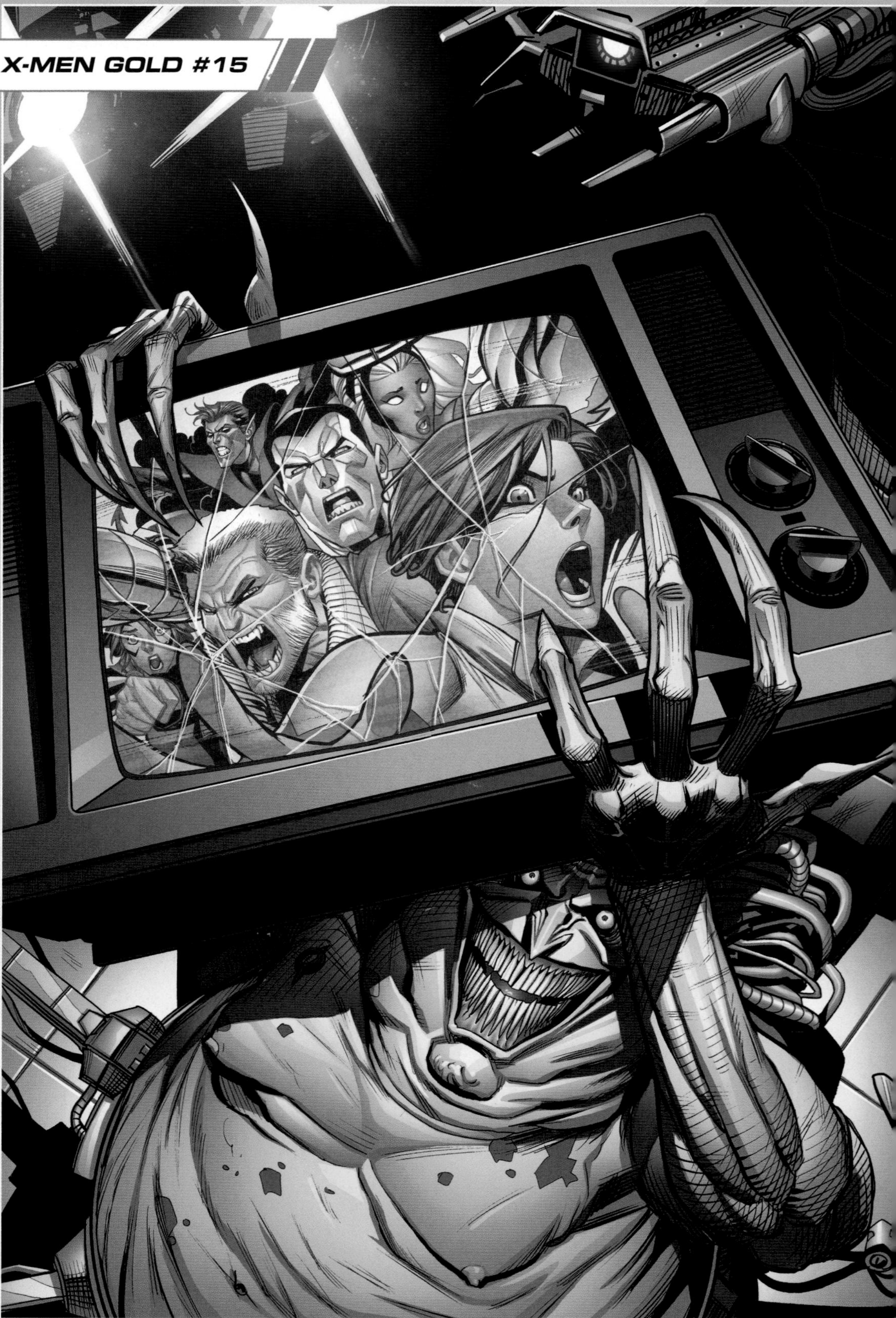

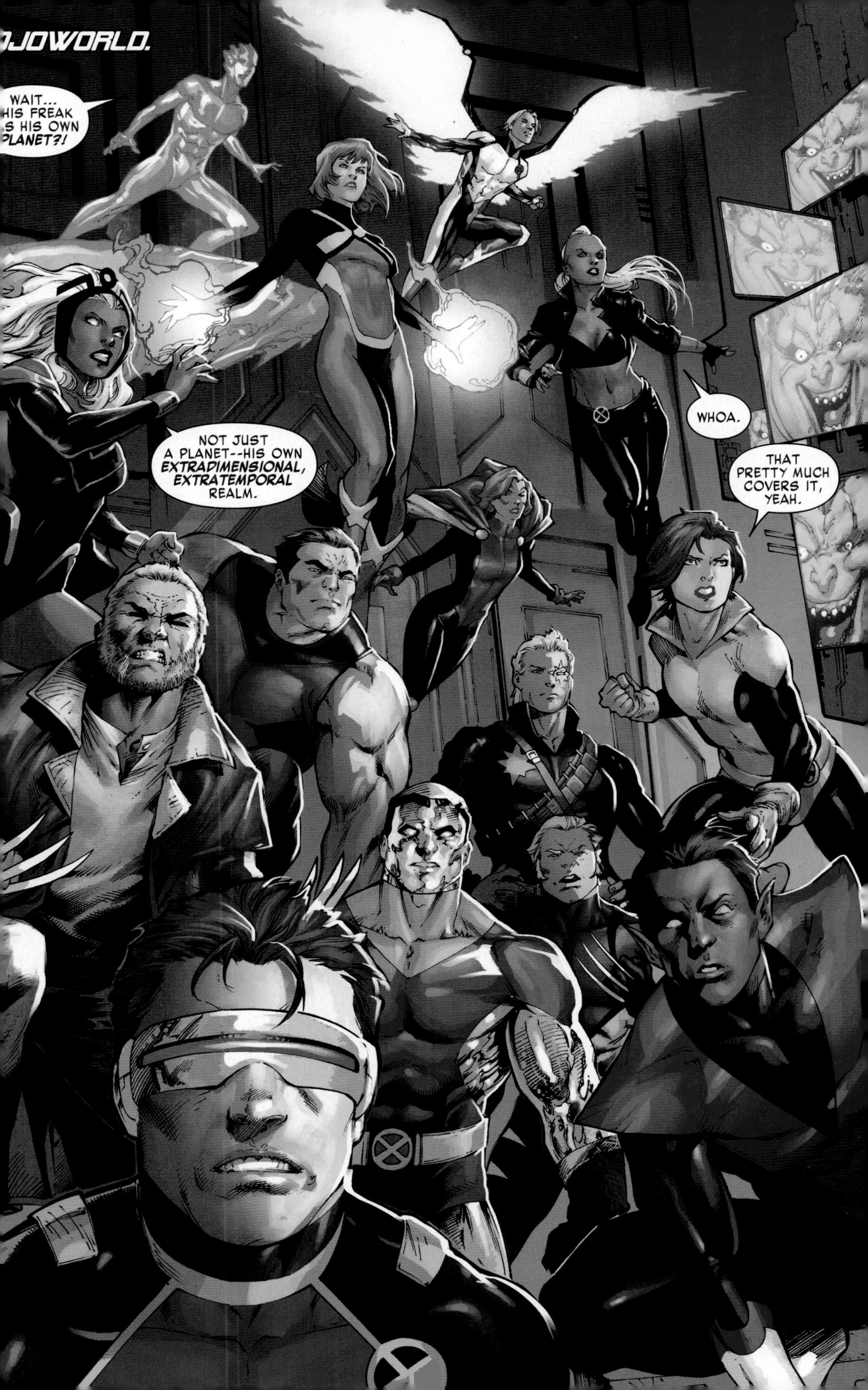
OJOWORLD.
WAIT... HIS FREAK S HIS OWN PLANET?!
NOT JUST A PLANET--HIS OWN EXTRADIMENSIONAL, EXTRATEMPORAL REALM.
WHOA.
THAT PRETTY MUCH COVERS IT, YEAH.

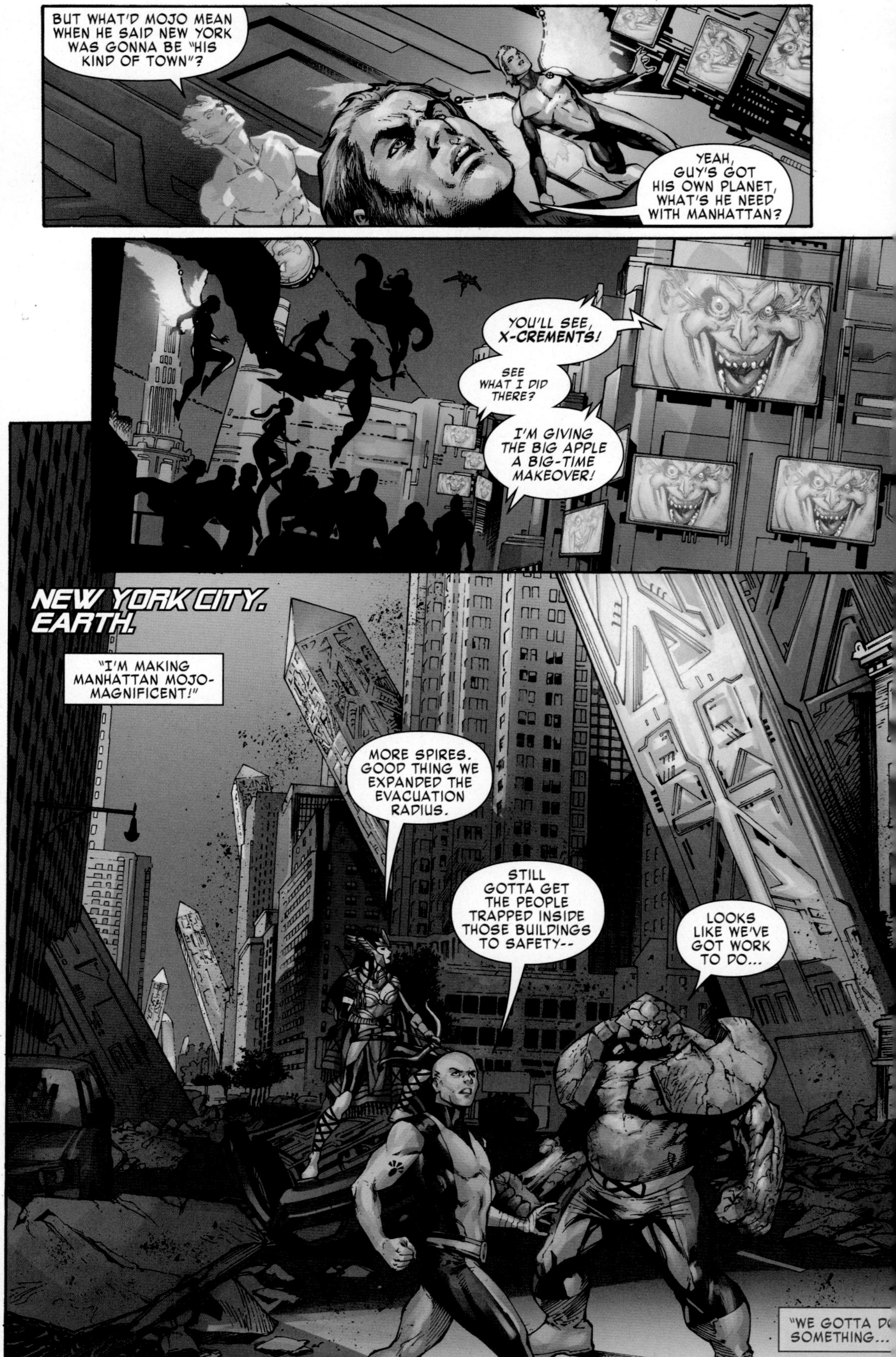
BUT WHAT'D MOJO MEAN WHEN HE SAID NEW YORK WAS GONNA BE "HIS KIND OF TOWN"?
YEAH, GUY'S GOT HIS OWN PLANET, WHAT'S HE NEED WITH MANHATTAN?
YOU'LL SEE, X-CREMENTS!
SEE WHAT I DID THERE?
I'M GIVING THE BIG APPLE A BIG-TIME MAKEOVER!
NEW YORK CITY. EARTH.
"I'M MAKING MANHATTAN MOJO-MAGNIFICENT!"
MORE SPIRES. GOOD THING WE EXPANDED THE EVACUATION RADIUS.
STILL GOTTA GET THE PEOPLE TRAPPED INSIDE THOSE BUILDINGS TO SAFETY--
LOOKS LIKE WE'VE GOT WORK TO DO...
"WE GOTTA DO SOMETHING...

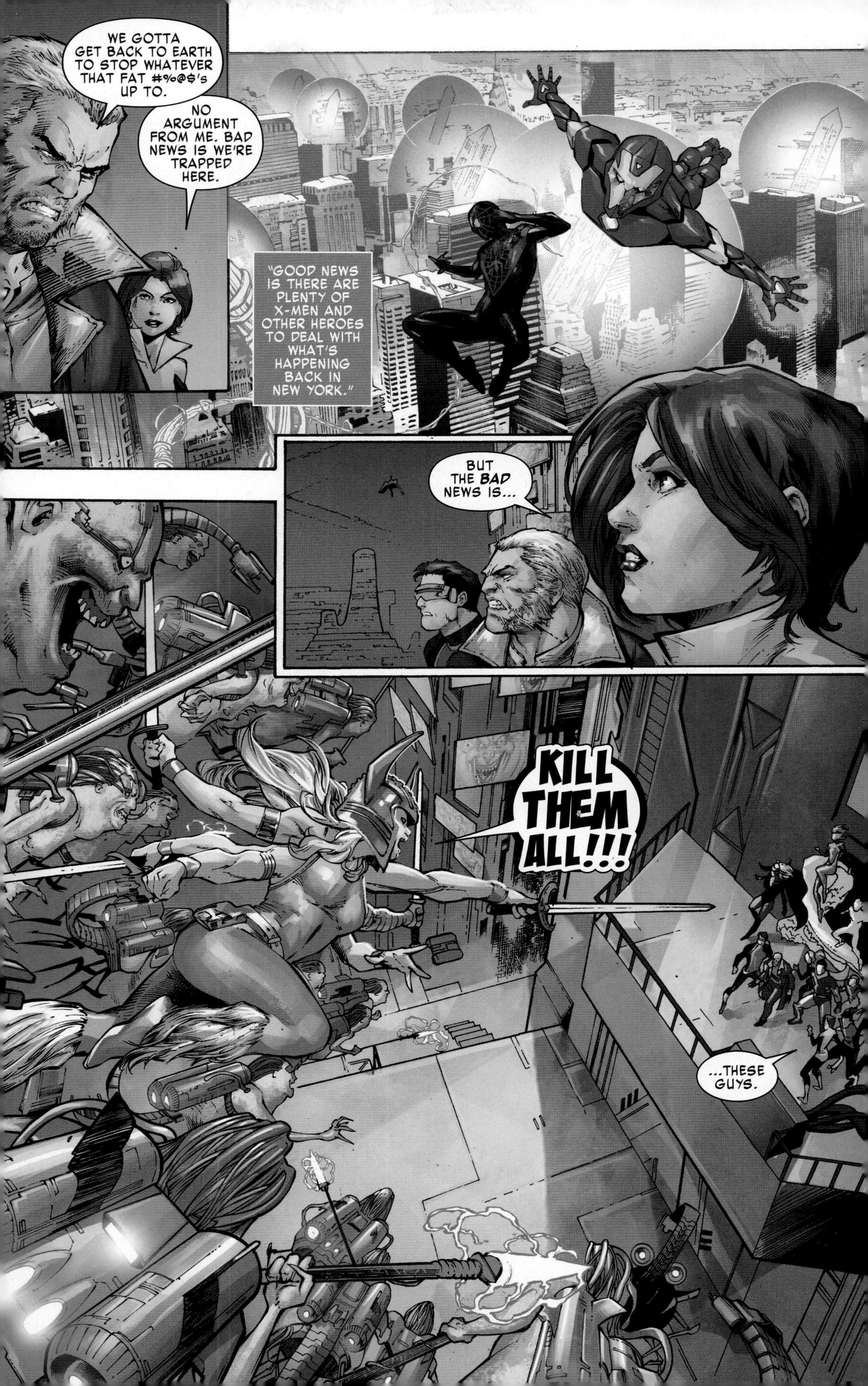
WE GOTTA GET BACK TO EARTH TO STOP WHATEVER THAT FAT #%@$'s UP TO.
NO ARGUMENT FROM ME. BAD NEWS IS WE'RE TRAPPED HERE.
"GOOD NEWS IS THERE ARE PLENTY OF X-MEN AND OTHER HEROES TO DEAL WITH WHAT'S HAPPENING BACK IN NEW YORK."
BUT THE BAD NEWS IS...
KILL THEM ALL!!!
...THESE GUYS.

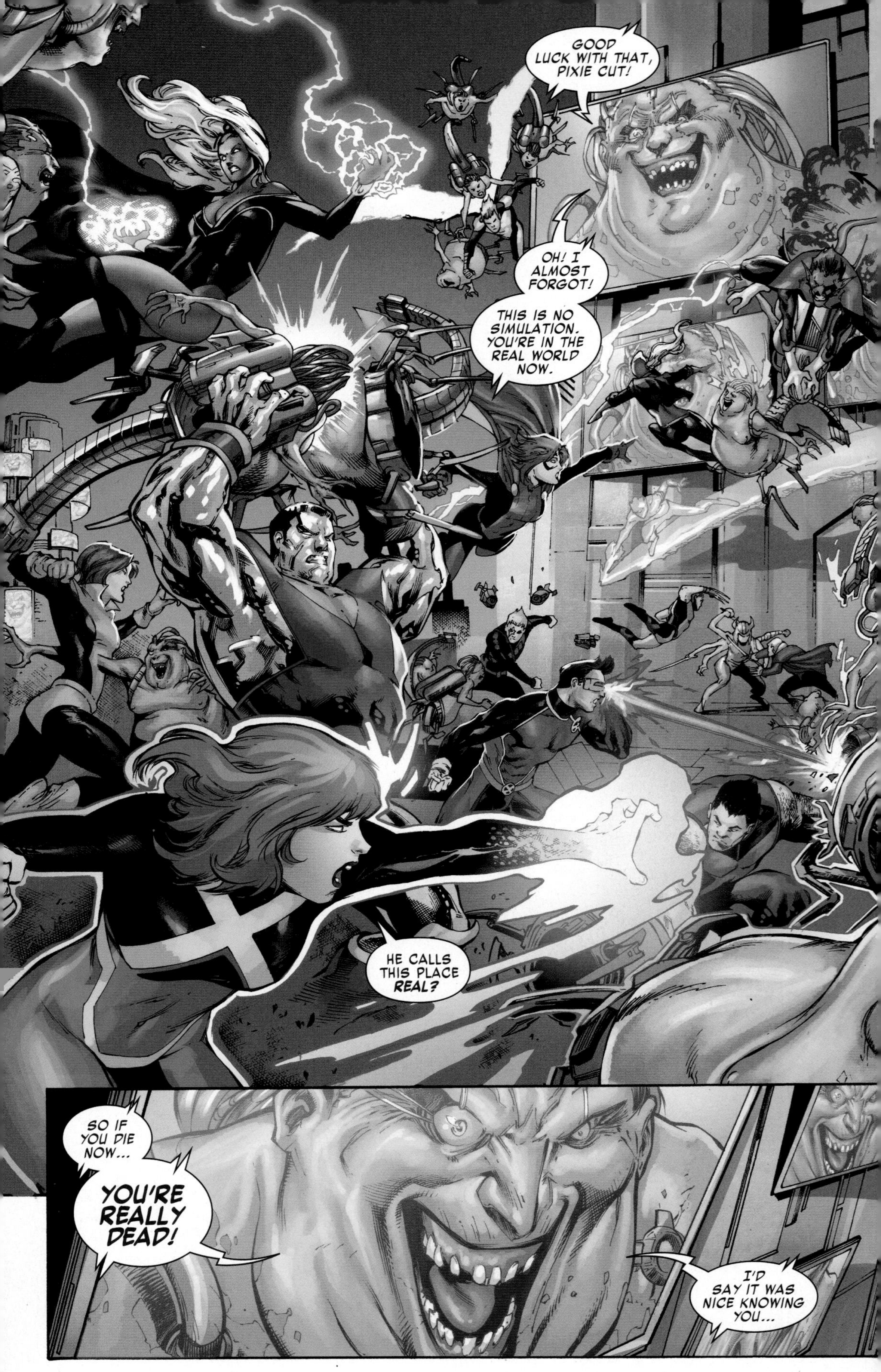
GOOD LUCK WITH THAT, PIXIE CUT!
OH! I ALMOST FORGOT!
THIS IS NO SIMULATION. YOU'RE IN THE REAL WORLD NOW.
HE CALLS THIS PLACE REAL?
SO IF YOU DIE NOW...
YOU'RE REALLY DEAD!
I'D SAY IT WAS NICE KNOWING YOU...

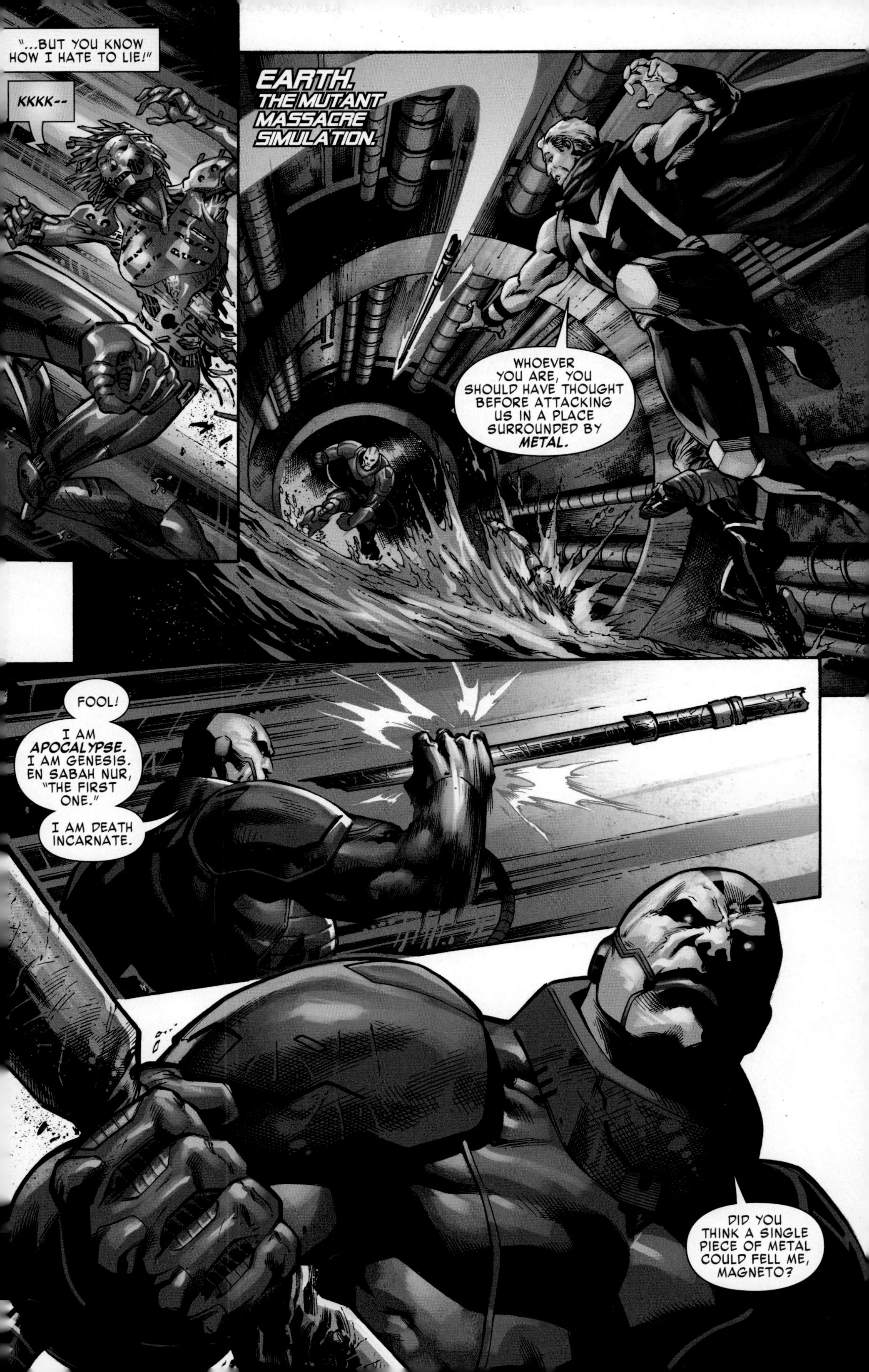
"...BUT YOU KNOW HOW I HATE TO LIE!"
KKKK--
EARTH. THE MUTANT MASSACRE SIMULATION.
WHOEVER YOU ARE, YOU SHOULD HAVE THOUGHT BEFORE ATTACKING US IN A PLACE SURROUNDED BY METAL.
FOOL!
I AM APOCALYPSE. I AM GENESIS. EN SABAH NUR, "THE FIRST ONE."
I AM DEATH INCARNATE.
DID YOU THINK A SINGLE PIECE OF METAL COULD FELL ME, MAGNETO?

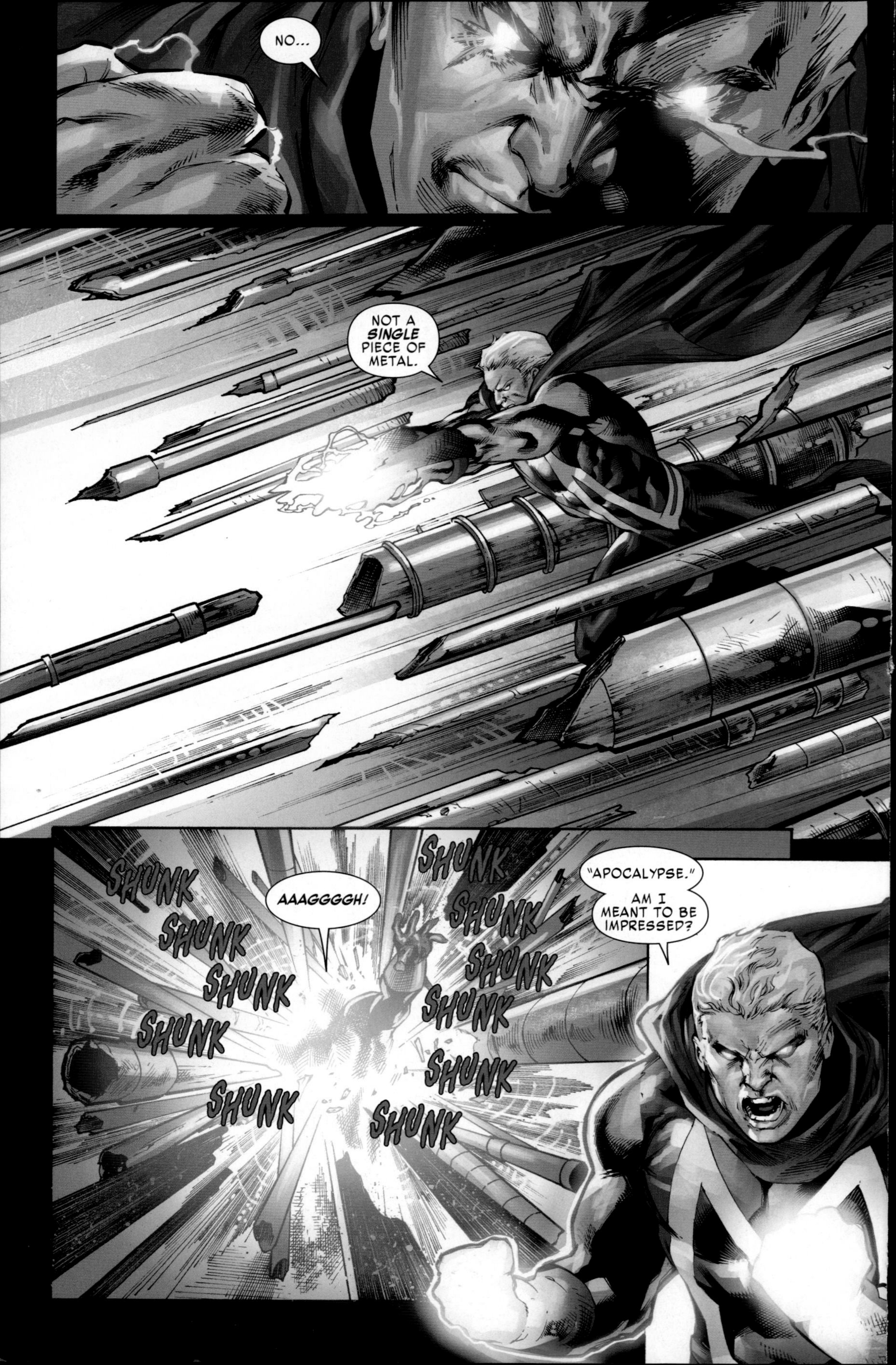
NO...
NOT A SINGLE PIECE OF METAL.
SHUNK
SHUNK
SHUNK
SHUNK
SHUNK
AAAGGGGH!
SHUNK
SHUNK
SHUNK
SHUNK
SHUNK
SHUNK
"APOCALYPSE."
AM I MEANT TO BE IMPRESSED?

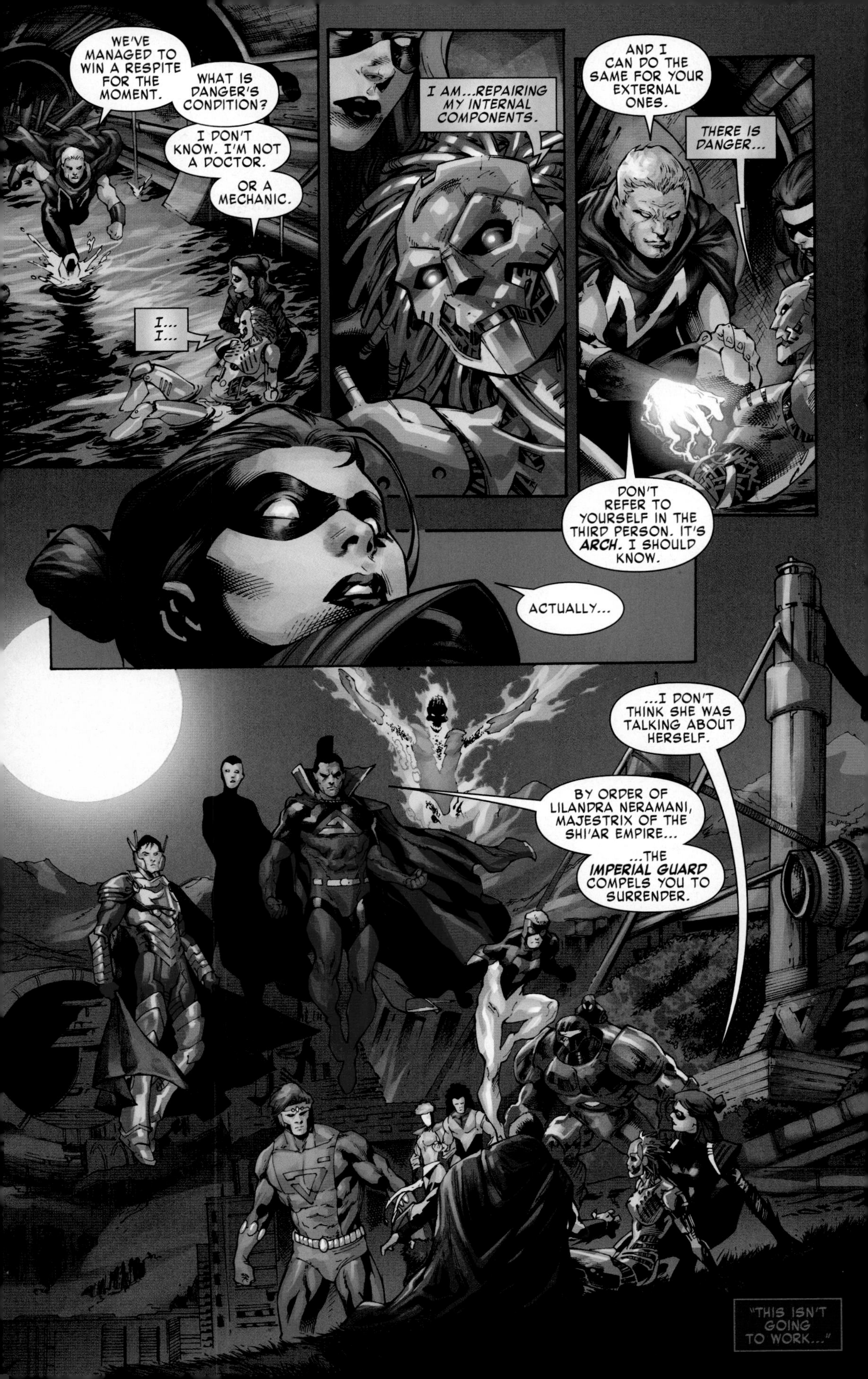
WE'VE MANAGED TO WIN A RESPITE FOR THE MOMENT.
WHAT IS DANGER'S CONDITION?
I DON'T KNOW. I'M NOT A DOCTOR.
OR A MECHANIC.
I... I...
I AM...REPAIRING MY INTERNAL COMPONENTS.
AND I CAN DO THE SAME FOR YOUR EXTERNAL ONES.
THERE IS DANGER...
DON'T REFER TO YOURSELF IN THE THIRD PERSON. IT'S ARCH. I SHOULD KNOW.
ACTUALLY...
...I DON'T THINK SHE WAS TALKING ABOUT HERSELF.
BY ORDER OF LILANDRA NERAMANI, MAJESTRIX OF THE SHI'AR EMPIRE...
...THE IMPERIAL GUARD COMPELS YOU TO SURRENDER.
"THIS ISN'T GOING TO WORK..."

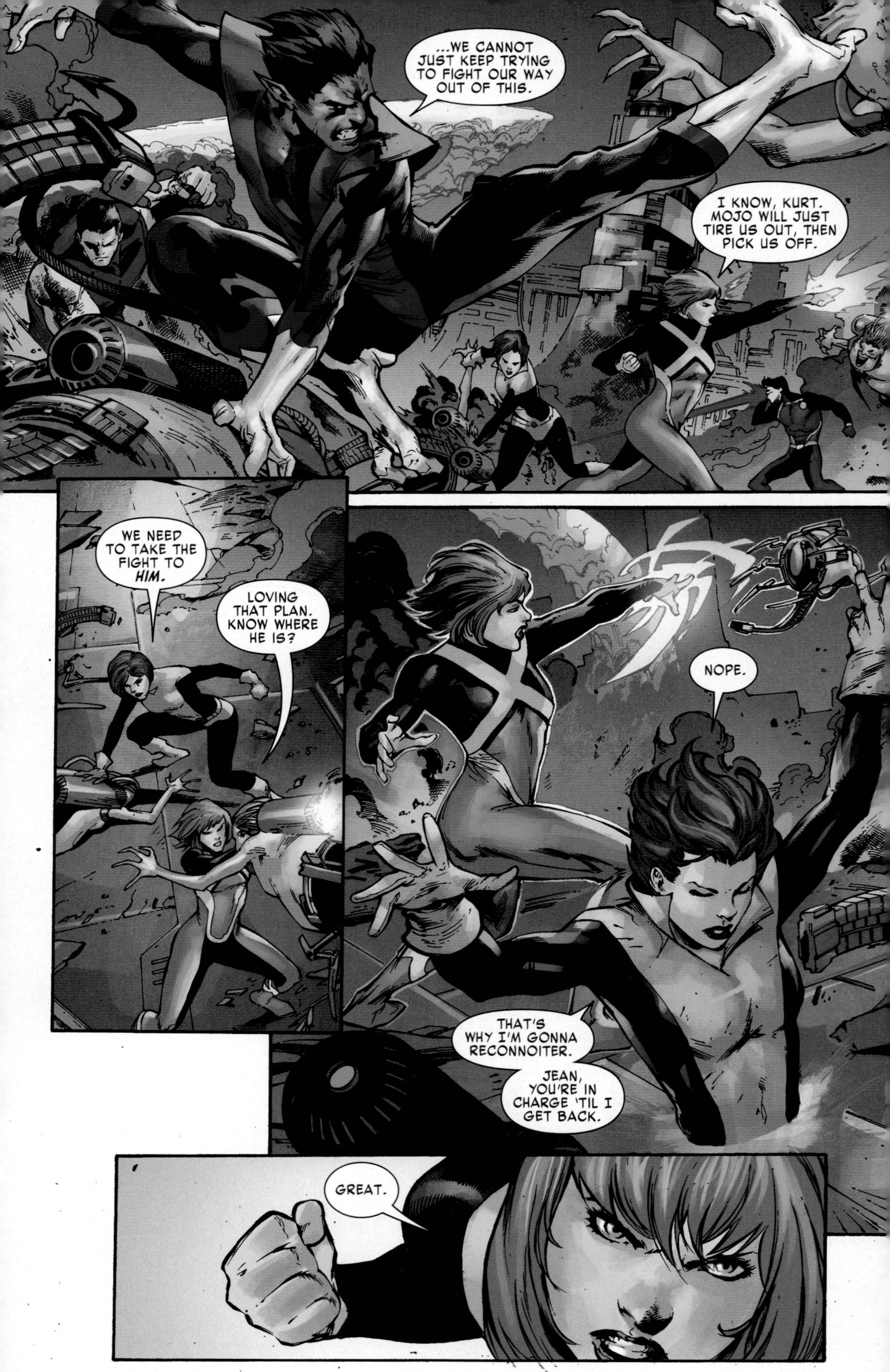
...WE CANNOT JUST KEEP TRYING TO FIGHT OUR WAY OUT OF THIS.
I KNOW, KURT. MOJO WILL JUST TIRE US OUT, THEN PICK US OFF.
WE NEED TO TAKE THE FIGHT TO *HIM*.
LOVING THAT PLAN. KNOW WHERE HE IS?
NOPE.
THAT'S WHY I'M GONNA RECONNOITER.
JEAN, YOU'RE IN CHARGE 'TIL I GET BACK.
GREAT.

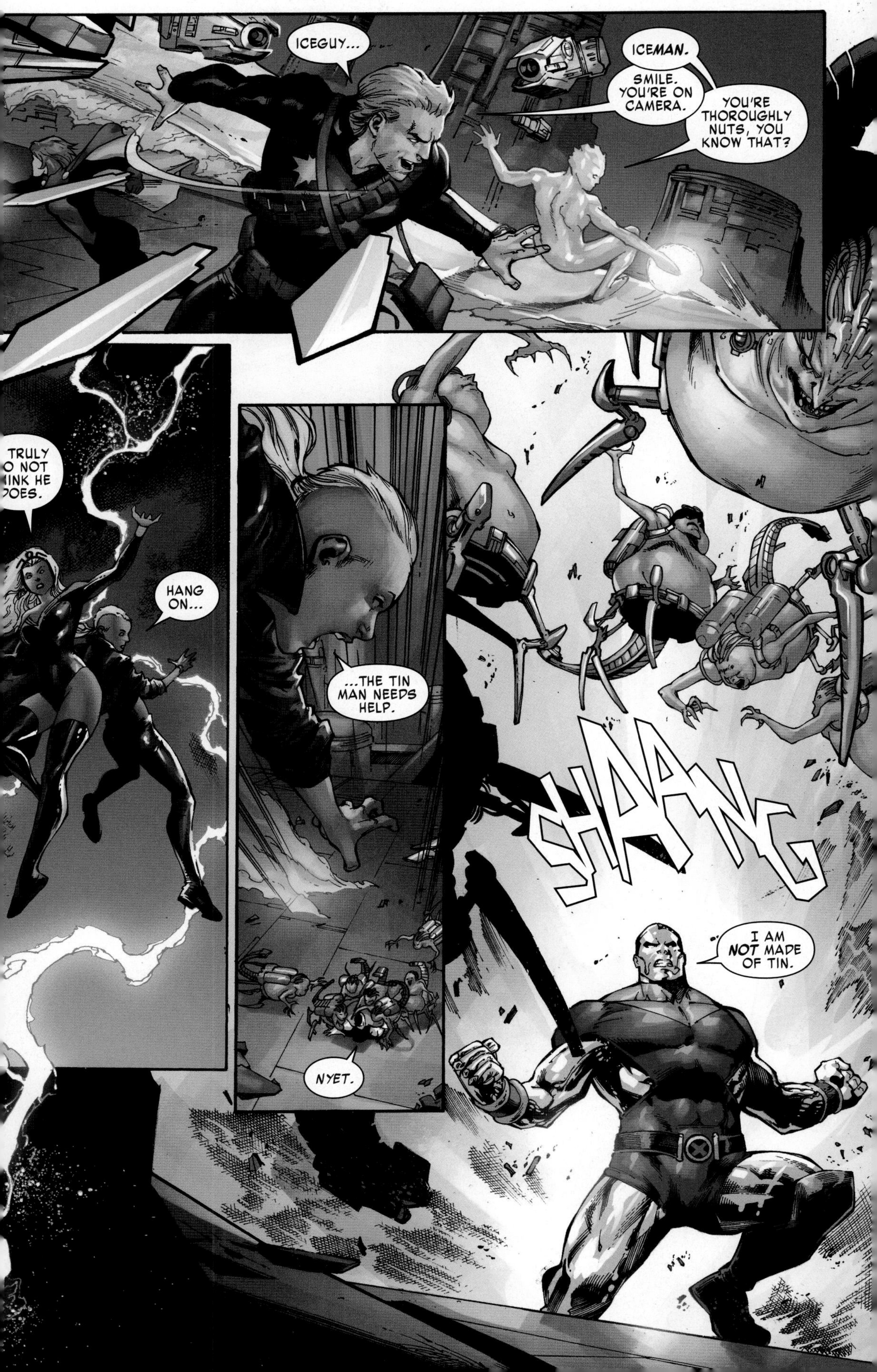
ICEGUY...
ICEMAN.
SMILE. YOU'RE ON CAMERA.
YOU'RE THOROUGHLY NUTS, YOU KNOW THAT?
TRULY O NOT INK HE OES.
HANG ON...
...THE TIN MAN NEEDS HELP.
NYET.
SHAAANG
I AM NOT MADE OF TIN.

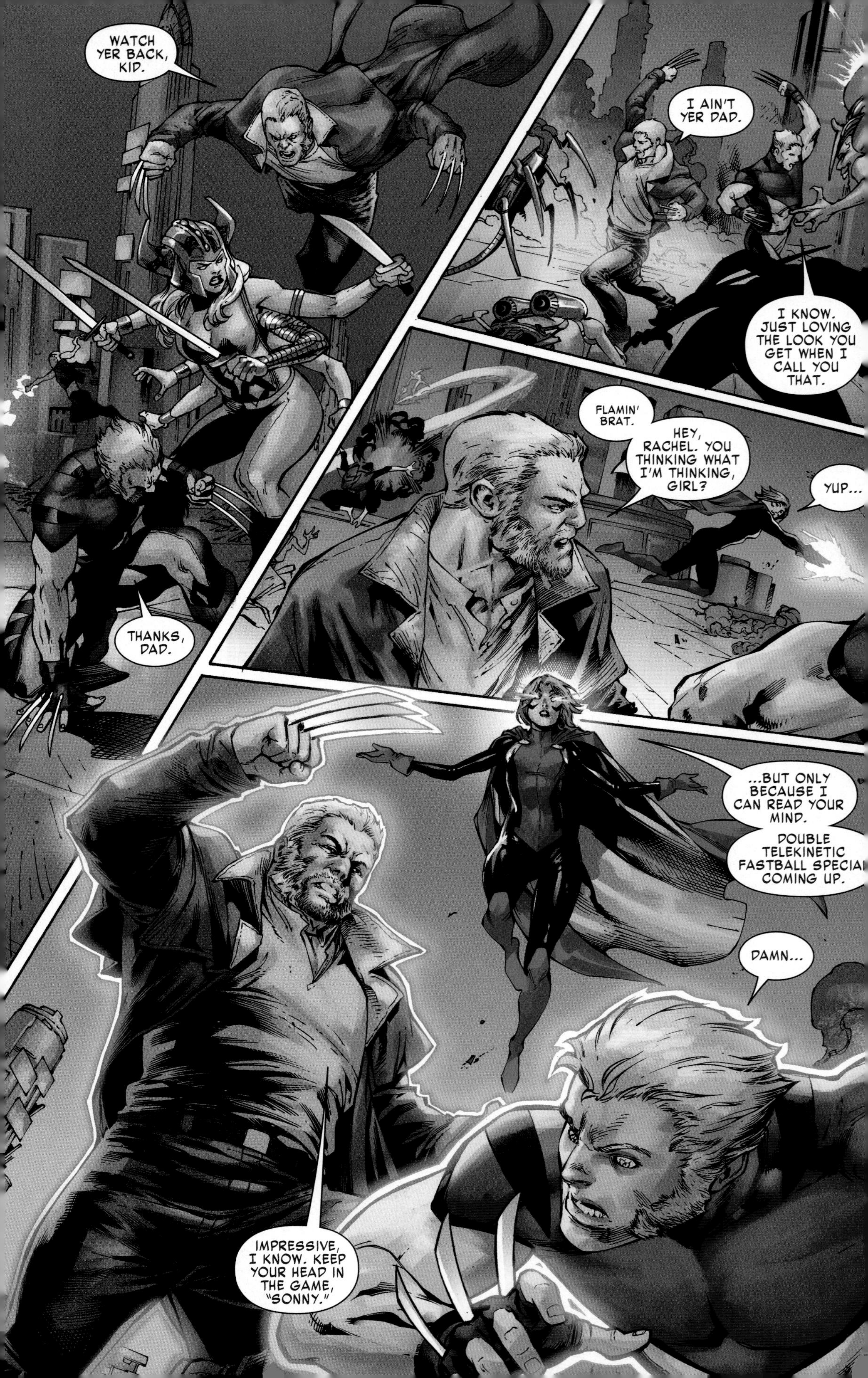
WATCH YER BACK, KID.
THANKS, DAD.
I AIN'T YER DAD.
I KNOW. JUST LOVING THE LOOK YOU GET WHEN I CALL YOU THAT.
FLAMIN' BRAT.
HEY, RACHEL. YOU THINKING WHAT I'M THINKING, GIRL?
YUP...
...BUT ONLY BECAUSE I CAN READ YOUR MIND.
DOUBLE TELEKINETIC FASTBALL SPECIAL COMING UP.
DAMN...
IMPRESSIVE, I KNOW. KEEP YOUR HEAD IN THE GAME, "SONNY."

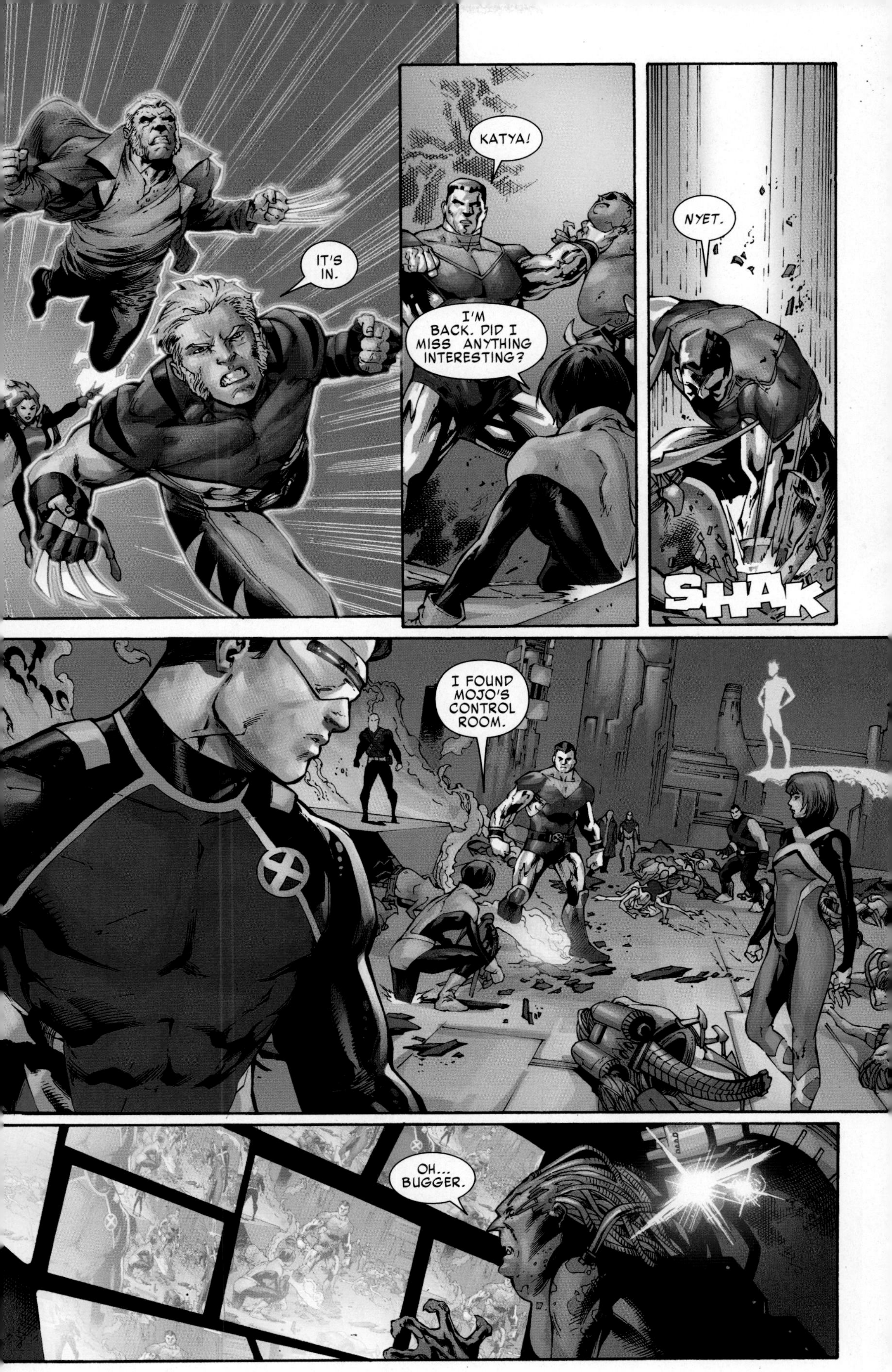
IT'S IN.
KATYA!
I'M BACK. DID I MISS ANYTHING INTERESTING?
NYET.
SHAK
I FOUND MOJO'S CONTROL ROOM.
OH... BUGGER.

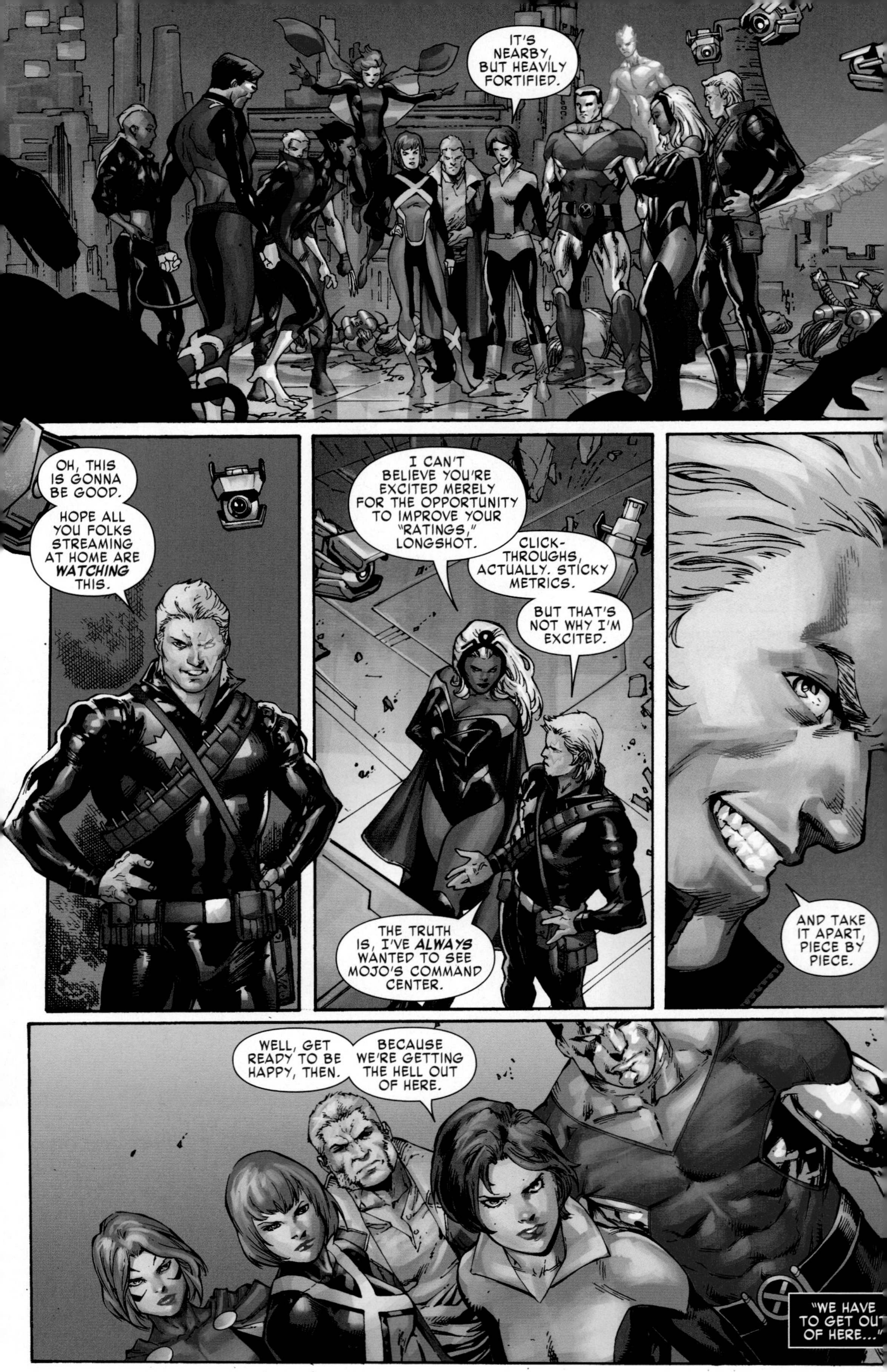

IT'S NEARBY, BUT HEAVILY FORTIFIED.
OH, THIS IS GONNA BE GOOD.
HOPE ALL YOU FOLKS STREAMING AT HOME ARE *WATCHING* THIS.
I CAN'T BELIEVE YOU'RE EXCITED MERELY FOR THE OPPORTUNITY TO IMPROVE YOUR "RATINGS," LONGSHOT.
CLICK-THROUGHS, ACTUALLY. STICKY METRICS.
BUT THAT'S NOT WHY I'M EXCITED.
THE TRUTH IS, I'VE *ALWAYS* WANTED TO SEE MOJO'S COMMAND CENTER.
AND TAKE IT APART, PIECE BY PIECE.
WELL, GET READY TO BE HAPPY, THEN.
BECAUSE WE'RE GETTING THE HELL OUT OF HERE.
"WE HAVE TO GET OUT OF HERE..."

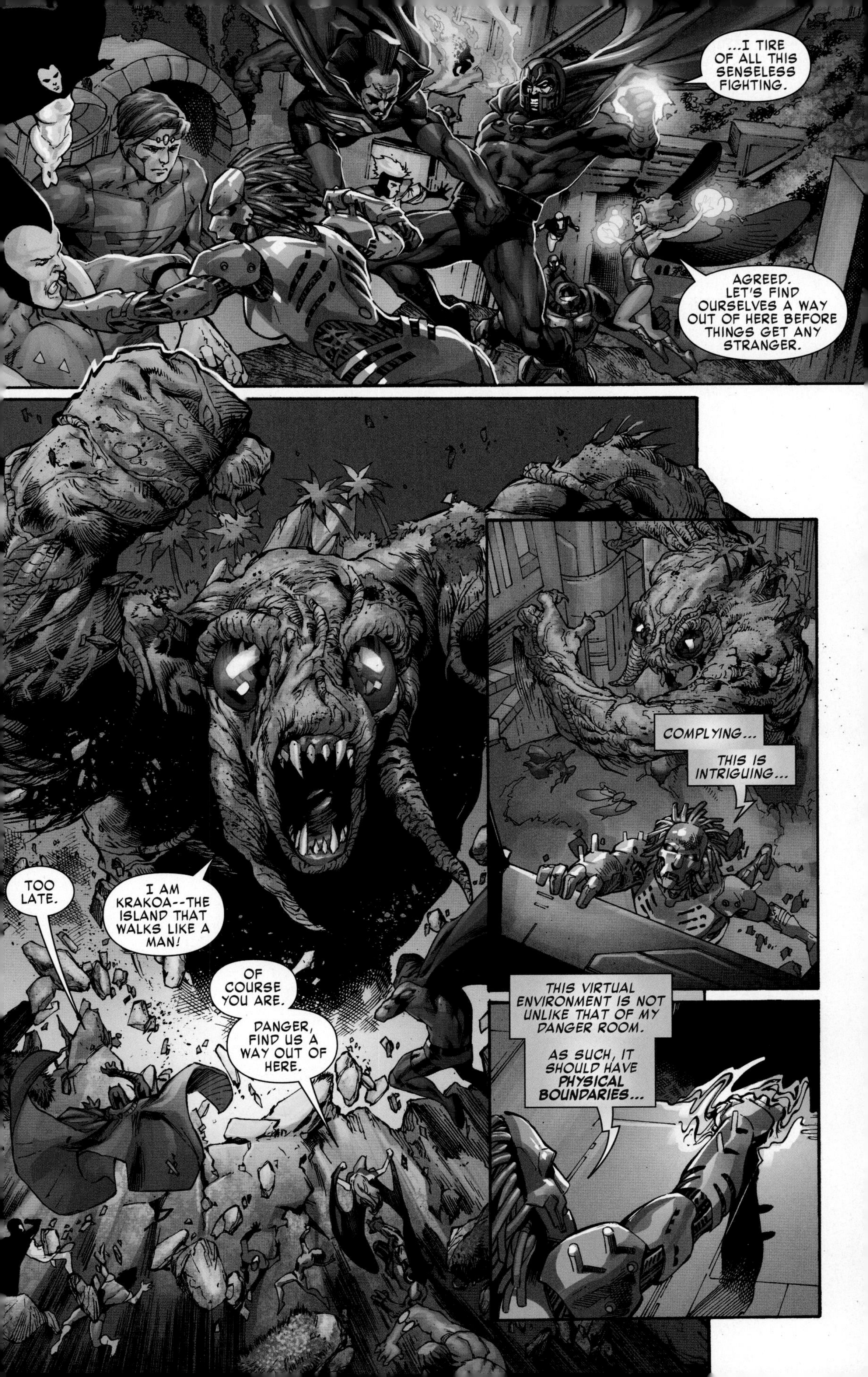
...I TIRE OF ALL THIS SENSELESS FIGHTING.
AGREED. LET'S FIND OURSELVES A WAY OUT OF HERE BEFORE THINGS GET ANY STRANGER.
TOO LATE.
I AM KRAKOA--THE ISLAND THAT WALKS LIKE A MAN!
OF COURSE YOU ARE.
DANGER, FIND US A WAY OUT OF HERE.
COMPLYING...
THIS IS INTRIGUING...
THIS VIRTUAL ENVIRONMENT IS NOT UNLIKE THAT OF MY DANGER ROOM.
AS SUCH, IT SHOULD HAVE PHYSICAL BOUNDARIES...

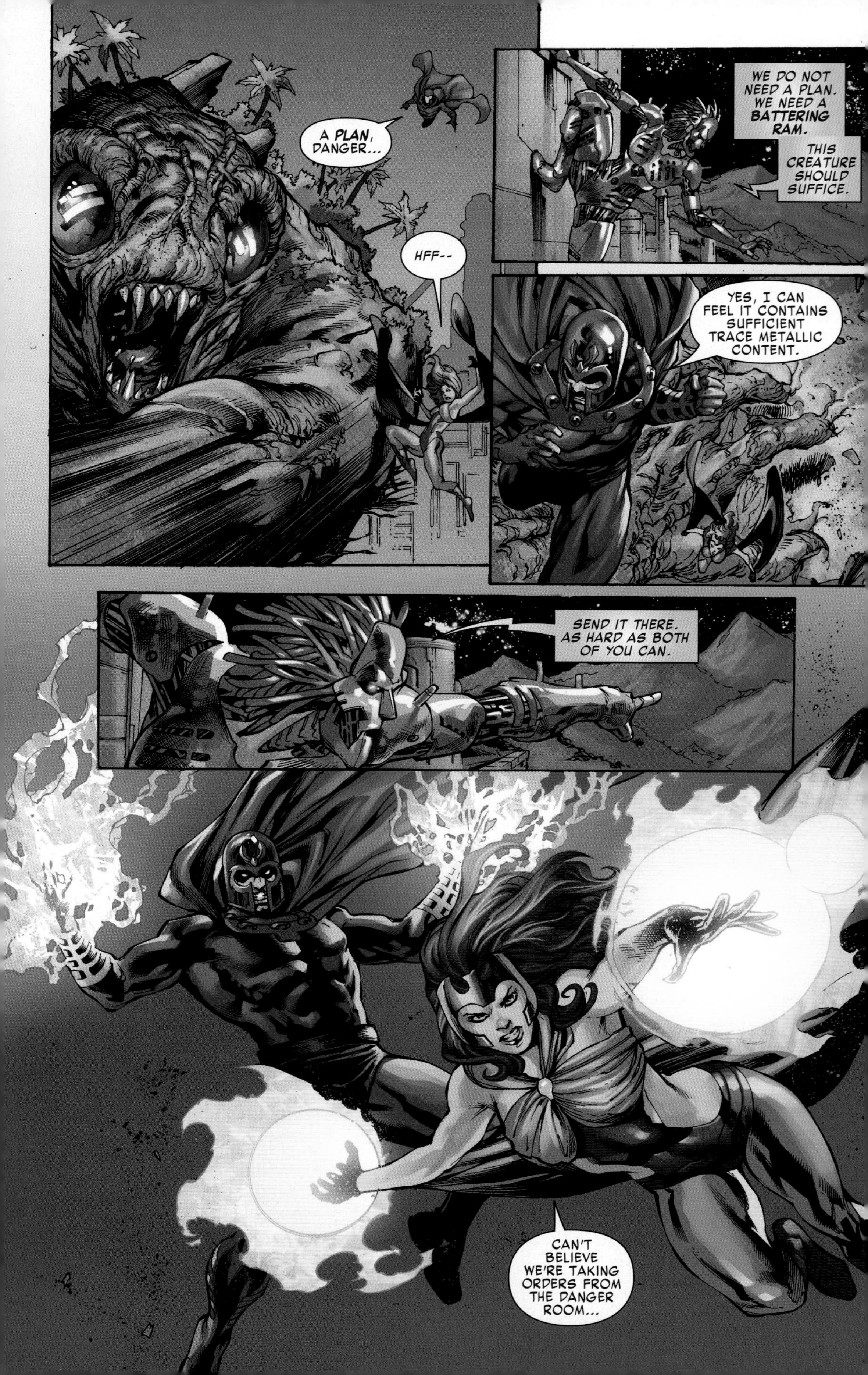

A PLAN, DANGER...
WE DO NOT NEED A PLAN. WE NEED A BATTERING RAM.
THIS CREATURE SHOULD SUFFICE.
HFF--
YES, I CAN FEEL IT CONTAINS SUFFICIENT TRACE METALLIC CONTENT.
SEND IT THERE. AS HARD AS BOTH OF YOU CAN.
CAN'T BELIEVE WE'RE TAKING ORDERS FROM THE DANGER ROOM...

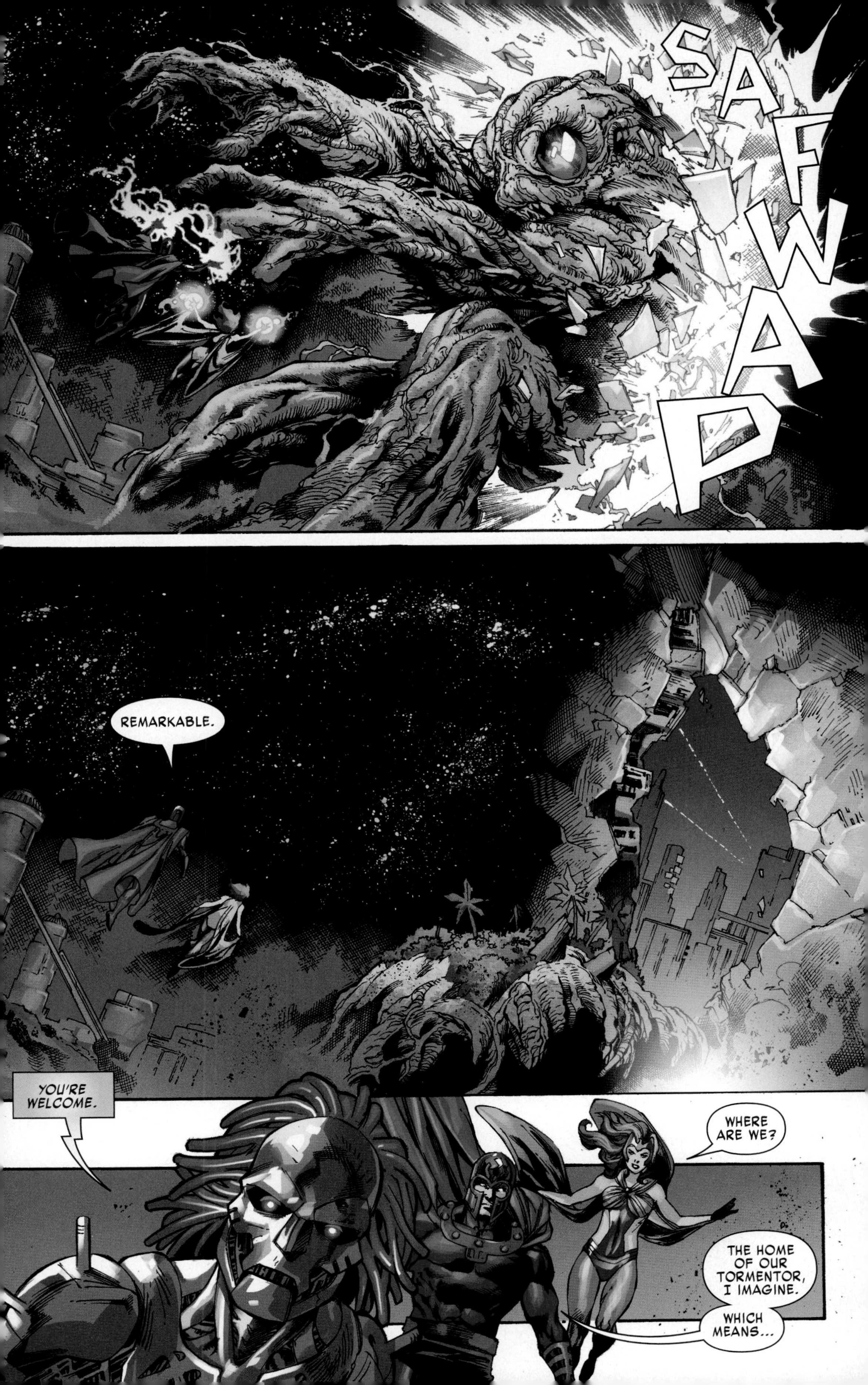
SAFWAP
REMARKABLE.
YOU'RE WELCOME.
WHERE ARE WE?
THE HOME OF OUR TORMENTOR, I IMAGINE.
WHICH MEANS...

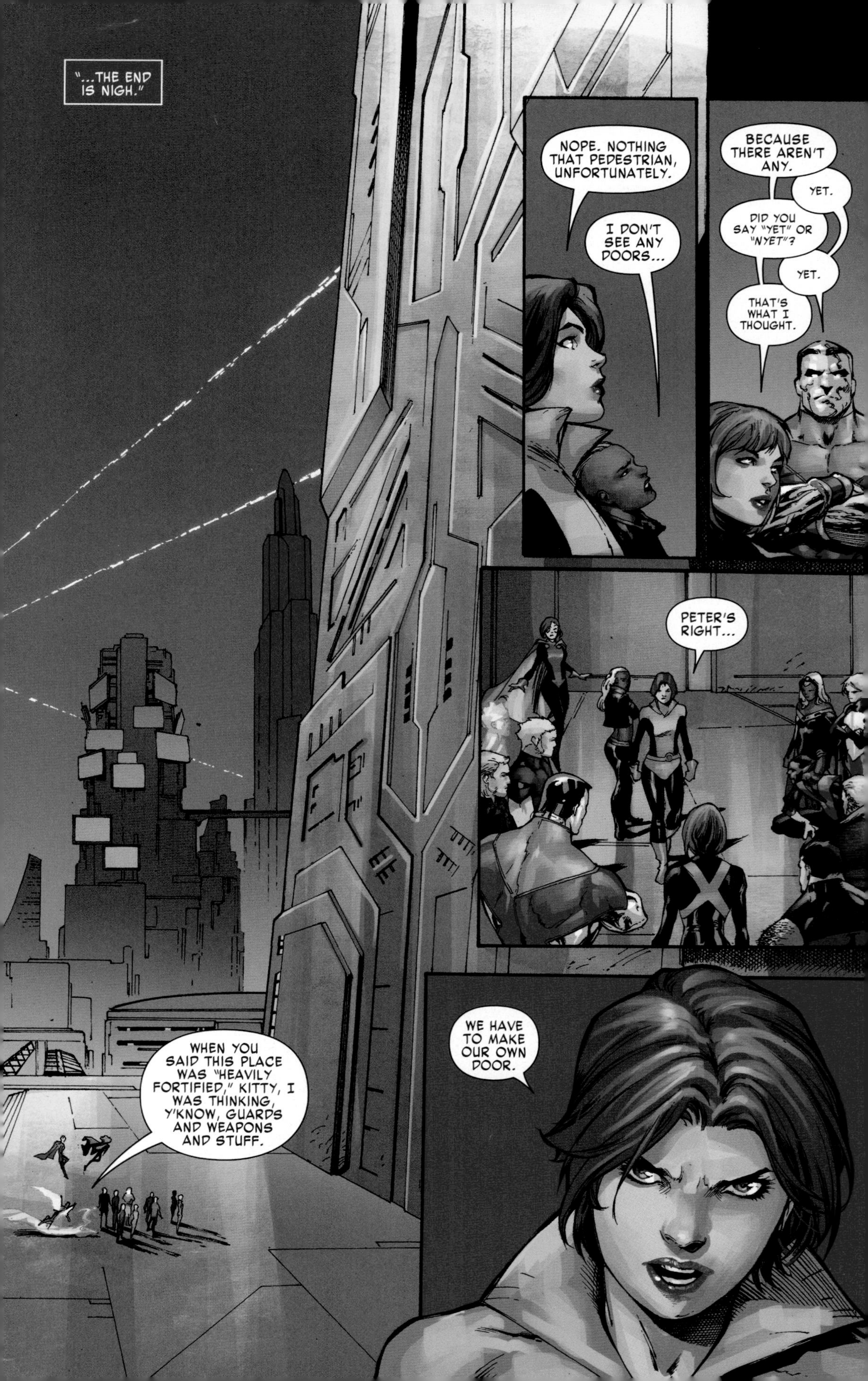
"...THE END IS NIGH."
NOPE. NOTHING THAT PEDESTRIAN, UNFORTUNATELY.
I DON'T SEE ANY DOORS...
BECAUSE THERE AREN'T ANY.
YET.
DID YOU SAY "YET" OR "NYET"?
YET.
THAT'S WHAT I THOUGHT.
PETER'S RIGHT...
WHEN YOU SAID THIS PLACE WAS "HEAVILY FORTIFIED," KITTY, I WAS THINKING, Y'KNOW, GUARDS AND WEAPONS AND STUFF.
WE HAVE TO MAKE OUR OWN DOOR.

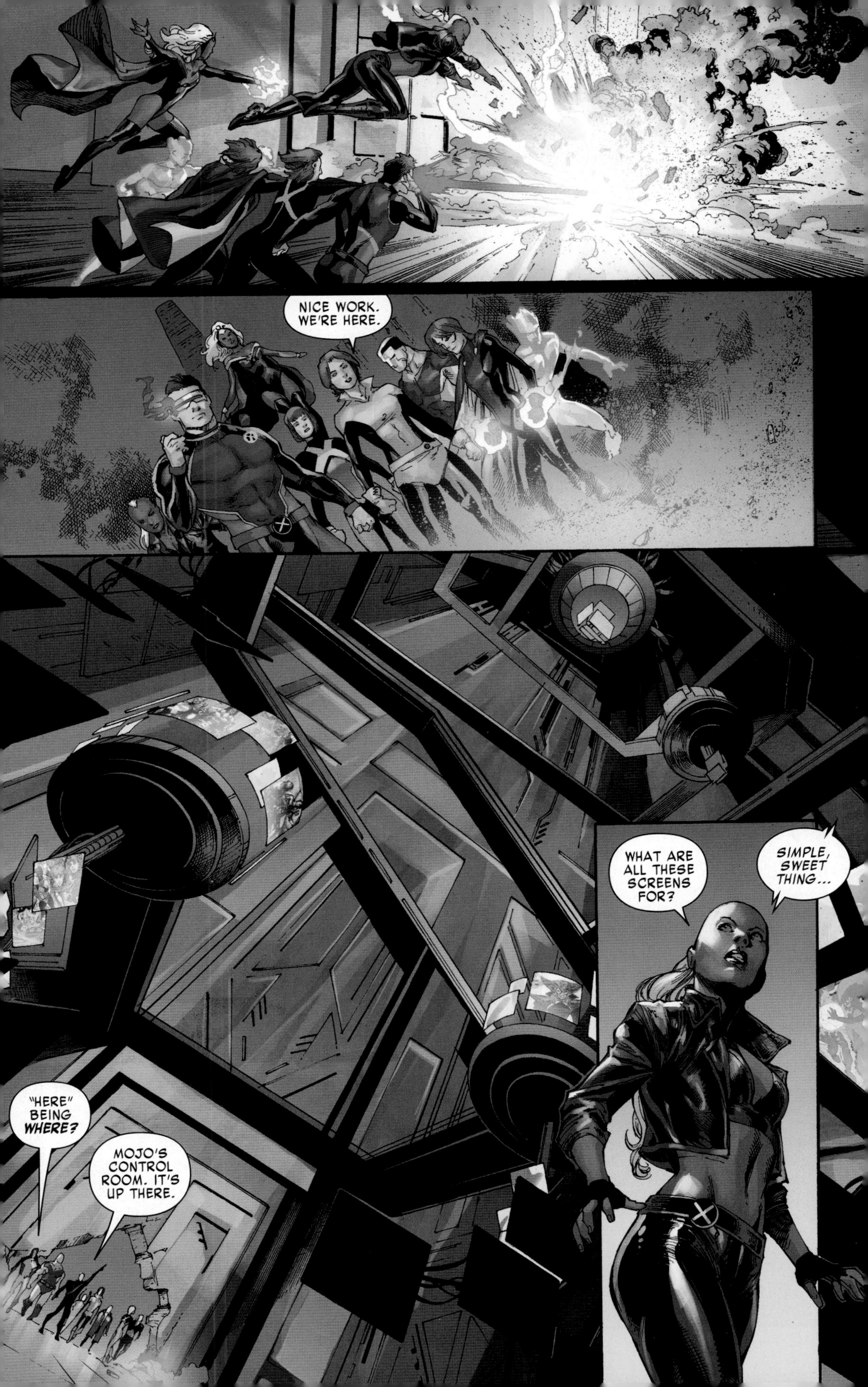
NICE WORK. WE'RE HERE.
"HERE" BEING WHERE?
MOJO'S CONTROL ROOM. IT'S UP THERE.
WHAT ARE ALL THESE SCREENS FOR?
SIMPLE, SWEET THING...

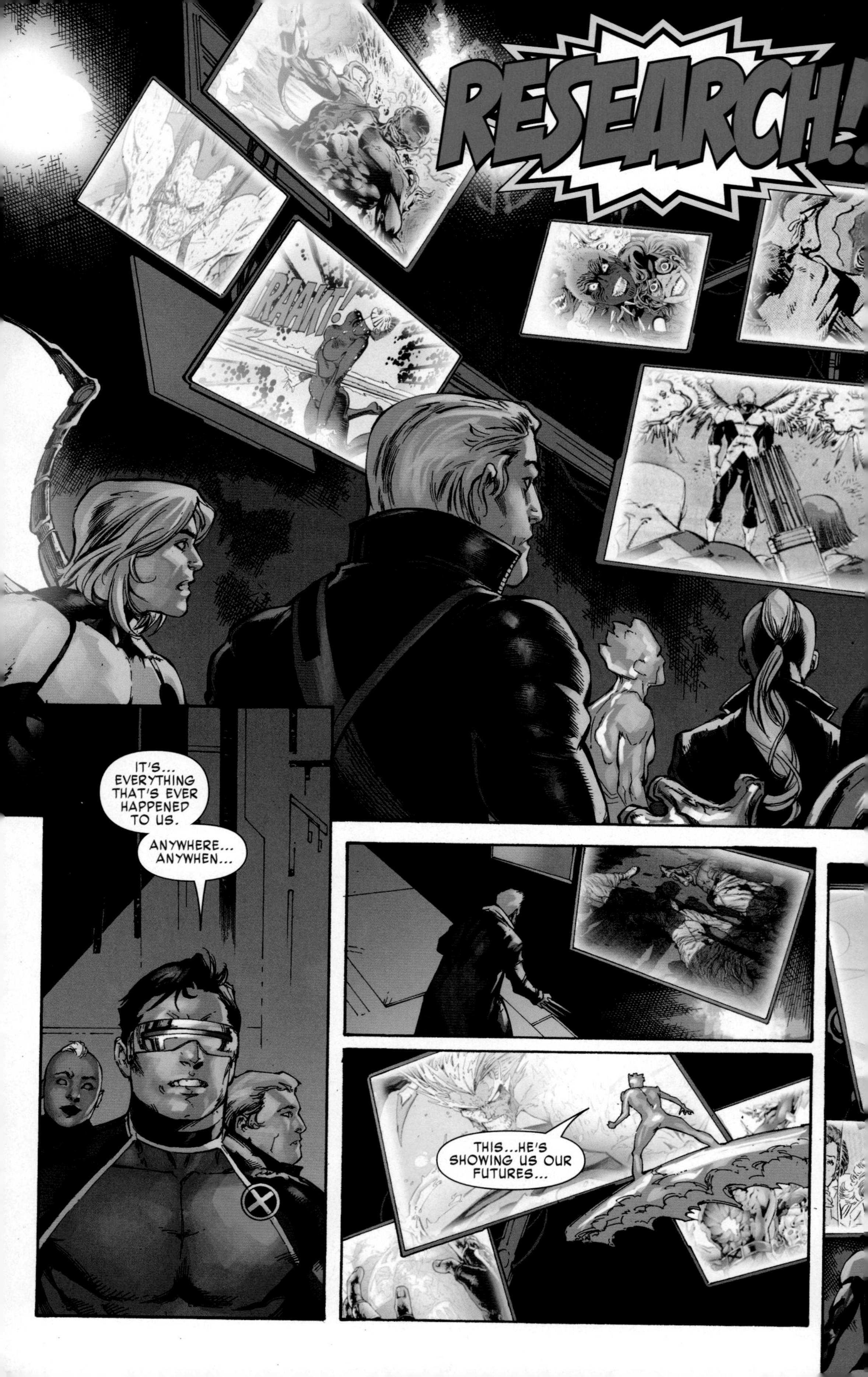
RESEARCH!!
RAAAKT!
IT'S... EVERYTHING THAT'S EVER HAPPENED TO US.
ANYWHERE... ANYWHEN...
THIS...HE'S SHOWING US OUR FUTURES...

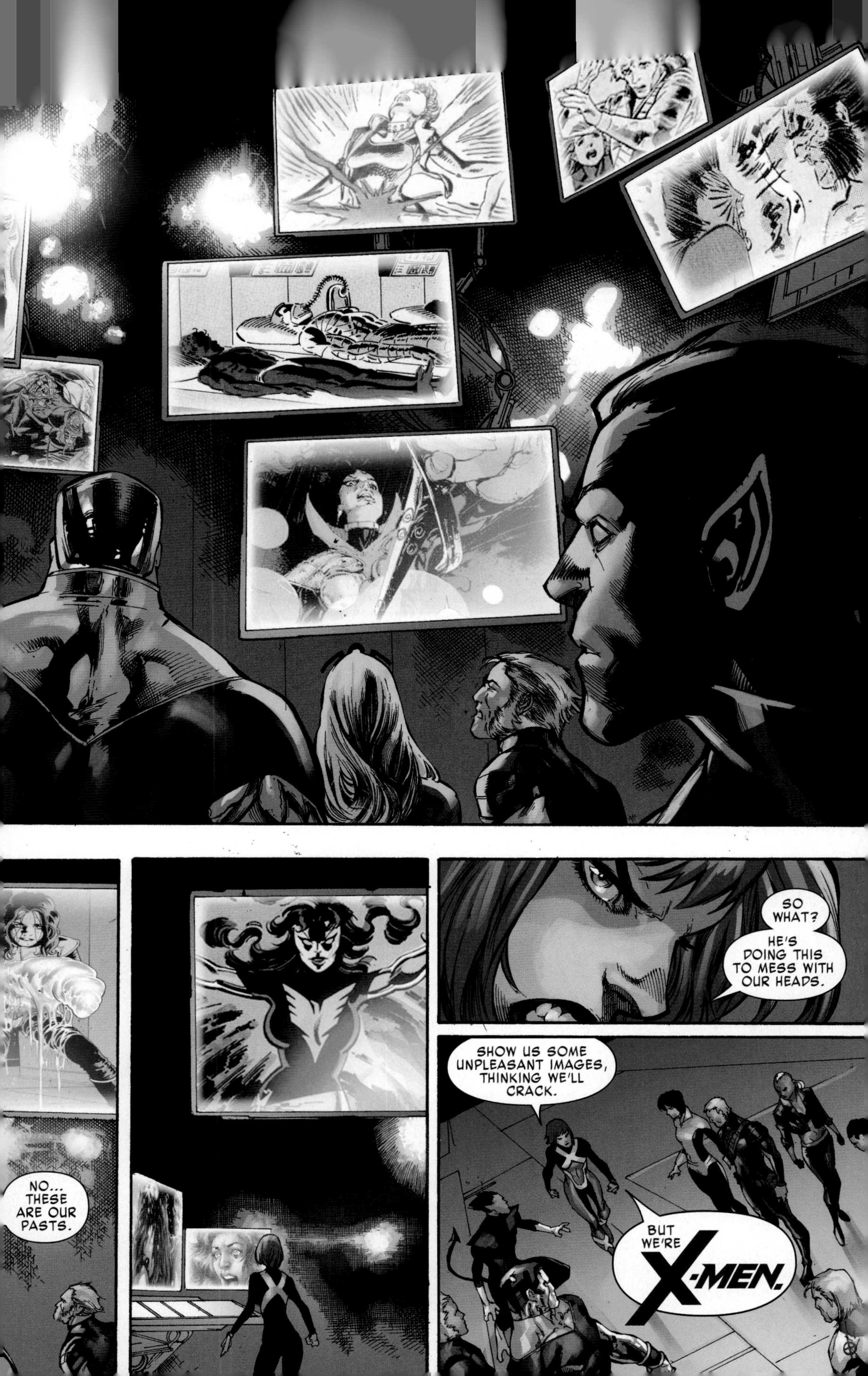
NO... THESE ARE OUR PASTS.
SO WHAT?
HE'S DOING THIS TO MESS WITH OUR HEADS.
SHOW US SOME UNPLEASANT IMAGES, THINKING WE'LL CRACK.
BUT WE'RE X-MEN.

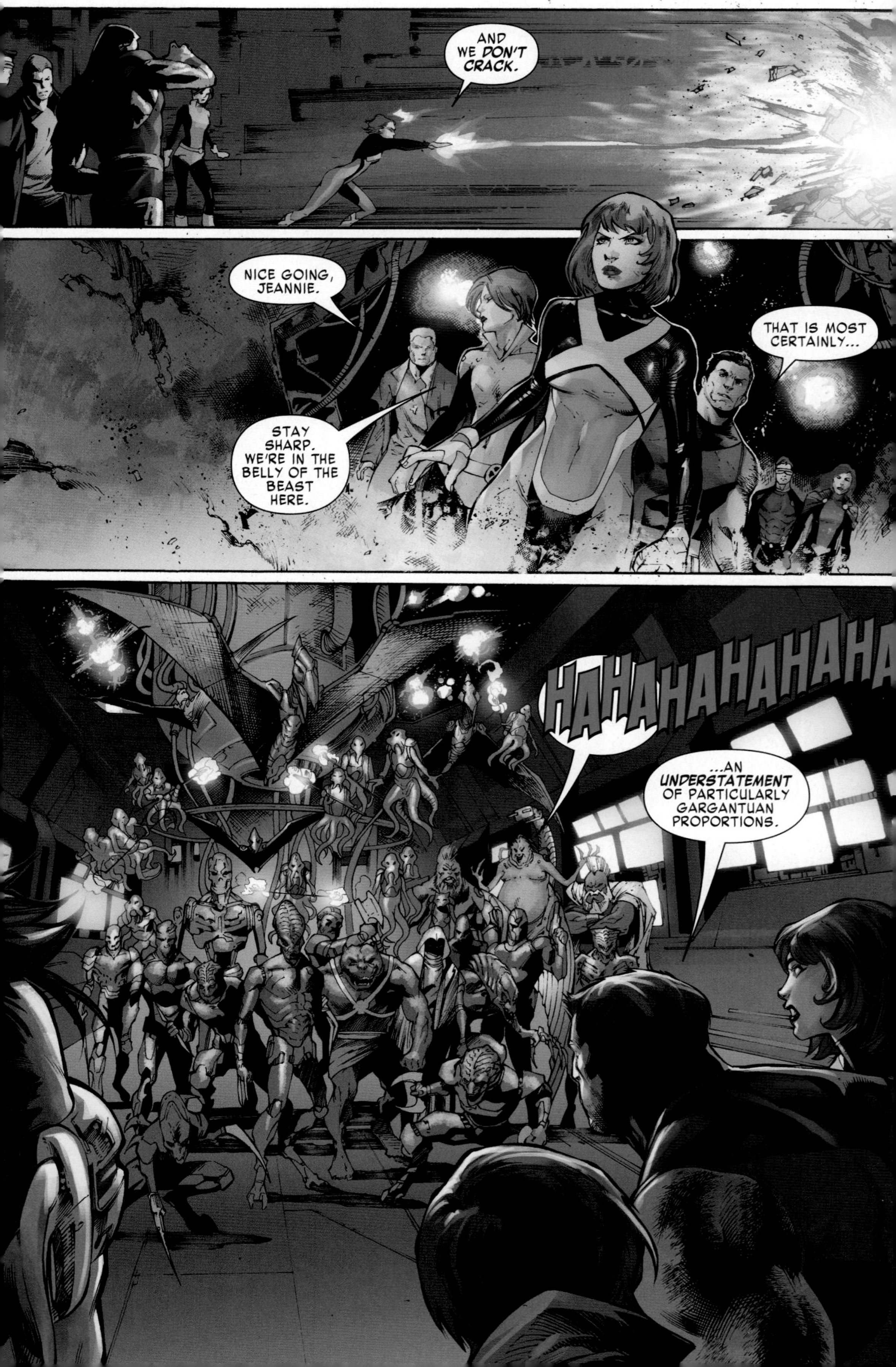
AND WE DON'T CRACK.
NICE GOING, JEANNIE.
STAY SHARP. WE'RE IN THE BELLY OF THE BEAST HERE.
THAT IS MOST CERTAINLY...
HAHAHAHAHAHA
...AN UNDERSTATEMENT OF PARTICULARLY GARGANTUAN PROPORTIONS.

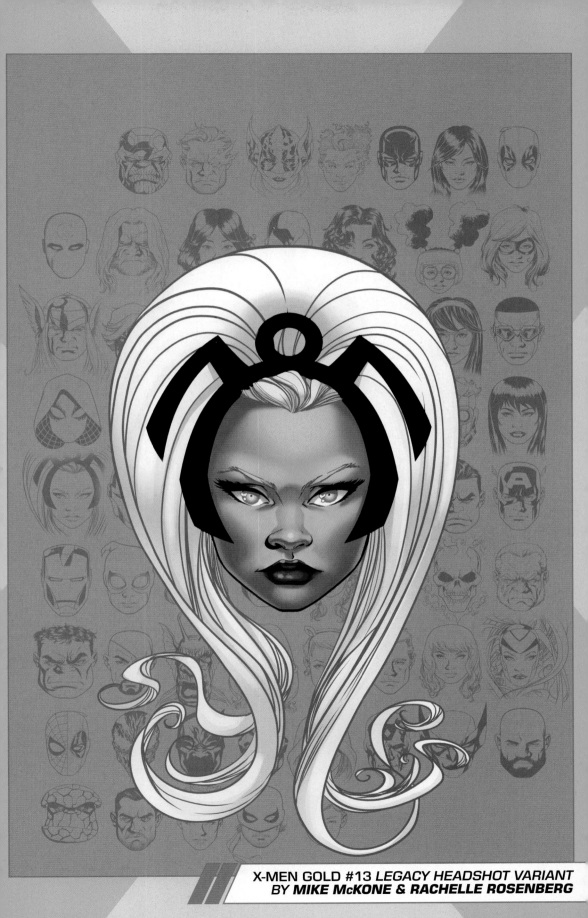

X-MEN GOLD #13 *LEGACY HEADSHOT VARIANT*
BY **MIKE McKONE** & **RACHELLE ROSENBERG**

X-MEN BLUE #15

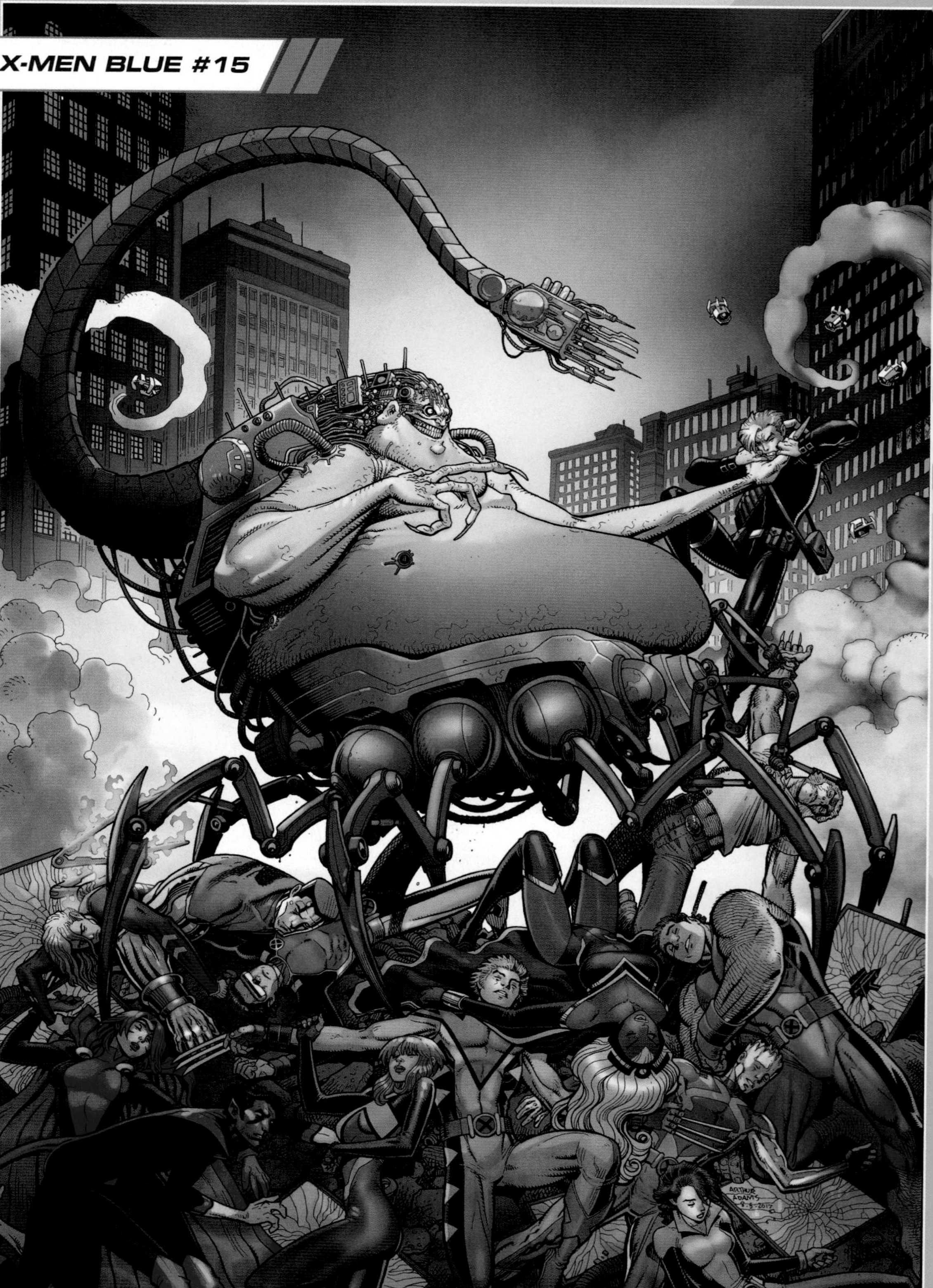

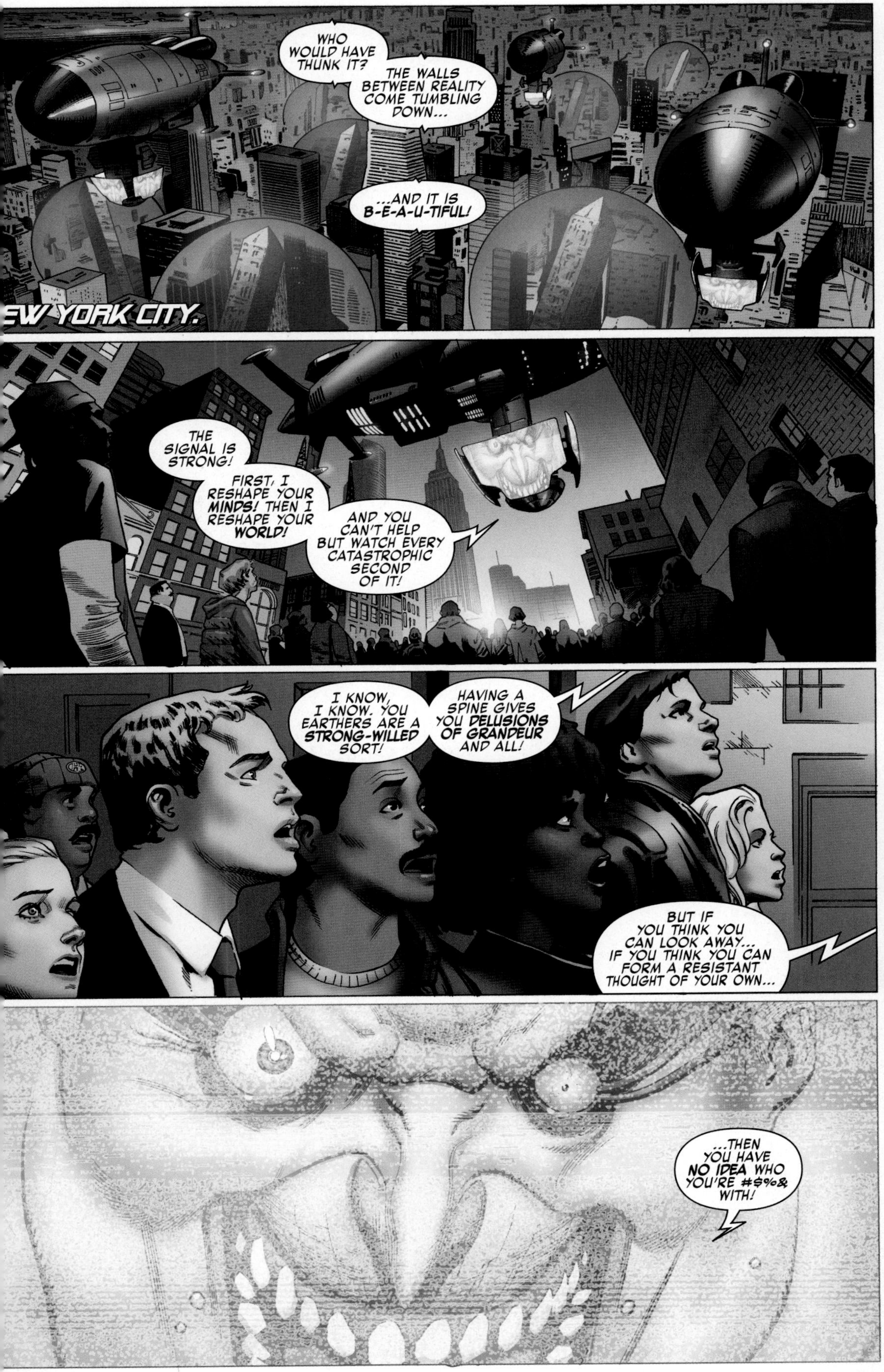
WHO WOULD HAVE THUNK IT?
THE WALLS BETWEEN REALITY COME TUMBLING DOWN...
...AND IT IS B-E-A-U-TIFUL!
EW YORK CITY.
THE SIGNAL IS STRONG!
FIRST, I RESHAPE YOUR MINDS! THEN I RESHAPE YOUR WORLD!
AND YOU CAN'T HELP BUT WATCH EVERY CATASTROPHIC SECOND OF IT!
I KNOW, I KNOW. YOU EARTHERS ARE A STRONG-WILLED SORT!
HAVING A SPINE GIVES YOU DELUSIONS OF GRANDEUR AND ALL!
BUT IF YOU THINK YOU CAN LOOK AWAY... IF YOU THINK YOU CAN FORM A RESISTANT THOUGHT OF YOUR OWN...
...THEN YOU HAVE NO IDEA WHO YOU'RE #$%& WITH!

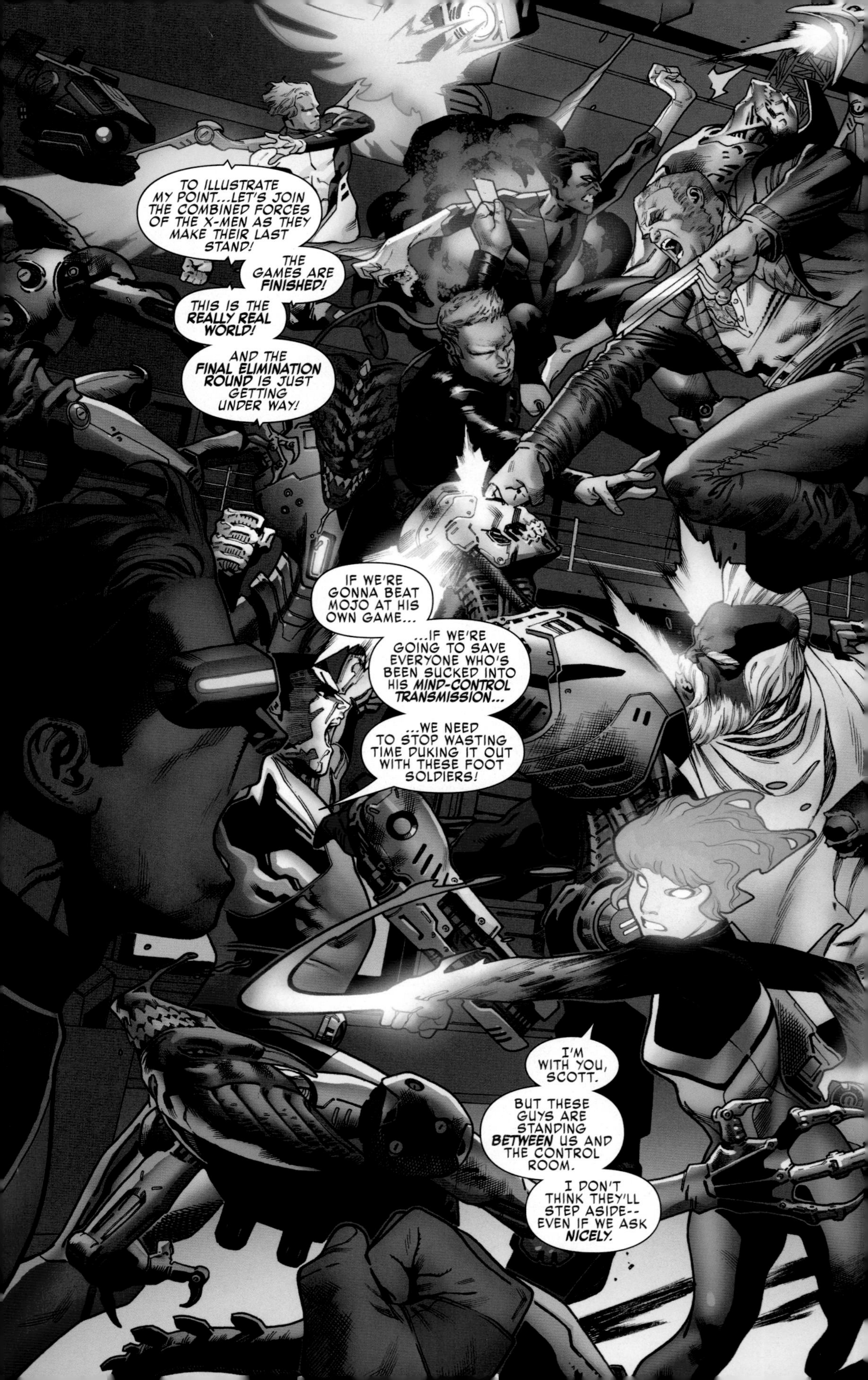
TO ILLUSTRATE MY POINT...LET'S JOIN THE COMBINED FORCES OF THE X-MEN AS THEY MAKE THEIR LAST STAND!
THE GAMES ARE FINISHED!
THIS IS THE REALLY REAL WORLD!
AND THE FINAL ELIMINATION ROUND IS JUST GETTING UNDER WAY!
IF WE'RE GONNA BEAT MOJO AT HIS OWN GAME...
...IF WE'RE GOING TO SAVE EVERYONE WHO'S BEEN SUCKED INTO HIS MIND-CONTROL TRANSMISSION...
...WE NEED TO STOP WASTING TIME DUKING IT OUT WITH THESE FOOT SOLDIERS!
I'M WITH YOU, SCOTT.
BUT THESE GUYS ARE STANDING BETWEEN US AND THE CONTROL ROOM.
I DON'T THINK THEY'LL STEP ASIDE-- EVEN IF WE ASK NICELY.

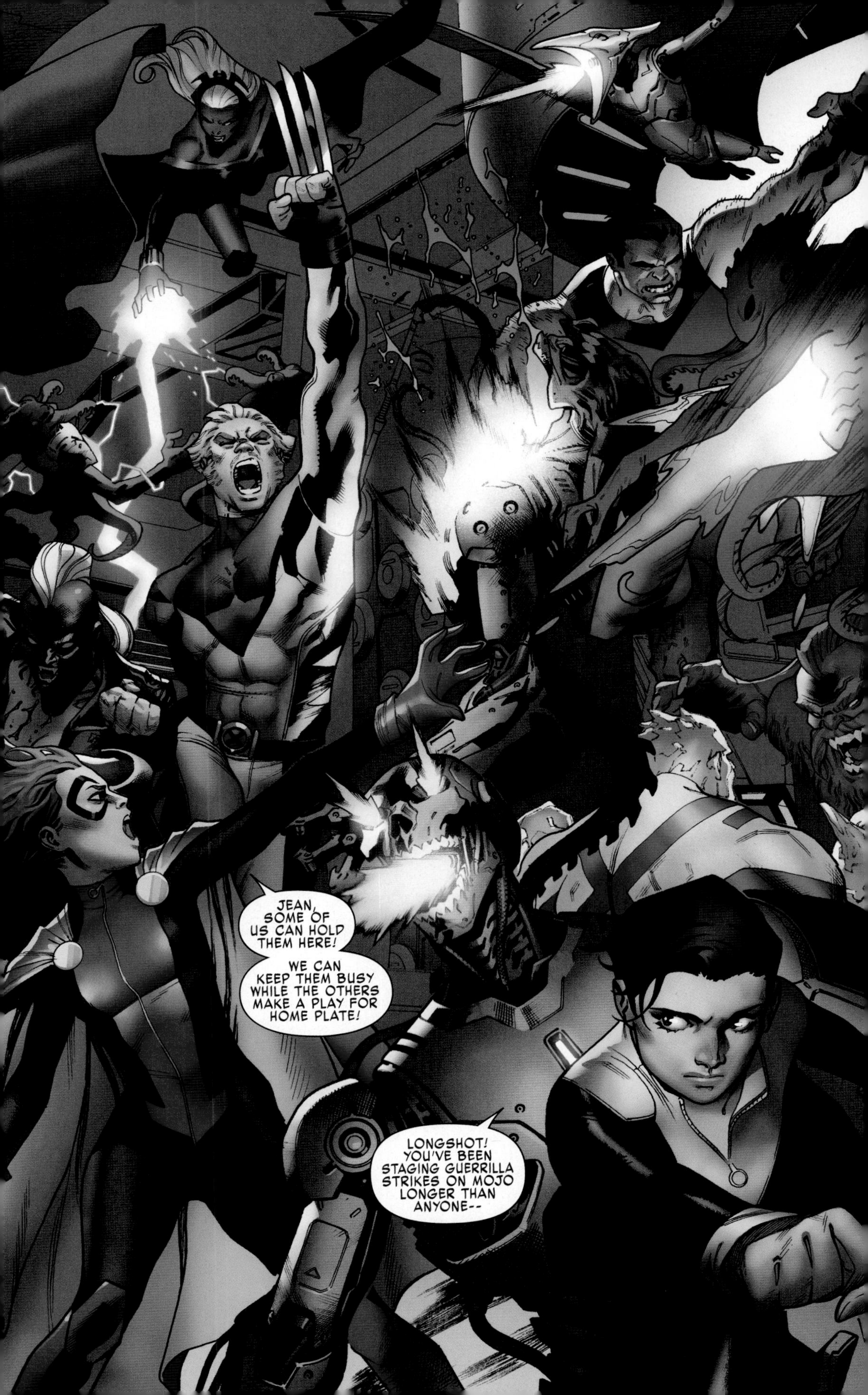
JEAN, SOME OF US CAN HOLD THEM HERE!
WE CAN KEEP THEM BUSY WHILE THE OTHERS MAKE A PLAY FOR HOME PLATE!
LONGSHOT! YOU'VE BEEN STAGING GUERRILLA STRIKES ON MOJO LONGER THAN ANYONE--

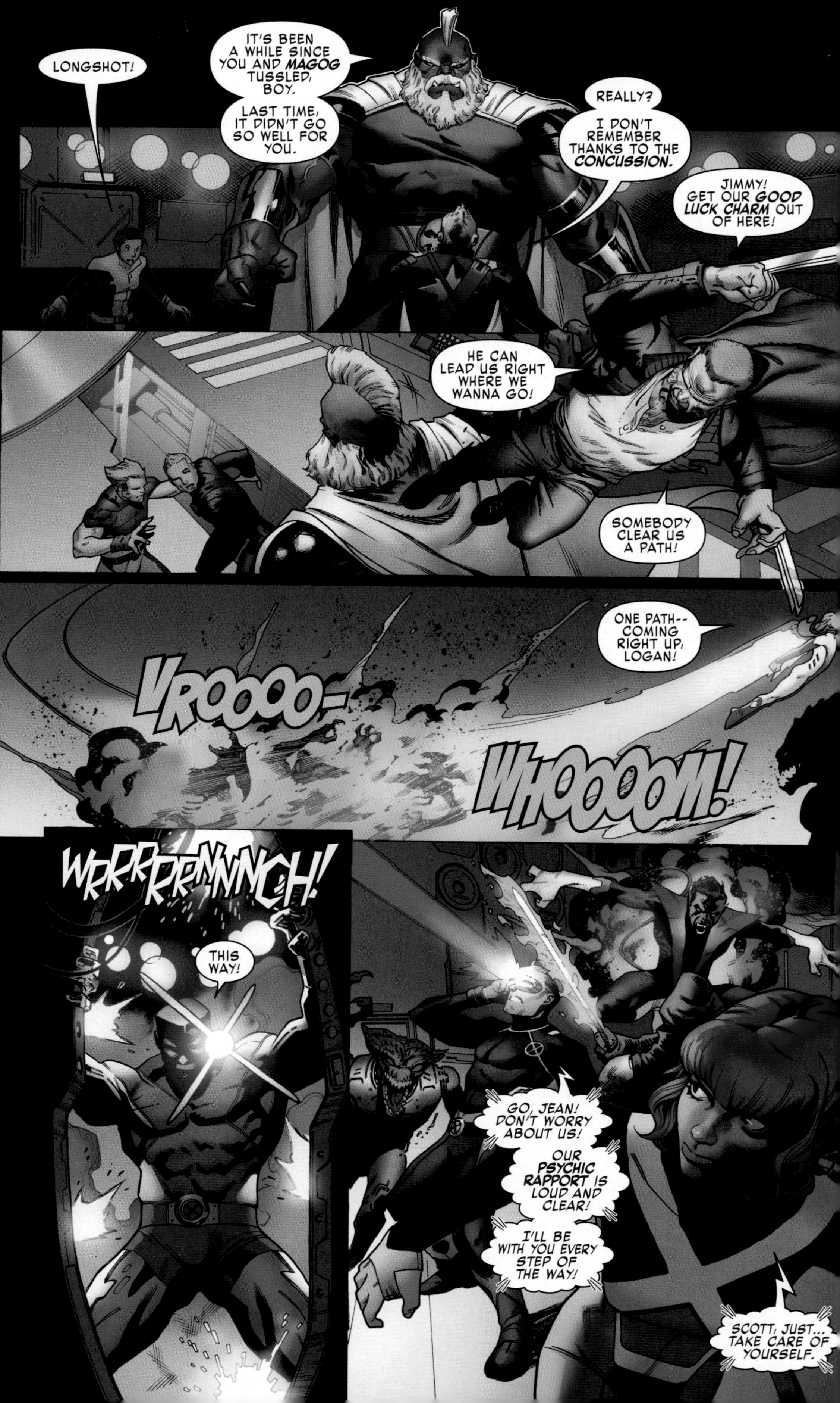
LONGSHOT!
IT'S BEEN A WHILE SINCE YOU AND MAGOG TUSSLED, BOY.
LAST TIME, IT DIDN'T GO SO WELL FOR YOU.
REALLY?
I DON'T REMEMBER THANKS TO THE CONCUSSION.
JIMMY! GET OUR GOOD LUCK CHARM OUT OF HERE!
HE CAN LEAD US RIGHT WHERE WE WANNA GO!
SOMEBODY CLEAR US A PATH!
ONE PATH-- COMING RIGHT UP, LOGAN!
VROOOO-
WHOOOOM!
WRRRRRNNNCH!
THIS WAY!
GO, JEAN! DON'T WORRY ABOUT US!
OUR PSYCHIC RAPPORT IS LOUD AND CLEAR!
I'LL BE WITH YOU EVERY STEP OF THE WAY!
SCOTT, JUST... TAKE CARE OF YOURSELF.

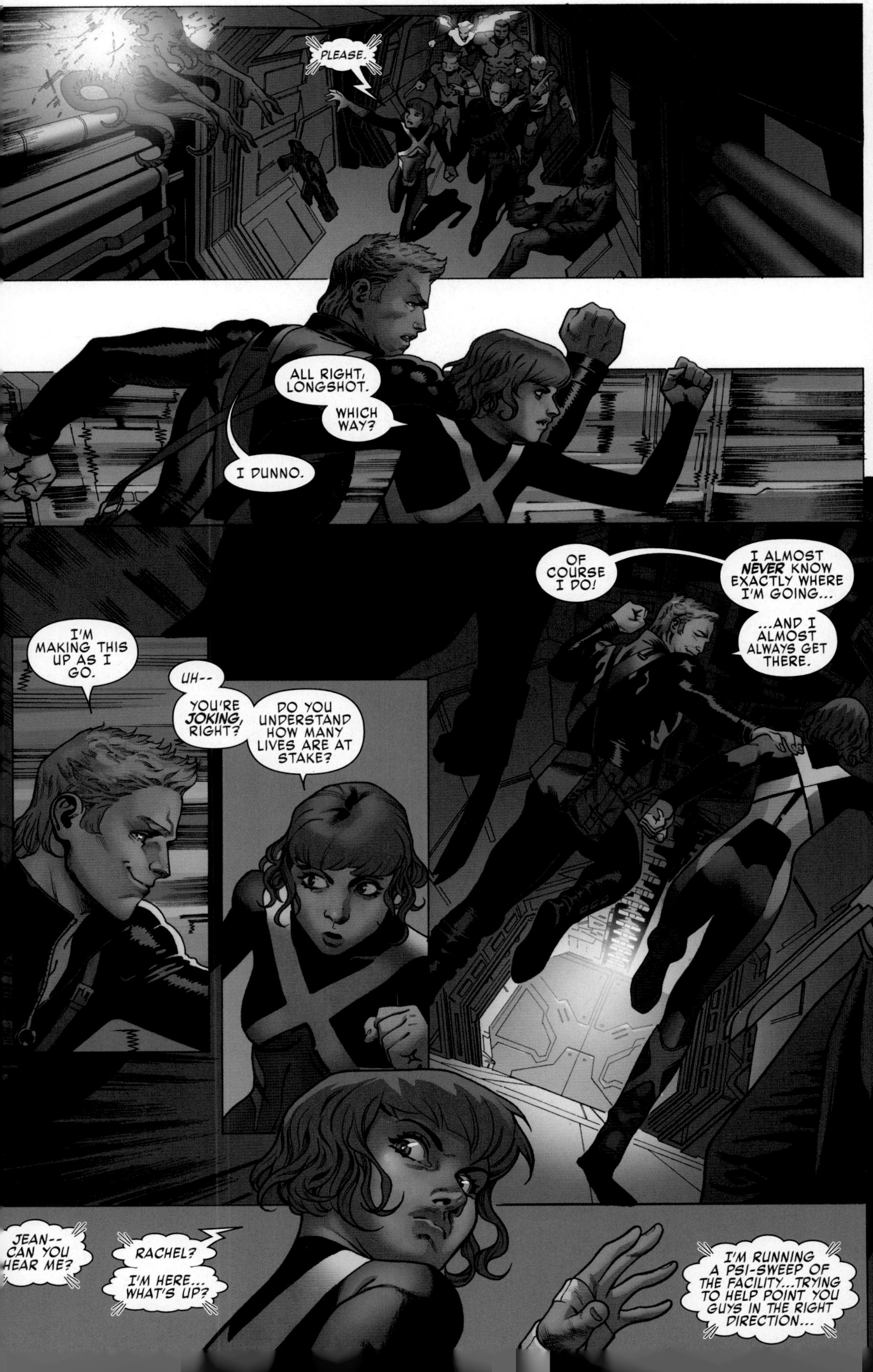
PLEASE.
ALL RIGHT, LONGSHOT.
WHICH WAY?
I DUNNO.
I'M MAKING THIS UP AS I GO.
UH--
YOU'RE JOKING, RIGHT?
DO YOU UNDERSTAND HOW MANY LIVES ARE AT STAKE?
OF COURSE I DO!
I ALMOST NEVER KNOW EXACTLY WHERE I'M GOING...
...AND I ALMOST ALWAYS GET THERE.
JEAN-- CAN YOU HEAR ME?
RACHEL?
I'M HERE... WHAT'S UP?
I'M RUNNING A PSI-SWEEP OF THE FACILITY...TRYING TO HELP POINT YOU GUYS IN THE RIGHT DIRECTION...

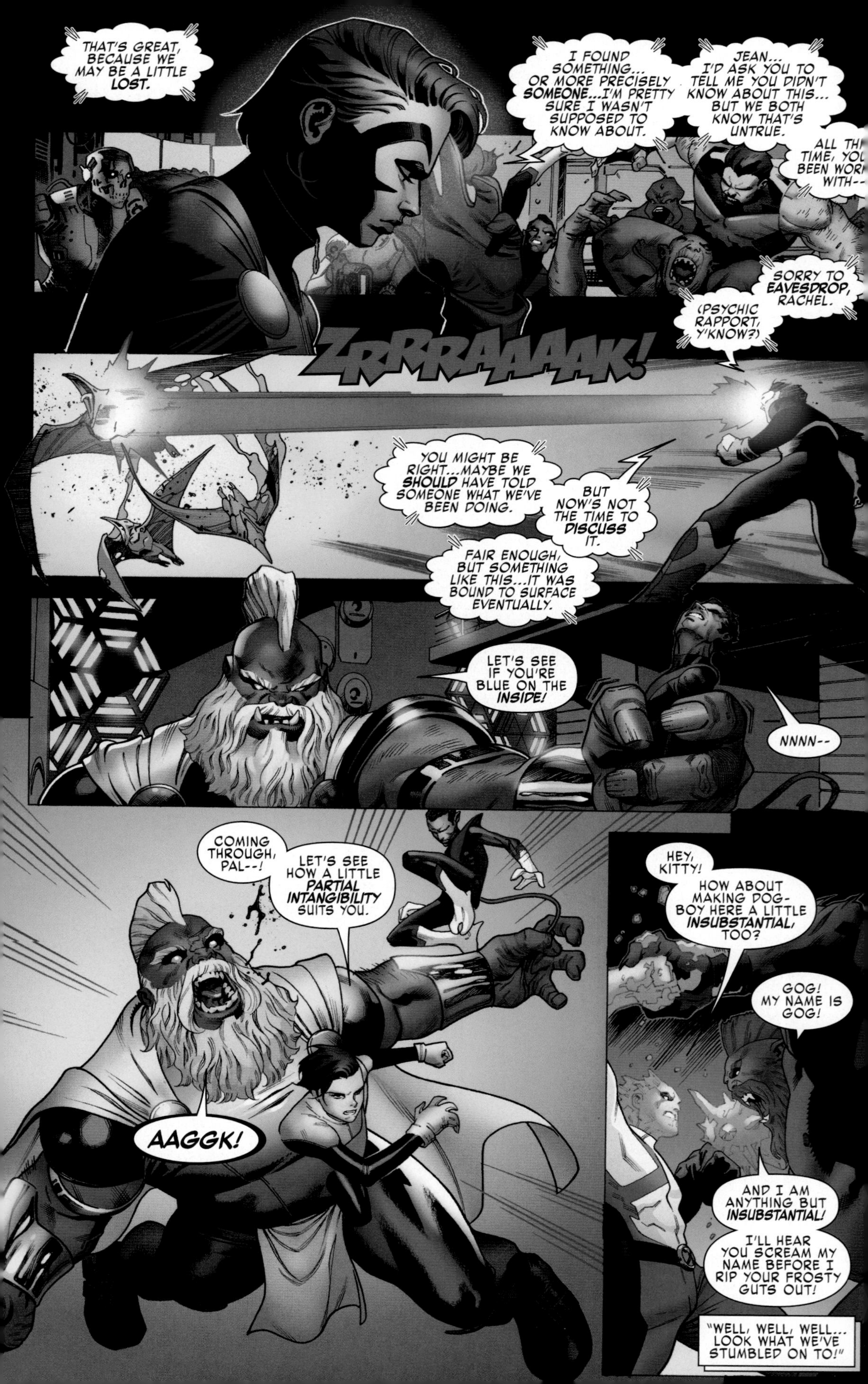
THAT'S GREAT, BECAUSE WE MAY BE A LITTLE LOST.
I FOUND SOMETHING... OR MORE PRECISELY SOMEONE...I'M PRETTY SURE I WASN'T SUPPOSED TO KNOW ABOUT.
JEAN... I'D ASK YOU TO TELL ME YOU DIDN'T KNOW ABOUT THIS... BUT WE BOTH KNOW THAT'S UNTRUE.
ALL THI TIME, YOU BEEN WORK WITH--
SORRY TO EAVESDROP, RACHEL.
(PSYCHIC RAPPORT, Y'KNOW?)
ZRRRAAAAK!
YOU MIGHT BE RIGHT...MAYBE WE SHOULD HAVE TOLD SOMEONE WHAT WE'VE BEEN DOING.
BUT NOW'S NOT THE TIME TO DISCUSS IT.
FAIR ENOUGH, BUT SOMETHING LIKE THIS...IT WAS BOUND TO SURFACE EVENTUALLY.
LET'S SEE IF YOU'RE BLUE ON THE INSIDE!
NNNN--
COMING THROUGH, PAL--!
LET'S SEE HOW A LITTLE PARTIAL INTANGIBILITY SUITS YOU.
AAGGK!
HEY, KITTY!
HOW ABOUT MAKING DOG-BOY HERE A LITTLE INSUBSTANTIAL, TOO?
GOG! MY NAME IS GOG!
AND I AM ANYTHING BUT INSUBSTANTIAL!
I'LL HEAR YOU SCREAM MY NAME BEFORE I RIP YOUR FROSTY GUTS OUT!
"WELL, WELL, WELL... LOOK WHAT WE'VE STUMBLED ON TO!"

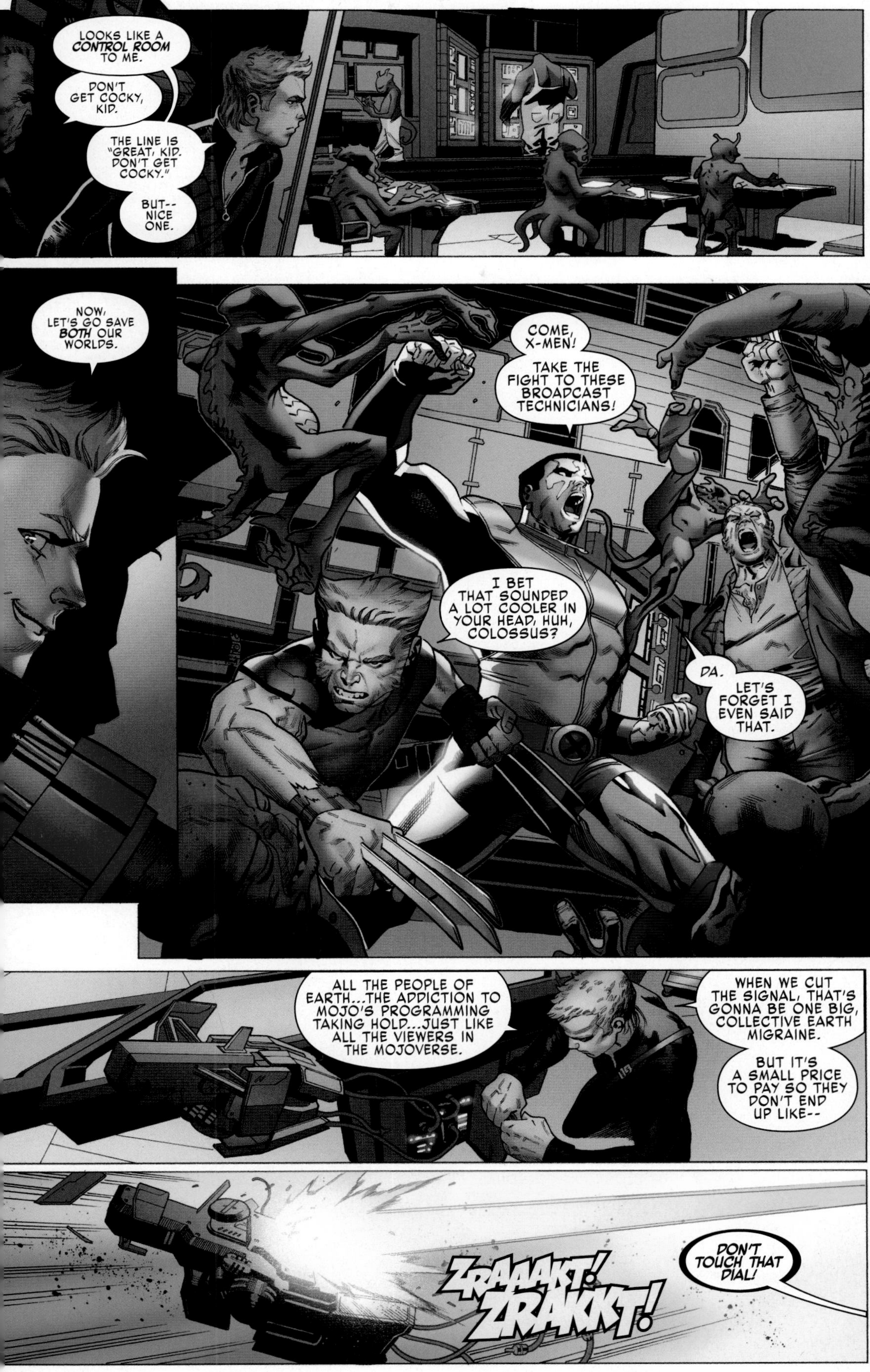
LOOKS LIKE A CONTROL ROOM TO ME.
DON'T GET COCKY, KID.
THE LINE IS "GREAT, KID. DON'T GET COCKY."
BUT-- NICE ONE.
NOW, LET'S GO SAVE BOTH OUR WORLDS.
COME, X-MEN!
TAKE THE FIGHT TO THESE BROADCAST TECHNICIANS!
I BET THAT SOUNDED A LOT COOLER IN YOUR HEAD, HUH, COLOSSUS?
DA.
LET'S FORGET I EVEN SAID THAT.
ALL THE PEOPLE OF EARTH...THE ADDICTION TO MOJO'S PROGRAMMING TAKING HOLD...JUST LIKE ALL THE VIEWERS IN THE MOJOVERSE.
WHEN WE CUT THE SIGNAL, THAT'S GONNA BE ONE BIG, COLLECTIVE EARTH MIGRAINE.
BUT IT'S A SMALL PRICE TO PAY SO THEY DON'T END UP LIKE--
ZRAAAKT! ZRAKKT!
DON'T TOUCH THAT DIAL!

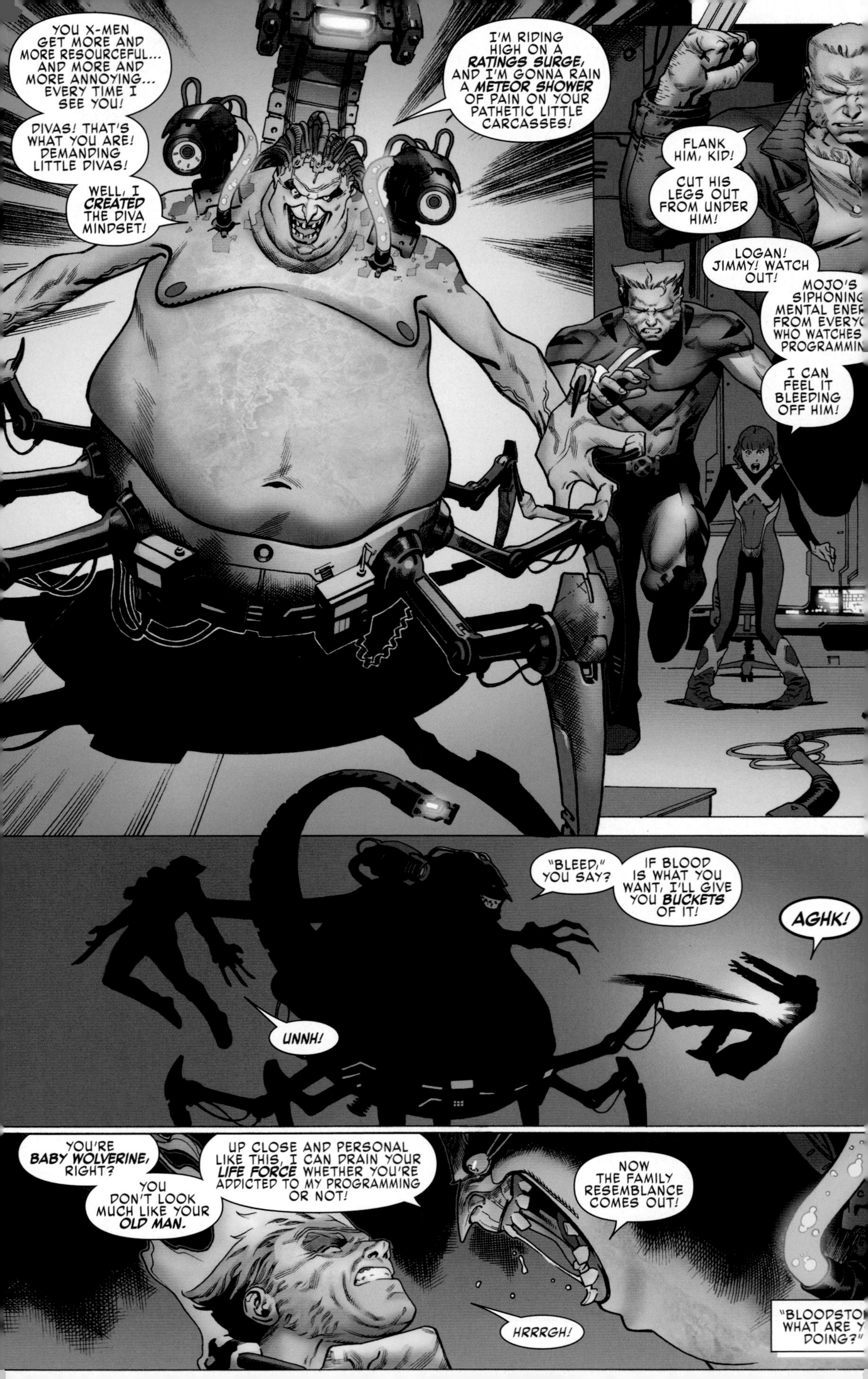
YOU X-MEN GET MORE AND MORE RESOURCEFUL... AND MORE AND MORE ANNOYING... EVERY TIME I SEE YOU!
DIVAS! THAT'S WHAT YOU ARE! DEMANDING LITTLE DIVAS!
WELL, I CREATED THE DIVA MINDSET!
I'M RIDING HIGH ON A RATINGS SURGE, AND I'M GONNA RAIN A METEOR SHOWER OF PAIN ON YOUR PATHETIC LITTLE CARCASSES!
FLANK HIM, KID!
CUT HIS LEGS OUT FROM UNDER HIM!
LOGAN! JIMMY! WATCH OUT!
MOJO'S SIPHONING MENTAL ENER
FROM EVERYO
WHO WATCHES
PROGRAMMIN
I CAN FEEL IT BLEEDING OFF HIM!
"BLEED," YOU SAY?
IF BLOOD IS WHAT YOU WANT, I'LL GIVE YOU BUCKETS OF IT!
AGHK!
UNNH!
YOU'RE BABY WOLVERINE, RIGHT?
YOU DON'T LOOK MUCH LIKE YOUR OLD MAN.
UP CLOSE AND PERSONAL LIKE THIS, I CAN DRAIN YOUR LIFE FORCE WHETHER YOU'RE ADDICTED TO MY PROGRAMMING OR NOT!
NOW THE FAMILY RESEMBLANCE COMES OUT!
HRRRGH!
"BLOODSTO
WHAT ARE Y
DOING?"

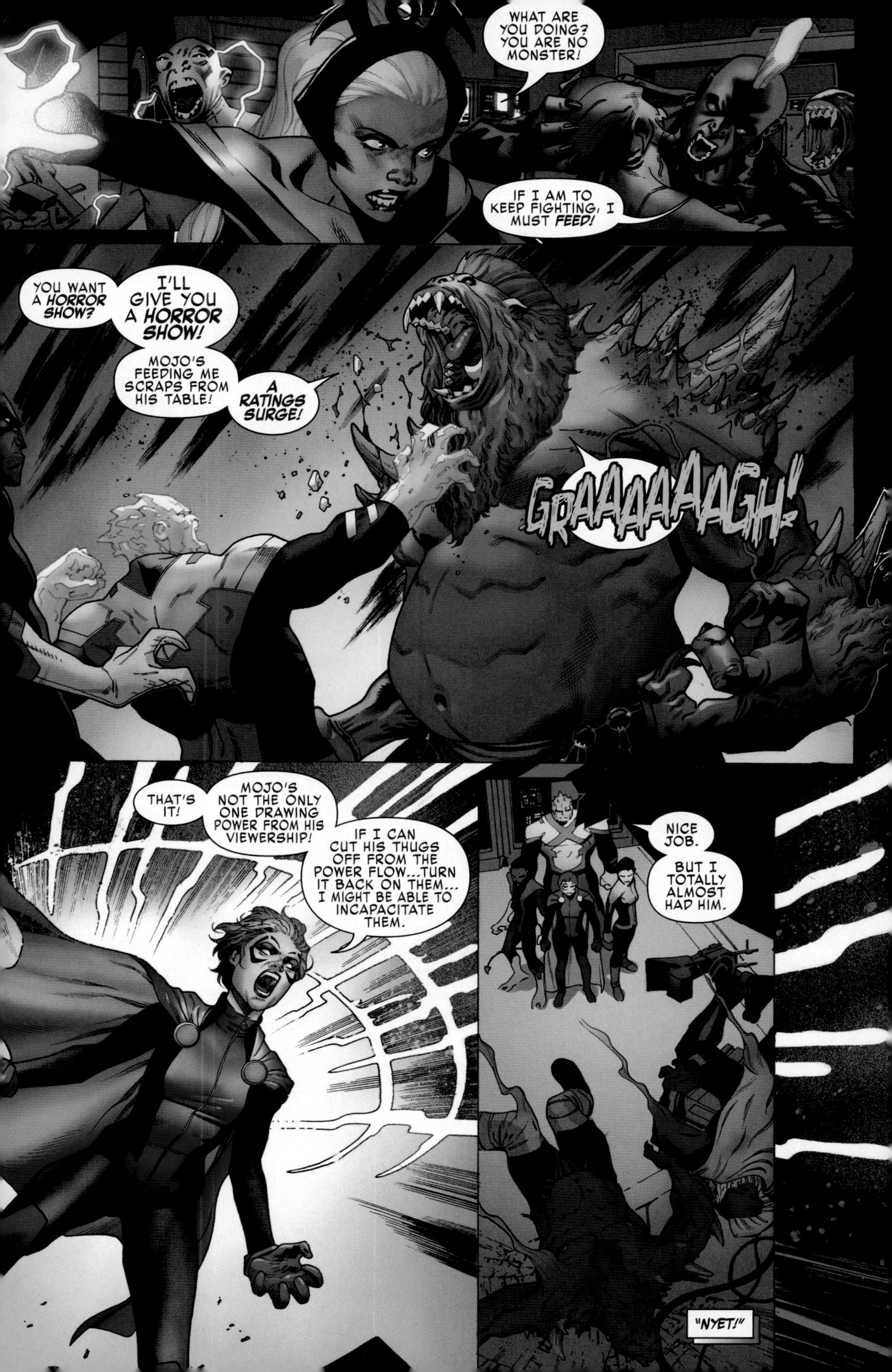
WHAT ARE YOU DOING? YOU ARE NO MONSTER!
IF I AM TO KEEP FIGHTING, I MUST FEED!
YOU WANT A HORROR SHOW?
I'LL GIVE YOU A HORROR SHOW!
MOJO'S FEEDING ME SCRAPS FROM HIS TABLE!
A RATINGS SURGE!
GRAAAAAAAGH!
THAT'S IT!
MOJO'S NOT THE ONLY ONE DRAWING POWER FROM HIS VIEWERSHIP!
IF I CAN CUT HIS THUGS OFF FROM THE POWER FLOW...TURN IT BACK ON THEM... I MIGHT BE ABLE TO INCAPACITATE THEM.
NICE JOB.
BUT I TOTALLY ALMOST HAD HIM.
"NYET!"

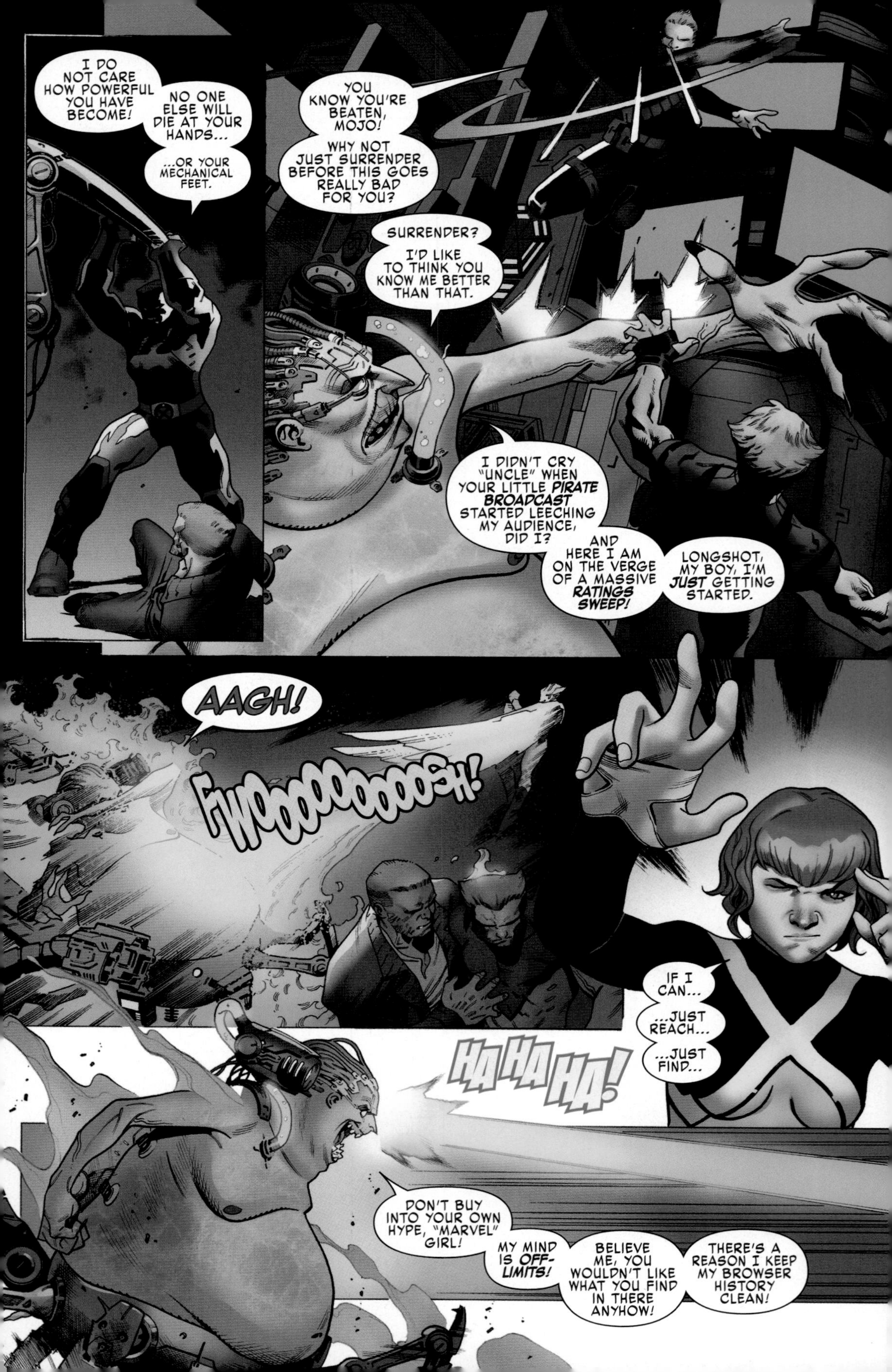
I DO NOT CARE HOW POWERFUL YOU HAVE BECOME!
NO ONE ELSE WILL DIE AT YOUR HANDS...
...OR YOUR MECHANICAL FEET.
YOU KNOW YOU'RE BEATEN, MOJO!
WHY NOT JUST SURRENDER BEFORE THIS GOES REALLY BAD FOR YOU?
SURRENDER?
I'D LIKE TO THINK YOU KNOW ME BETTER THAN THAT.
I DIDN'T CRY "UNCLE" WHEN YOUR LITTLE PIRATE BROADCAST STARTED LEECHING MY AUDIENCE, DID I?
AND HERE I AM ON THE VERGE OF A MASSIVE RATINGS SWEEP!
LONGSHOT, MY BOY, I'M JUST GETTING STARTED.
AAGH!
FWOOOOOOOOOSH!
IF I CAN...
...JUST REACH...
...JUST FIND...
HA HA HA!
DON'T BUY INTO YOUR OWN HYPE, "MARVEL" GIRL!
MY MIND IS OFF-LIMITS!
BELIEVE ME, YOU WOULDN'T LIKE WHAT YOU FIND IN THERE ANYHOW!
THERE'S A REASON I KEEP MY BROWSER HISTORY CLEAN!

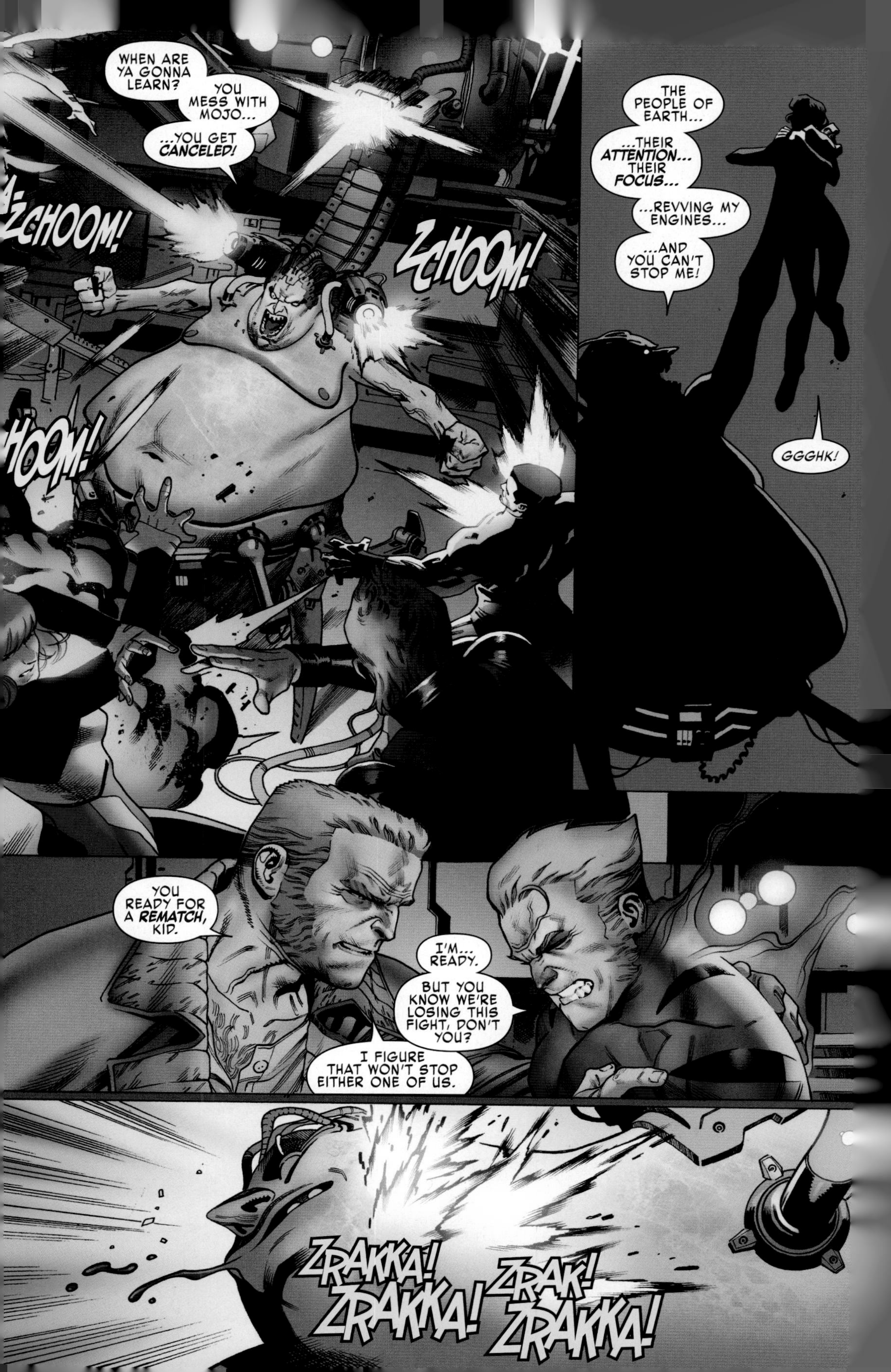
WHEN ARE YA GONNA LEARN?
YOU MESS WITH MOJO...
...YOU GET CANCELED!
ZCHOOM!
ZCHOOM!
HOOM!
THE PEOPLE OF EARTH...
...THEIR ATTENTION... THEIR FOCUS...
...REVVING MY ENGINES...
...AND YOU CAN'T STOP ME!
GGGHK!
YOU READY FOR A REMATCH, KID.
I'M... READY.
BUT YOU KNOW WE'RE LOSING THIS FIGHT, DON'T YOU?
I FIGURE THAT WON'T STOP EITHER ONE OF US.
ZRAKKA! ZRAKKA! ZRAK! ZRAKKA!

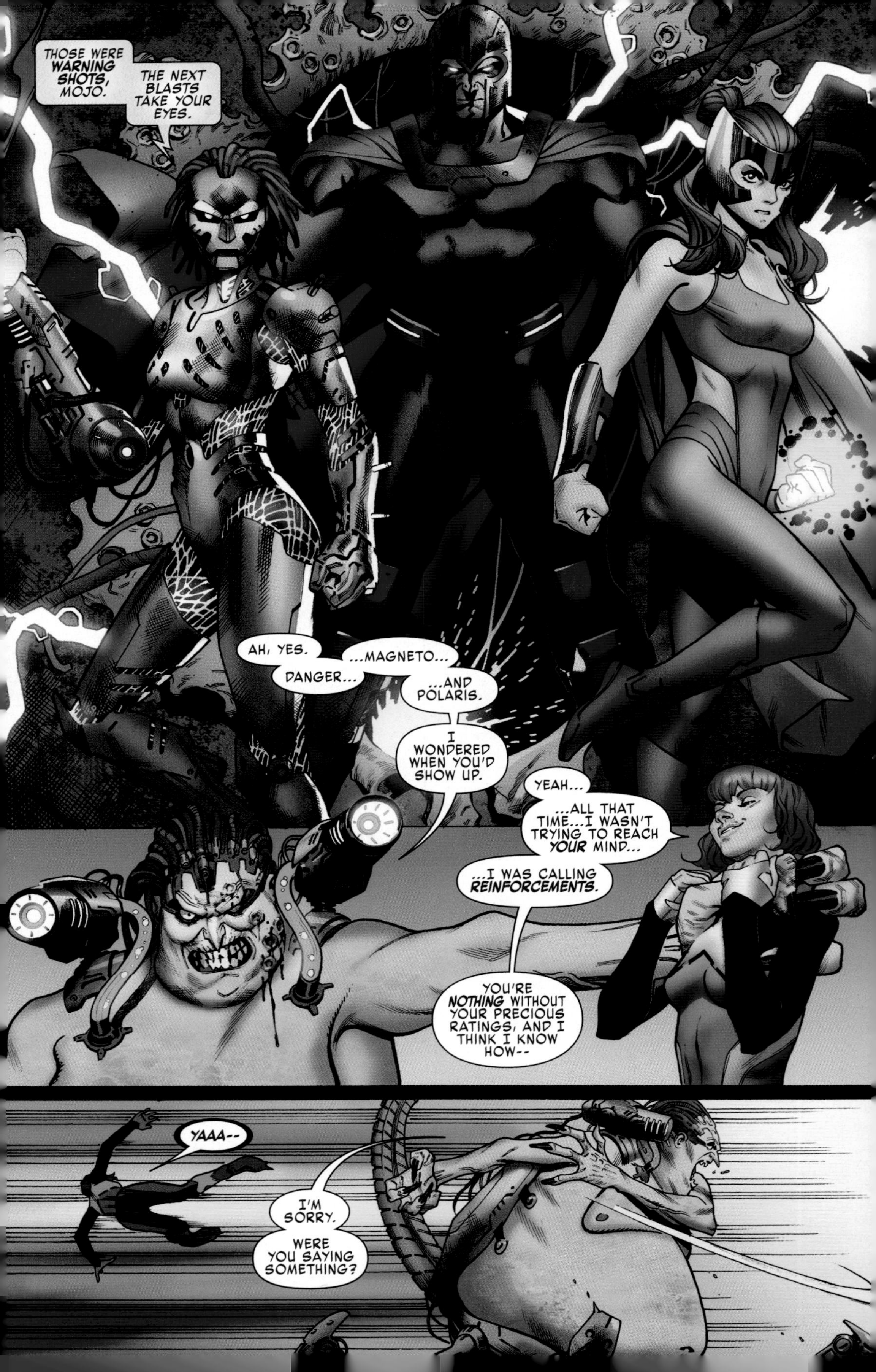
THOSE WERE WARNING SHOTS, MOJO.
THE NEXT BLASTS TAKE YOUR EYES.
AH, YES.
DANGER...
...MAGNETO...
...AND POLARIS.
I WONDERED WHEN YOU'D SHOW UP.
YEAH...
...ALL THAT TIME...I WASN'T TRYING TO REACH YOUR MIND...
...I WAS CALLING REINFORCEMENTS.
YOU'RE NOTHING WITHOUT YOUR PRECIOUS RATINGS, AND I THINK I KNOW HOW--
YAAA--
I'M SORRY.
WERE YOU SAYING SOMETHING?

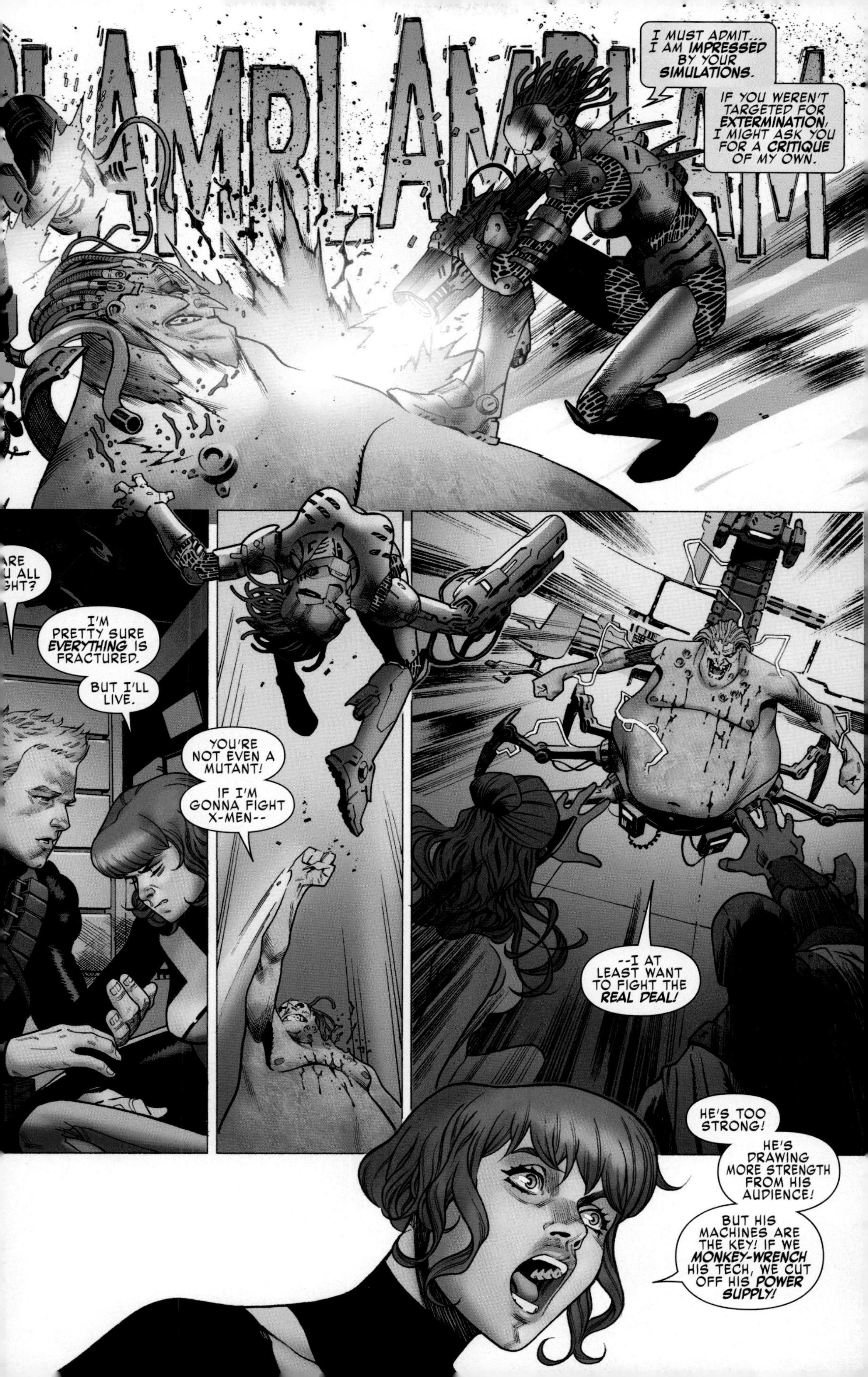
AMRLAMRLAMRLAM
I MUST ADMIT... I AM IMPRESSED BY YOUR SIMULATIONS.
IF YOU WEREN'T TARGETED FOR EXTERMINATION, I MIGHT ASK YOU FOR A CRITIQUE OF MY OWN.
ARE U ALL GHT?
I'M PRETTY SURE EVERYTHING IS FRACTURED.
BUT I'LL LIVE.
YOU'RE NOT EVEN A MUTANT!
IF I'M GONNA FIGHT X-MEN--
--I AT LEAST WANT TO FIGHT THE REAL DEAL!
HE'S TOO STRONG!
HE'S DRAWING MORE STRENGTH FROM HIS AUDIENCE!
BUT HIS MACHINES ARE THE KEY! IF WE MONKEY-WRENCH HIS TECH, WE CUT OFF HIS POWER SUPPLY!

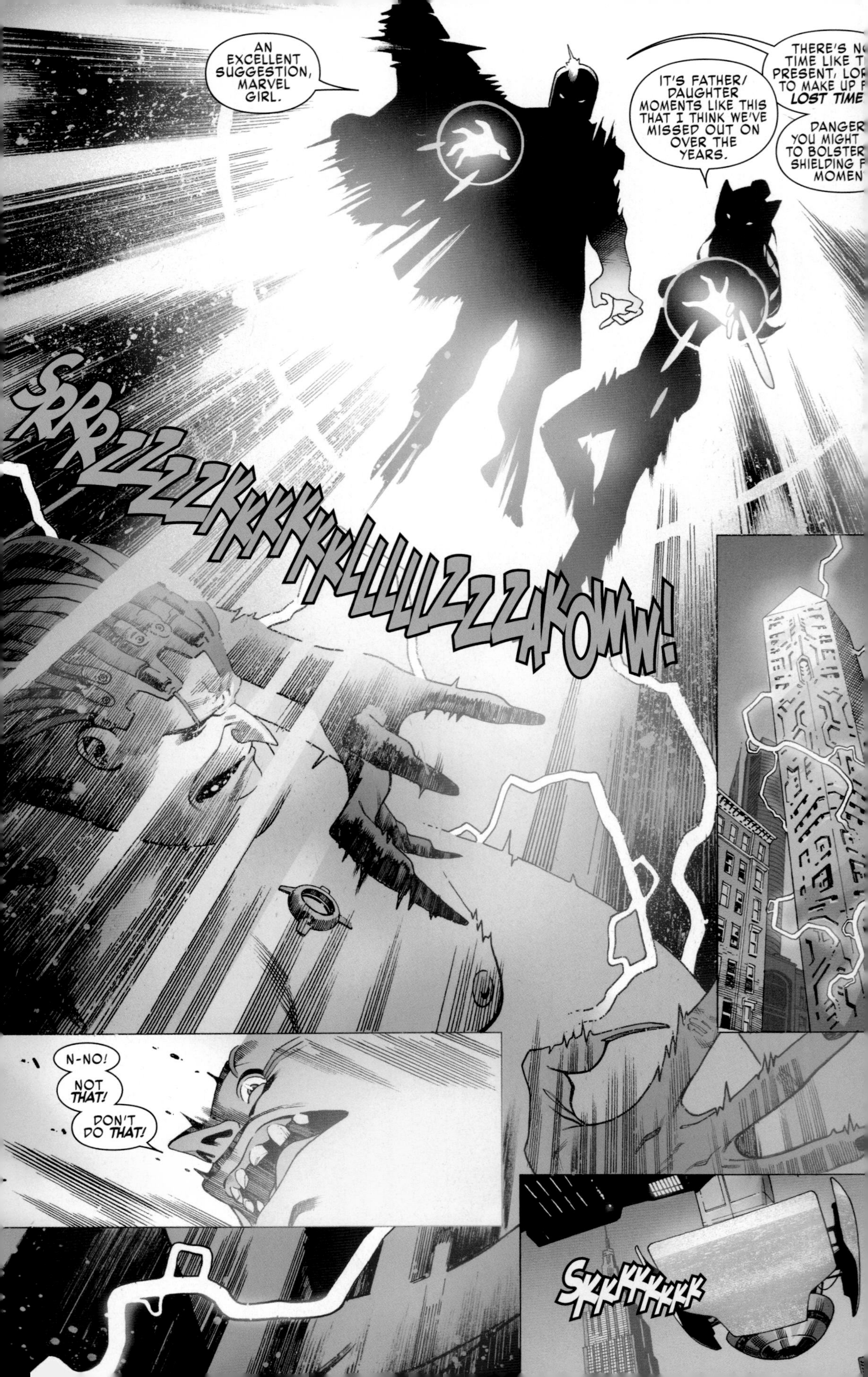

AN EXCELLENT SUGGESTION, MARVEL GIRL.
IT'S FATHER/ DAUGHTER MOMENTS LIKE THIS THAT I THINK WE'VE MISSED OUT ON OVER THE YEARS.
SRRRZZZZZKKKKKKLLLLLLZZZAKOWW!
N-NO!
NOT THAT!
DON'T DO THAT!
SKKKKKKKK

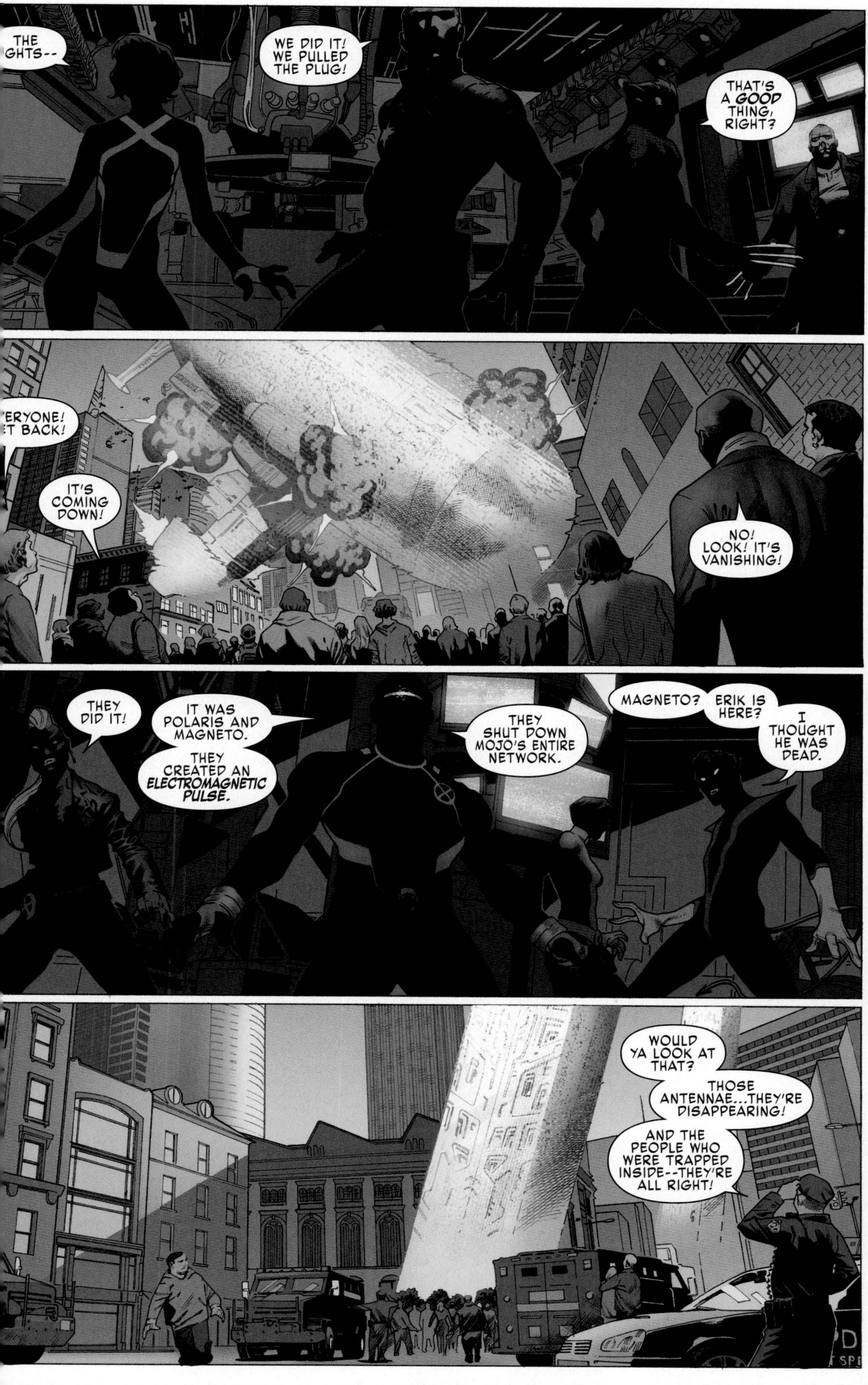
THE
GHTS--
WE DID IT! WE PULLED THE PLUG!
THAT'S A GOOD THING, RIGHT?
ERYONE!
T BACK!
IT'S COMING DOWN!
NO! LOOK! IT'S VANISHING!
THEY DID IT!
IT WAS POLARIS AND MAGNETO.
THEY CREATED AN ELECTROMAGNETIC PULSE.
THEY SHUT DOWN MOJO'S ENTIRE NETWORK.
MAGNETO?
ERIK IS HERE?
I THOUGHT HE WAS DEAD.
WOULD YA LOOK AT THAT?
THOSE ANTENNAE...THEY'RE DISAPPEARING!
AND THE PEOPLE WHO WERE TRAPPED INSIDE--THEY'RE ALL RIGHT!

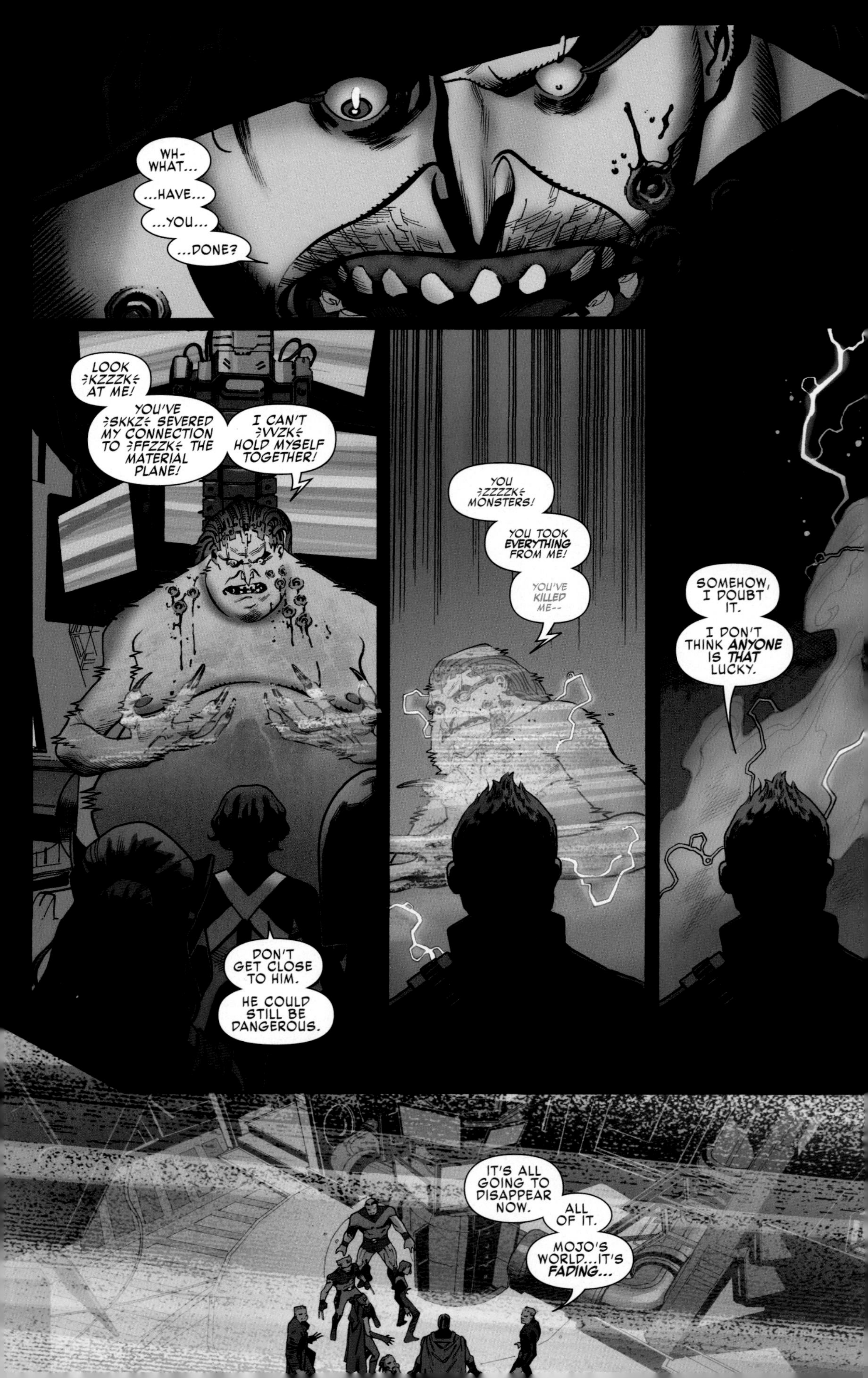

WH- WHAT... ...HAVE... ...YOU... ...DONE?
LOOK ⫘KZZZK⫘ AT ME!
YOU'VE ⫘SKKZ⫘ SEVERED MY CONNECTION TO ⫘FFZZK⫘ THE MATERIAL PLANE!
I CAN'T ⫘VVZK⫘ HOLD MYSELF TOGETHER!
DON'T GET CLOSE TO HIM.
HE COULD STILL BE DANGEROUS.
YOU ⫘ZZZZK⫘ MONSTERS!
YOU TOOK EVERYTHING FROM ME!
YOU'VE KILLED ME--
SOMEHOW, I DOUBT IT.
I DON'T THINK ANYONE IS THAT LUCKY.
IT'S ALL GOING TO DISAPPEAR NOW.
ALL OF IT.
MOJO'S WORLD...IT'S FADING...

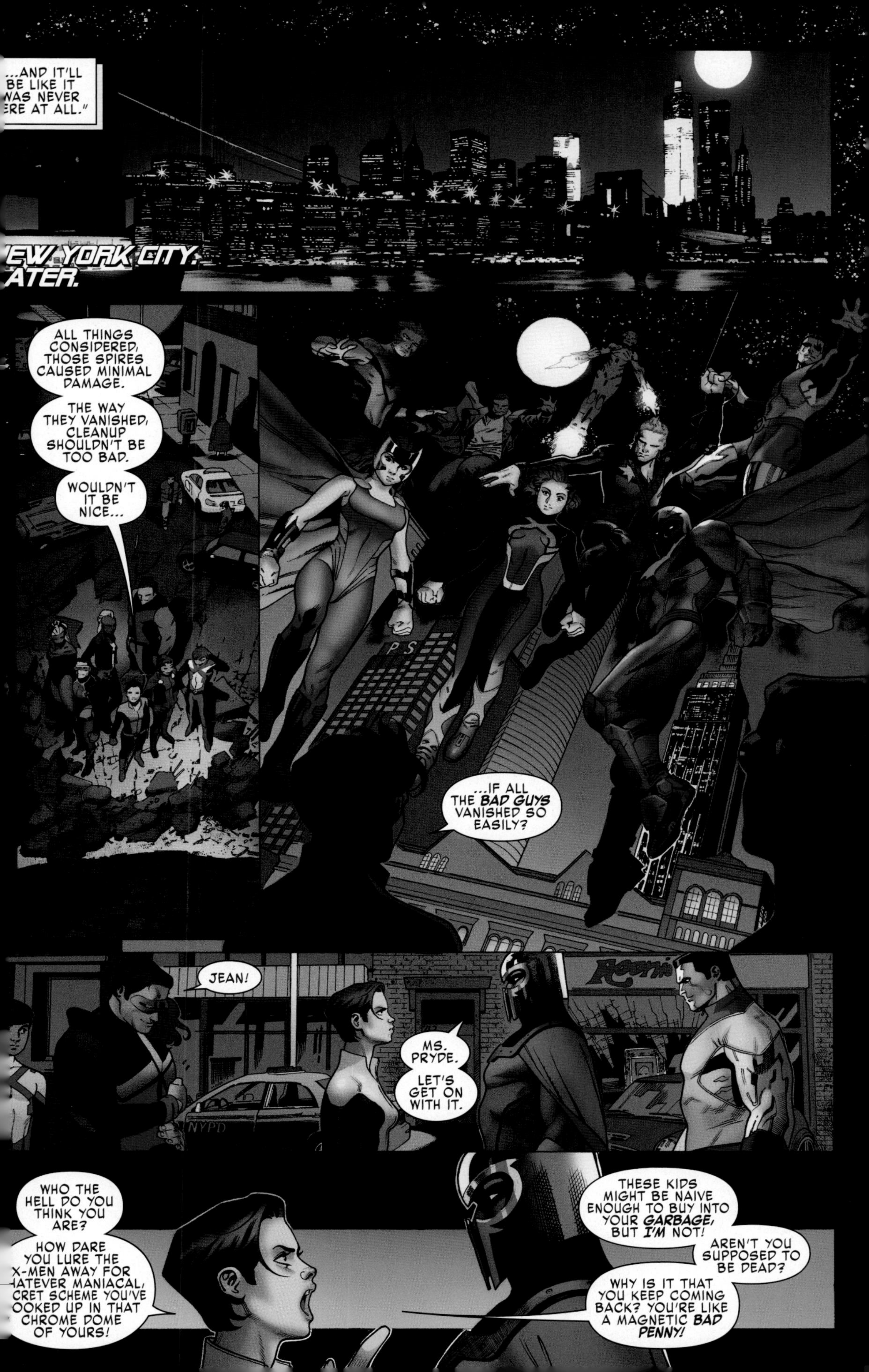
...AND IT'LL BE LIKE IT WAS NEVER ERE AT ALL."
EW YORK CITY. ATER.
ALL THINGS CONSIDERED, THOSE SPIRES CAUSED MINIMAL DAMAGE.
THE WAY THEY VANISHED, CLEANUP SHOULDN'T BE TOO BAD.
WOULDN'T IT BE NICE...
...IF ALL THE BAD GUYS VANISHED SO EASILY?
JEAN!
MS. PRYDE.
LET'S GET ON WITH IT.
NYPD
WHO THE HELL DO YOU THINK YOU ARE?
HOW DARE YOU LURE THE X-MEN AWAY FOR HATEVER MANIACAL, CRET SCHEME YOU'VE OOKED UP IN THAT CHROME DOME OF YOURS!
THESE KIDS MIGHT BE NAIVE ENOUGH TO BUY INTO YOUR GARBAGE, BUT I'M NOT!
AREN'T YOU SUPPOSED TO BE DEAD?
WHY IS IT THAT YOU KEEP COMING BACK? YOU'RE LIKE A MAGNETIC BAD PENNY!

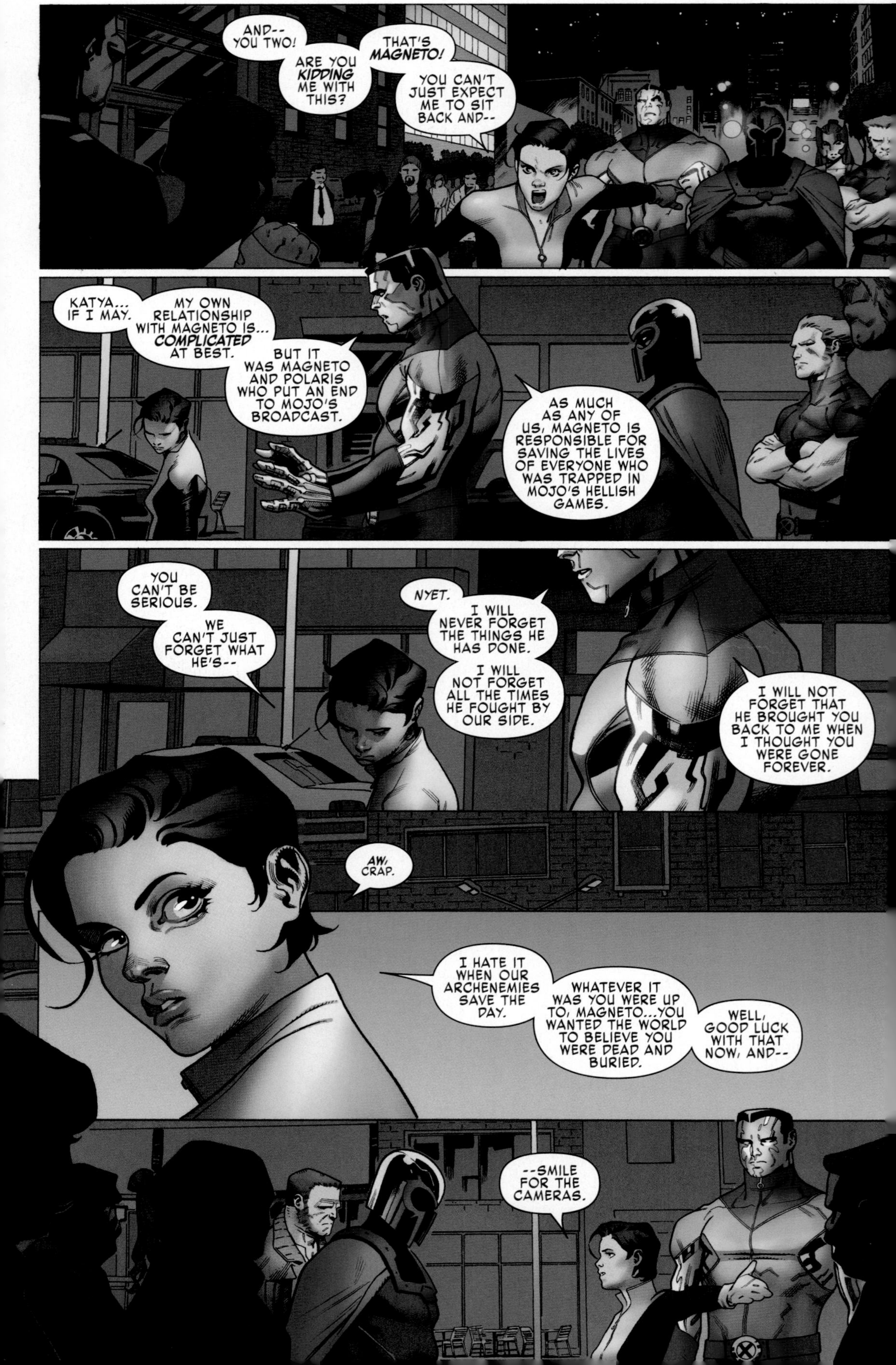
AND-- YOU TWO!
ARE YOU KIDDING ME WITH THIS?
THAT'S MAGNETO!
YOU CAN'T JUST EXPECT ME TO SIT BACK AND--
KATYA... IF I MAY.
MY OWN RELATIONSHIP WITH MAGNETO IS... COMPLICATED AT BEST.
BUT IT WAS MAGNETO AND POLARIS WHO PUT AN END TO MOJO'S BROADCAST.
AS MUCH AS ANY OF US, MAGNETO IS RESPONSIBLE FOR SAVING THE LIVES OF EVERYONE WHO WAS TRAPPED IN MOJO'S HELLISH GAMES.
YOU CAN'T BE SERIOUS.
WE CAN'T JUST FORGET WHAT HE'S--
NYET.
I WILL NEVER FORGET THE THINGS HE HAS DONE.
I WILL NOT FORGET ALL THE TIMES HE FOUGHT BY OUR SIDE.
I WILL NOT FORGET THAT HE BROUGHT YOU BACK TO ME WHEN I THOUGHT YOU WERE GONE FOREVER.
AW, CRAP.
I HATE IT WHEN OUR ARCHENEMIES SAVE THE DAY.
WHATEVER IT WAS YOU WERE UP TO, MAGNETO...YOU WANTED THE WORLD TO BELIEVE YOU WERE DEAD AND BURIED.
WELL, GOOD LUCK WITH THAT NOW, AND--
--SMILE FOR THE CAMERAS.

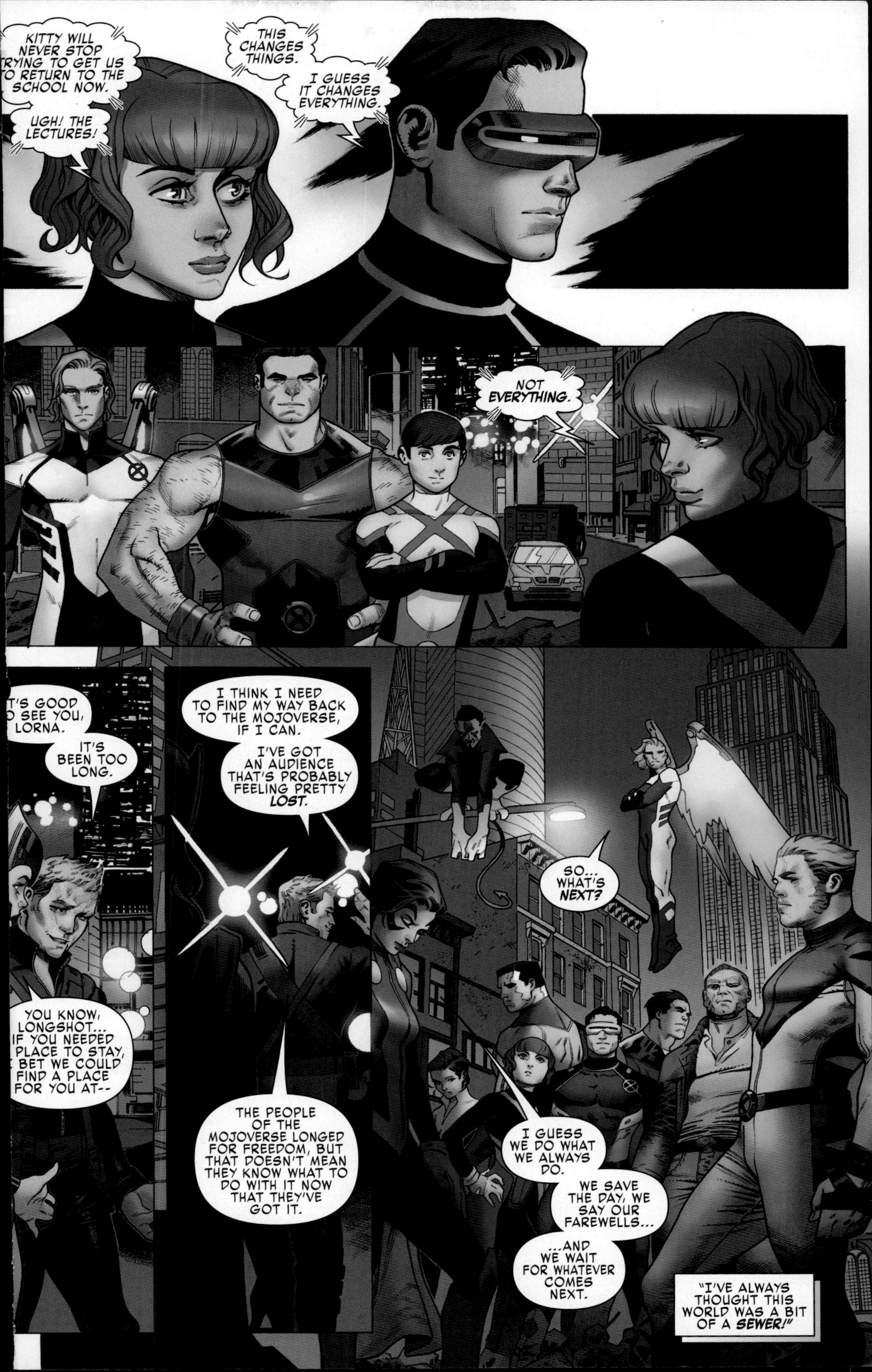
KITTY WILL NEVER STOP TRYING TO GET US TO RETURN TO THE SCHOOL NOW.
UGH! THE LECTURES!
THIS CHANGES THINGS.
I GUESS IT CHANGES EVERYTHING.
NOT EVERYTHING.
IT'S GOOD TO SEE YOU, LORNA.
IT'S BEEN TOO LONG.
YOU KNOW, LONGSHOT... IF YOU NEEDED A PLACE TO STAY, I BET WE COULD FIND A PLACE FOR YOU AT--
I THINK I NEED TO FIND MY WAY BACK TO THE MOJOVERSE, IF I CAN.
I'VE GOT AN AUDIENCE THAT'S PROBABLY FEELING PRETTY LOST.
THE PEOPLE OF THE MOJOVERSE LONGED FOR FREEDOM, BUT THAT DOESN'T MEAN THEY KNOW WHAT TO DO WITH IT NOW THAT THEY'VE GOT IT.
SO... WHAT'S NEXT?
I GUESS WE DO WHAT WE ALWAYS DO.
WE SAVE THE DAY, WE SAY OUR FAREWELLS...
...AND WE WAIT FOR WHATEVER COMES NEXT.
"I'VE ALWAYS THOUGHT THIS WORLD WAS A BIT OF A SEWER!"

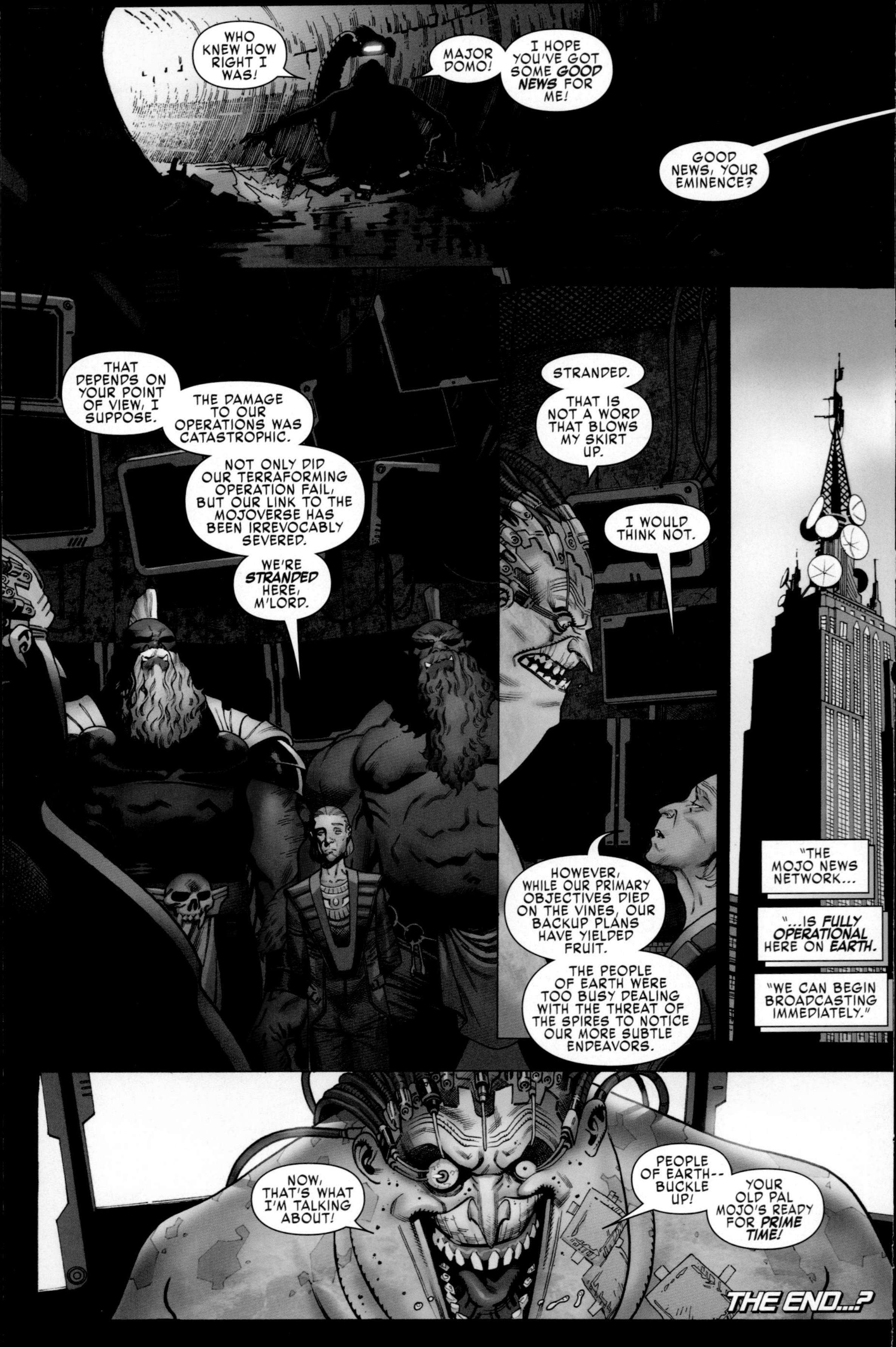
WHO KNEW HOW RIGHT I WAS!
MAJOR DOMO!
I HOPE YOU'VE GOT SOME GOOD NEWS FOR ME!
GOOD NEWS, YOUR EMINENCE?
THAT DEPENDS ON YOUR POINT OF VIEW, I SUPPOSE.
THE DAMAGE TO OUR OPERATIONS WAS CATASTROPHIC.
NOT ONLY DID OUR TERRAFORMING OPERATION FAIL, BUT OUR LINK TO THE MOJOVERSE HAS BEEN IRREVOCABLY SEVERED.
WE'RE STRANDED HERE, M'LORD.
STRANDED.
THAT IS NOT A WORD THAT BLOWS MY SKIRT UP.
I WOULD THINK NOT.
HOWEVER, WHILE OUR PRIMARY OBJECTIVES DIED ON THE VINES, OUR BACKUP PLANS HAVE YIELDED FRUIT.
THE PEOPLE OF EARTH WERE TOO BUSY DEALING WITH THE THREAT OF THE SPIRES TO NOTICE OUR MORE SUBTLE ENDEAVORS.
"THE MOJO NEWS NETWORK...
"...IS FULLY OPERATIONAL HERE ON EARTH.
"WE CAN BEGIN BROADCASTING IMMEDIATELY."
NOW, THAT'S WHAT I'M TALKING ABOUT!
PEOPLE OF EARTH-- BUCKLE UP!
YOUR OLD PAL MOJO'S READY FOR PRIME TIME!
THE END...?

X-MEN GOLD

HOW TO DRAW THE X-MEN
IN SIX EASY STEPS!
BY CHIP "WHOA, MORE MUTANTS" ZDARSKY

Wow! A "sketch variant cover"! Your path to drawing for MARVEL COMICS, I guess! Anyway, here's a fun and informative step-by-step guide!

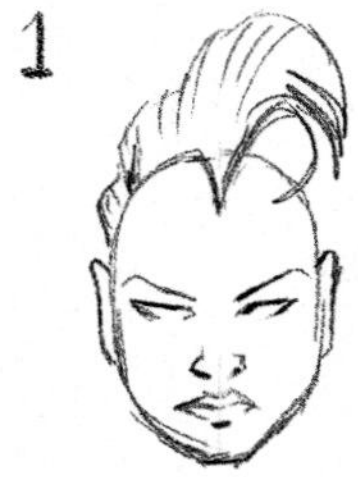
1

The X-Men! So many great members to choose from, but if I were to choose the best starting point, it would have to be with the best X-Man: STORM! So let's begin by drawing her!

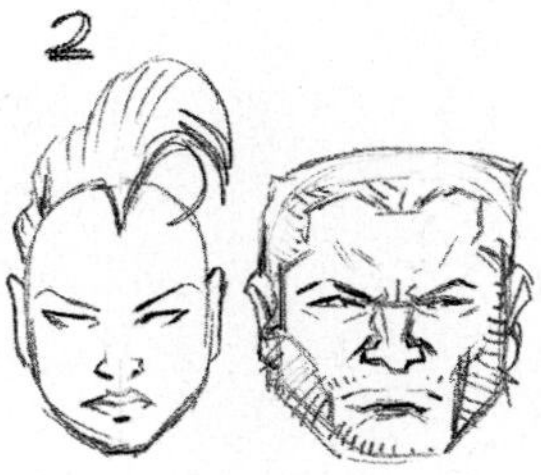
2

And of course the name "X-Men" is synonymous with LOGAN! His current incarnation is an older version of him, so keep his hair white and shorter! Don't be afraid to add some wrinkles!

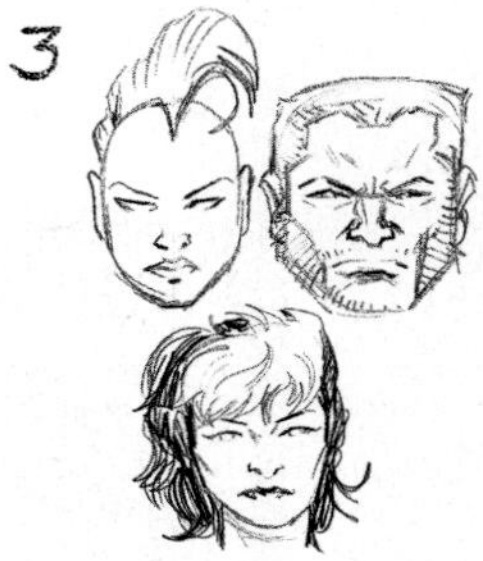
3

Then ROGUE, with her trademark white streak! But if we're making an X-MEN team, we should include some original members...

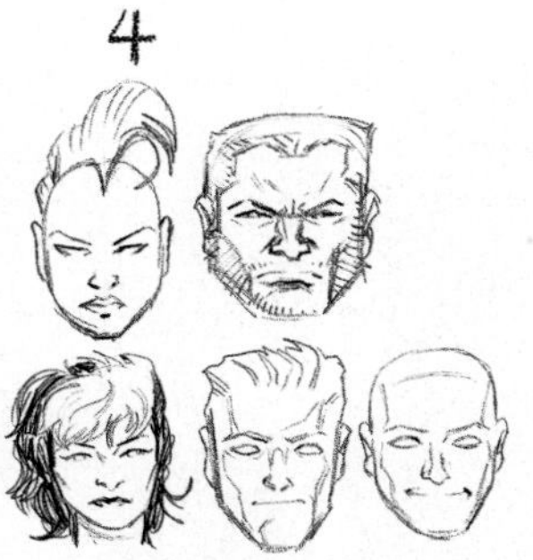
4

...like ICEMAN! He's a great fit for—oh, wait. There's TWO guys who are ICEMAN. They're technically the same, just one has time-traveled. LOTS of time travel in X-Men, heh. Well, let's just include both of them!

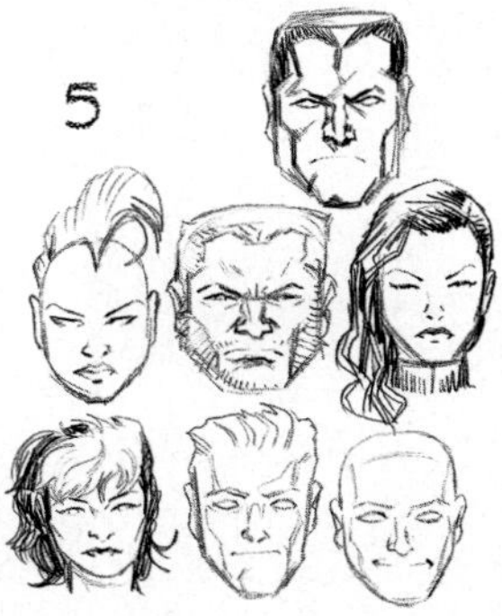
5

Gonna want a strong guy on the team, so COLOSSUS it is! That way he and LOGAN can do "fastball specials." And we should also include PSYLOCKE, for her telepathy and telekinesis!

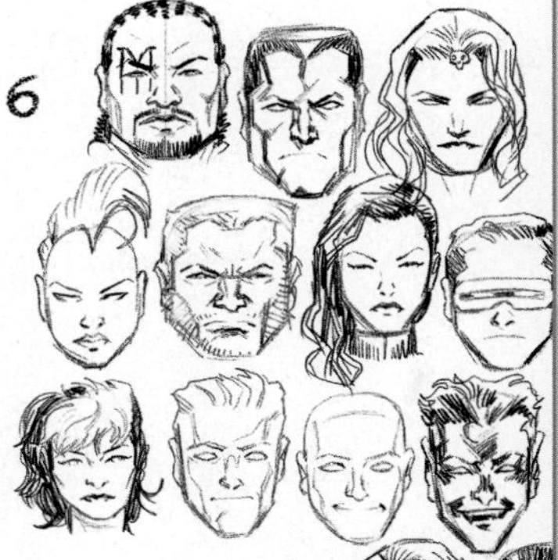
6

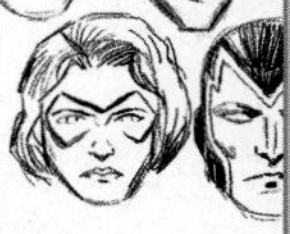

No X-Men team is complete without someone from the future! So let's put BISHOP in here! Oh! Also, RACHEL SUMMERS! I guess her new code name is PRESTIGE! And you can never have too many villains turned heroes on the team, so let's add the shape-changer MYSTIQUE! I like an X-MEN team that has CYCLOPS on it so let's include him as well! Oh, wait, he's dead. But his teen version isn't! Perfect! May as well expand the original members as well with ARCHANGEL! And for a sense of fun, let's put NIGHTCRAWLER on the team as well! And everyone loves GAMBIT, so we should try and find some room for him as

X-MEN GOLD #13 *HOW TO DRAW VARIANT*
BY ***CHIP ZDARSKY***

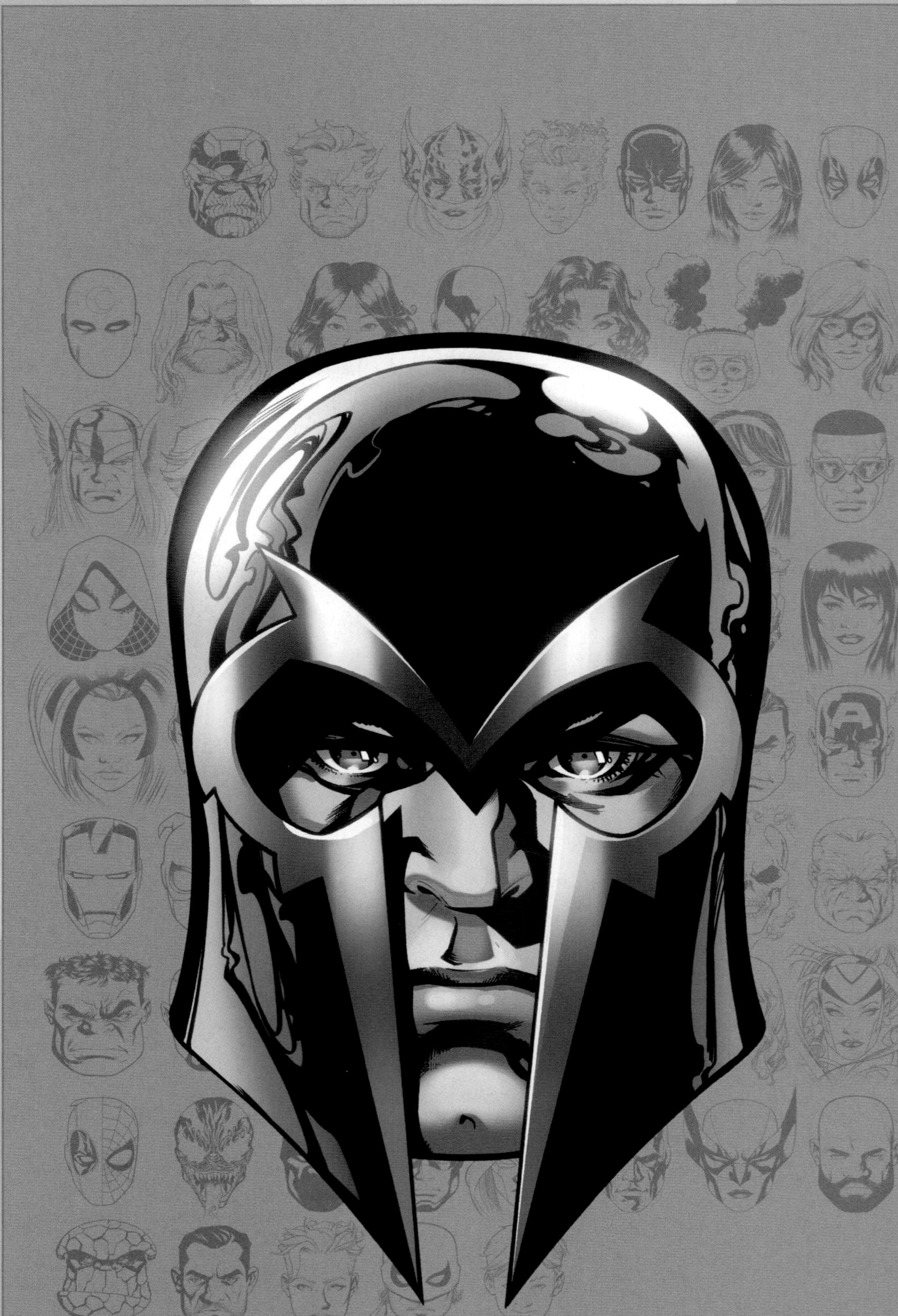

X-MEN BLUE #13 *LEGACY HEADSHOT VARIANT*
BY ***MIKE McKONE & RACHELLE ROSENBERG***